Anne Samson completed her PhD at Royal Holloway, University of London in 2004, the outcome of which was published by I.B.Tauris in 2006 as *Britain, South Africa and the East Africa Campaign: The Union Comes of Age*. Anne has written a number of chapters and papers related to the East Africa campaign and South Africa's involvement in Africa. She works as an independent historian and is currently, collaborating with the Great War in East Africa Association on various events. In her other life, she works in education in the lifelong learning sector in the UK and with state primary school education in Tanzania. She currently lives in the UK but spends as much time in Africa as possible.

WORLD WAR I IN AFRICA

The Forgotten Conflict Among
the European Powers

ANNE SAMSON

I.B.TAURIS
LONDON • NEW YORK • OXFORD • NEW DELHI • SYDNEY

I.B. TAURIS
Bloomsbury Publishing Plc
50 Bedford Square, London, WC1B 3DP, UK
1385 Broadway, New York, NY 10018, USA

BLOOMSBURY, I.B. TAURIS and the I.B. Tauris logo are
trademarks of Bloomsbury Publishing Plc

First published in Great Britain 2015
Paperback edition first published 2019

A catalogue record for this book is available from the British Library.

ISBN: 978 1 78076 119 0
   PB: 978 1 78831 444 2

A full CIP record is available from the Library of Congress

International Library of Twentieth Century History, vol. 50

Typeset by Newgen Publishers, Chennai, India

To find out more about our authors and books visit
www.bloomsbury.com and sign up for our newsletters.

Dedicated to all those past and present affected
by the campaigns in East and southern Africa
and in loving memory of
'Pa' Gerry Stilwell

CONTENTS

ACKNOWLEDGEMENTS

The following people have been instrumental in enabling this book to be completed. A special thanks to Harry Fecitt MBE TD for his patience in correcting my many campaign errors, for explaining various military terms and his generosity in sharing information. His outspoken and direct approach has been instrumental in helping me clarify my thinking. He is, however, in no way responsible for any errors which remain in this text – they are purely my own. Other special thanks are due to Suryakanthie Chetty, a fellow South African whom I met in Berlin. Thank you for your early proofreading, insights and challenges too, and to Alan Carter for correcting my grammar, punctuation and logic at a particularly busy time. Daniel Steinbeck for sharing his findings on prisoners of war during the campaign, Filippe de Meneses, Pedro Aires Oliveira and Doug Wheeler for their pointers to Portugal's involvement in Angola and other sources and all those I met along the way who listened, questioned and passed on tit-bits, including those on the Great War Forum and the Great War in East Africa Association. The writing of this book would not have been possible without the support and understanding of my family in South Africa who helped track down books and allowed me to spend time in the archives on our short annual visits home. Also, friends Katy and Dilly in Marangu, Tanzania, who in between our education work, helped me find places and nuggets of information. Not least, the trustees, archivists and librarians who enabled my research to be conducted as painlessly as possible, both in South Africa and in the UK. In particular, I am grateful to the following who permitted me to consult original documents: Bodleian Library, Oxford; Department of Special Collections and Western Manuscripts; New College, Oxford; Rhodes House Library (Lucy McCann); British Library, India Office Records, Manuscripts Department; Cambridge University Library Archive, Churchill Archives Centre, Cambridge; Liddell Hart Centre for Military Research, King's College London; Imperial War Museum Archive; Parliamentary Archive, Houses of Parliament; The National Archives, Kew; Wiltshire and Swindon Archives; Colindale Newspaper Library; South African Defence Force Archive; South African National Archive and South Africa National Library, Cape Town. Ran Meinertzhagen gave me permission to look at his father's papers and to reference them in this text. The following have kindly granted permission for me to quote and reference from the sources over which they hold copyright. The British Library Board for Arthur James Balfour; Trustees of the Liddell Hart Centre for Military Archives for WR Robertson, Trustees of the Imperial War Museum for Henry Wilson, The Bodleian Library for Lewis Harcourt, Parliamentary Archives for David Lloyd George, Andrew Bonar Law and JCC Davidson, Patricia King for Norman King, Carolann Smith-Dorrien for Horace Smith-Dorrien, Neil Armstrong for an unknown Petty Officer Stoker on HMS Weymouth, Jean Robjant for LES Ward, Michael Barrow for Edmund Barrow, Sara Morrison for Walter Long and Brian Drummond Smith for Noel Smith. Maurice Hankey's papers have been reproduced with permission of the Master and Fellows of Churchill College, Cambridge, whilst Crown Copyright documents in the India Office Private Papers of the British Library, The National Archives, Kew, and within other private collections appear by permission of the Controller of Her Majesty's Stationery Office. Every effort was made to trace other copyright holders prior to publication.

Thank you to Tony Stockwell for your constant support and encouragement and to all my education colleagues for your support and understanding. I am grateful to Lester Crook at I.B.Tauris for prompting me to write the book and to Tomasz Hoskins also at Tauris for his support and guidance. Final thanks, is to John for joining me in my research safaris and excursions around Africa, all in the name of history.

INTRODUCTION

'Whenever in these present momentous times I read some laconic paragraph indicating that the Navy has attacked and sunk some enemy ship, I wonder how much scheming and dare-devil courage have gone to achieve that three-line result.'[1] So wrote Piet Pretorius about tracking down and sinking the *Königsberg*. His statement is just as pertinent for the non-military historian reading a book or article on life or some campaign in any war. Realising, through discussion with military experts and travelling through the East African countryside, that bland acknowledgements of success or defeat cover a whole interplay of individuals and organisations inspired this book.

The book does not aim to tell the military story as that has been done elsewhere. However, it draws on these narratives and original documents to show the interrelatedness of policy and strategy with what was happening on the ground and in-between. It attempts to shed some light on the influence of the individual politician, official, commander, soldier and civilian, in determining the direction of war. As a British Staff College lecturer summed up in 1901, 'War is a contest between two human intelligences rather than between two bodies of men.'[2] In telling the story of the First World War in East and southern Africa, this book will hopefully show some of the 'humanness' of war and that not all military men were keen on fighting for fighting's sake.

One of the challenges in writing such a history is that the historian is reliant on what other people have remembered and chosen to record. 'Memories are pictures, and they form haphazardly on the mental screen.'[3] Memories are personal and only those which are recorded and made public are available, if found, to create the mosaic. This means, that no story is ever complete. Even the official histories which aimed to give a complete picture do not. These official stories are based on the information available at the time as well as the dominant ideology at the time of writing. The result of these extraneous factors is that the second volume of the official history of the East African campaign was never completed while that of the German South West Africa campaign only contains one-third of the story.[4] This is not surprising given the nature of war and that the nature of the terrain in East and southern Africa made the recording of events erratic.[5] There are no records of the East African Mounted Rifles who were never disbanded, yet the unit consisting of 85 per cent of the population in the first days of the war, had only one major, one sergeant and two troopers at the end.[6] Reading the Belgian official history of the war makes the reader wonder if it is the same war that is being spoken about. It is clearly written to the glory of 'little' Belgium fighting against the super powers and succeeding. Reference to its dependency on Britain is almost unmentioned.[7] In addition, little if anything was recorded of the Indian, black and coloured involvement in the East and southern theatres despite these groups contributing the greatest proportion of manpower. This is not to say that the historians of the time were slack. They were writing for specific purposes and with the information they had, as noted by the Historical Department letter to General Wapshare's widow asking her not to destroy any papers now that he had died.[8] This book, too, is written in a specific time and context with the information available and as a result will have its own flaws.

The campaign

The 1914–1918 war was between European powers about power. So why involve subordinate countries outside of Europe? This question has no doubt inspired a renewed interest in the East Africa campaign, as seen by the increased number of publications on the subject: Ross Anderson's *The Forgotten Front*, Hew Strachan's *The First World War in*

Africa, Edward Paice's *Tip and Run* and Giles Foden's *Mimi and Toutou Go Forth*, being the most popular.[9] Interest in the East Africa campaign is fuelled by the number of first claims the campaign makes. It was the longest lasting of the war and according to *The Times* had the first naval engagement on 13 August 1914 on Lake Nyasa. The first naval Victoria Cross (VC) of the war was won during an attack on Dar-es-Salaam by Captain Henry Peel Ritchie.[10] Hostilities started with a bombardment of Dar-es-Salaam on 8 August 1914 before those in Europe, and ended on 25 November 1918, fourteen days after the armistice in Europe was signed. Trench warfare was to all intents and purposes non-existent. Emil Paul von Lettow-Vorbeck, German commander in East Africa, was the only German general to occupy British territory and was also the only undefeated German general of the war. He led a force of 260 Germans and up to 12,000 askaris against a total allied force of around 100,000 soldiers and one million porters.

The campaign in East Africa was, and still is, important for various reasons. As Francis Brett Young, in his foreword to Thornhill's *Taking Tanganyika*, notes: 'that campaign was unique of its kind: the first tropical warfare waged under modern conditions of transport and armament, and the first in which organized native troops on either side fought with white men and against them'.[11] Similarly, the campaign in South West Africa was of significance. Britain asked South Africa, a country which had fought against it fifteen years before, to undertake the task. This remarkable undertaking was reinforced by Prime Minister Louis Botha leading the South African forces into the German colony after putting down a rebellion in his own country which had been initiated by senior military men opposing the campaign. Following South Africa's involvement in German South West Africa, the country, under the command of General Jan Christian Smuts, took on the German forces in East Africa, linking the two campaigns and bringing cohesion to the First World War in southern, central and eastern Africa.

The advent of the centenary of the outbreak of the Great War seems an opportune moment for the campaigns in Africa to be reconsidered and acknowledged in their own right, not as side-shows of the European War. Individually, each campaign might be regarded as a side-show, however, collectively they achieve a significance not usually associated with the African continent. In telling the story of the war in East and southern Africa, the contributions of Smuts and Lettow-Vorbeck, two men who were both politicians and military men, admired and despised by their fellow countrymen yet had a huge regard for each other and became friends, will be assessed. This can only be done by looking at their relationships with those around them and the context in which these took place.

This book expands on my thesis published by I.B.Tauris in 2005 under the title *Britain, South Africa and the East Africa Campaign, 1914–1918: The Union Comes of Age* whilst correcting the errors which managed to slip through. It does not aim to explore the military aspects of the campaign as that has been admirably done by others.[12] However, it does aim to explore why the war was taken to East Africa and why it progressed the way it did. In essence, it looks at the interplay of individuals at all levels and how they contributed to the outcome of the war. Strong personalities directed various aspects of the war. This was understandable as war requires strong individuals to make difficult decisions. Issues arise, and invariably will, when those personalities clash, each believing that their perception of the situation is the right one. It becomes more complex when politicians believe that 'war is too serious to be left to the Generals' and have to have their say.[13] By exploring the interplay of the main individual players involved, southern Africa, as a whole, is drawn into the discussion, not least because from 1916 the Union of South Africa was to play a dominant role in the campaign and the country's deputy Prime Minister, General Jan Christian Smuts, commanded the forces there for a year. In addition, Southern and Northern Rhodesia as well as Nyasaland, Portuguese East Africa and Congo were drawn in by virtue of being neighbouring countries. Through South Africa's pre-1916 involvement in the wider war and the internal political situation, the campaigns in German South West Africa and Angola became involved in the story.

The politics of the campaigns in East and southern Africa played out at various levels, locally within each territory, at individual country level, within the various colonial empires (Strachan's 'sub-imperialism')[14] and across powers in Europe. It was in effect a 'war between empires'.[15] Twenty-eight countries were involved in the campaign, some subordinate to others, but each integrally linked and influencing the war on the ground.

In 1914 when war broke out in Europe, sub-Saharan Africa was divided under the control of five European powers – Britain, Germany, Portugal, Belgium and France. Of the territories, Britain controlled the majority in some form – either directly or through chartered companies. British influence dominated southern and eastern Africa except for German South West Africa and Portuguese Angola in the south-west and Portuguese and German East Africa on the eastern side. The centre of the continent was dominated by Belgium which controlled the Congo while West Africa was relatively evenly split between Britain and France with some German and Portuguese influence.

In Africa, there tended to be some co-operation between the European powers to protect the position of the white man who was outnumbered by black, Indian and Arab. The years prior to the outbreak of war had seen numerous wars to subjugate the recalcitrant masses and force subservience. In Europe, the powers worked together to support the position of their citizens in Africa but were also prepared to undermine each other for territorial and economic advantage wherever possible. Of the southern and eastern African territories, those of South Africa, German and British East Africa, Uganda and the Congo were seen as most valuable to the European countries with Britain desiring German East Africa and the Portuguese territories in particular so as to own a continuous strip of land from Cape Town to Cairo. Competing against British interests was the German desire for either British or Belgian and Portuguese territory to join its two sub-Saharan German colonies across the breadth of Africa. The most developed territory under discussion, South Africa, was interested in incorporating neighbouring German, Portuguese and British territories into its fold, at least to the Zambezi River. This, no doubt, resulted in increased tensions in the area as well as between the associated European powers.

Lettow-Vorbeck and Smuts

Before looking at the background of each of the territories directly involved in the campaign to understand why they would consider taking up arms in the great conflict at the risk of undermining the position of the white man, it seems opportune to introduce the two lead protagonists: General Paul von Lettow-Vorbeck and his 1916 adversary, General Jan Smuts, Deputy Prime Minister of South Africa and Minister of Defence. Although they only got to meet in 1929 for the first time, their paths had overlapped since 1903 when Lettow-Vorbeck was posted to South West Africa and 'gained abundant personal experience [...] of Boers, both on the Staff of General von [sic] Botha and as an independent Company and Detachment Commander.'[16]

Lettow-Vorbeck was born on 20 March 1870 in Saarlouis, Germany, and having spent some years at Oxford University (his mother was Scottish) followed his father into the German War Academy in 1888. His adversary Smuts, two months his junior, was born on 24 May 1870 in Malmesbury, Cape Colony, studied law and became a Boer commander in 1900/1 during the Anglo-Boer or South African War. Lettow-Vorbeck was posted to Africa in 1903, although Dolbey claims that he was involved in southern Africa even earlier: 'Before the war in South Africa, rumour says, he was instructor to the "Staats Artillerie," which Kruger [President of the Zuid-Afrikaanse Republiek] raised to stay the storm that he knew inevitably would overwhelm him. Serving, with Smuts and Botha themselves in the early months of the Boer war, he joined the inglorious procession of foreigners that fled across the bridge at Komati Poort after Pretoria fell, and left the Boer to fight it out unaided for two long and weary years more.'[17] Evidence and timeframes suggest, however, that he was on the German General Staff based in Berlin, updating the German government on what was happening during the 1899–1901 war.[18] A short sojourn in Germany saw Lettow-Vorbeck return to Africa, firstly for a brief period in the Cameroons in 1913 and then to East Africa in 1914. During this time, Smuts and his colleague and friend, Louis Botha worked to obtain independence for their defeated country, which they did in 1906, followed by the formation of Union in 1910. In 1910, Botha became Prime Minister and Smuts his deputy with responsibility for the Union's armed forces.

When war broke out in 1914, Lettow-Vorbeck gathered together the troops he had and set about attracting as many allied forces to East Africa as possible to assist Germany's struggle in Europe. The war in East Africa officially ended on 25 November 1918 when Lettow-Vorbeck surrendered in accordance with the armistice instructions from Germany. In March 1919, he returned to Germany, the only undefeated German general of the First World War and retired from the army in 1920, to enter politics as a parliamentary deputy for the right wing or conservative German National People's Party.

Smuts started the war in the political arena helping to guide South Africa to declare war on German South West Africa in 1914 and where he took up arms in 1915 before returning to the political scene and taking the field in German East Africa. He went to London in 1917 to attend the British Imperial War meetings and stayed there for the remainder of the war and peace discussions, returning to South Africa as premier in 1919 following Louis Botha's death from the influenza on 27 August 1919.

The campaign in East Africa started when the port of Dar-es-Salaam was shelled on 8 August 1914. Despite this attack and the German occupation of the British town of Taveta later in the month, a period of calm ensued whilst both colonies and their home governments took stock of the war on land. In November 1914, Britain attempted to re-launch the campaign with an attack on Tanga and Longido. But, for various reasons, mainly the lack of available manpower, the theatre quietened down again until February 1916 when Jan Smuts took command of the combined British forces and started his chase after Lettow-Vorbeck. The chase lasted a year before Smuts left for South Africa and Europe. In London he continued to influence the campaign, bringing about a change in commander from his successor General Hoskins to the South African van Deventer. The latter, having been absent from the campaign for about five months, saw the campaign move into Portuguese East Africa and to its end in Northern Rhodesia.

There is no record of Smuts and Lettow-Vorbeck meeting apart from in 1929 in London. However, their paths continued to cross. In 1945 Smuts and others were sending Lettow-Vorbeck food parcels after the latter was put on the Nazi blacklist following the 20 July 1944 bomb plot against Hitler.[19] In 1953, after Smuts' death, Lettow-Vorbeck visited the battlegrounds of South West Africa, then under South African rule, and East Africa renamed Tanganyika and under British mandate. Listowell maintains it was Smuts who invited Lettow-Vorbeck to visit Africa in 1953 after tracking him down in Hamburg in 1951.[20] This is unlikely as Smuts died on 11 September 1950 at the age of 87, although he did write to Lettow-Vorbeck on 15 May 1950.[21] Lettow-Vorbeck died in Hamburg on 9 March 1964 at the age of 98. The lifetime of these two men, whose paths crossed at various times over the African continent, saw the dividing of Africa between the European powers, a redefining of these relationships and at the time of Lettow-Vorbeck's death, the first African colonies achieve independence.

Terminology

One of the difficulties many authors of African history face is that of terminology, especially when dealing with pre- and post-colonial periods. Over time various terms and descriptors have been used for different groups of people at different times. In an attempt to reduce confusion and to stay true to the period, the terms used at the time being written about have been maintained. Although these terms are not necessarily those in use today and in some cases are frowned upon, their use in no way has any political or other connotation. Therefore the words black, white, native, Indian, South African (English, Afrikaans, British), Boer and non-white used in this text are purely descriptors to aid the understanding of the period.

In the text, reference has been made to the 1899–1901 war between Britain and the two southern African Boer Republics, although on occasion Southern African, Anglo-Boer and Boer War have been used. In current South African texts the war is referred to as the South African War, but, it does not appear that this practice has extended to the United Kingdom.

Composition of the forces

The composition below is based on what the British army worked to during World War One. However, the circumstances of the campaign in East Africa meant there were variations depending on what manpower could be raised. Nevertheless, the table in next page gives some idea of how the different military ranks linked together.[22] The German forces or *Schutztruppe* were organised into fourteen Field Companies (*Feldkompagnien*). These were made up of mobile company columns, each column having 2 officers, 1 doctor, 2 German non-commissioned officers, 150 askari, 2 machine guns, 322 carriers, 100 askari 'boys' and 13 European 'boys'. European volunteers formed *Schutzkompagnie* of 40–120 men.[23]

	Consisting of	Leader/commander
Section	6–8 privates, riflemen or guardsmen	Corporal Lance Corporal (deputy)
Platoon or Troop (Mounted Infantry & Cavalry, Engineers, Artillery)	4 Sections Total of 32 men	Subaltern (Lieutenant or 2nd Lieutenant) Sergeant in support NCO – NonCommissioned Officer
Company or Squadron (Mounted Infantry & Cavalry, Engineers) or Battery (Artillery)	3 or 4 Platoons, troops or sections of machine guns Total of up to 130 men Transport for a Machine Gun Company in EA: 4 porters to carry gun parts and ammunition 15 porters per gun to carry ammunition 3 mules per gun to carry reserve ammunition	Major Captain = 2nd in command Company Sergeant Major (Warrant Officer Class 2) Company Quartermaster Sergeant
Battalion or Regiment (Indian Army, Mounted Infantry & Cavalry, Engineers, Artillery)	4 Companies Machine Gun Section Head Quarters (signallers, cooks, drivers, regimental police, clerks, storemen, medical personnel) Total between 500 and 800 men	Lieutenant Colonel (Commanding Officer) Senior Major = 2nd in command Adjutant (senior Captain) Regimental Sergeant Major (Warrant Officer Class 1) Quartermaster (Lieutenant or Captain) Regimental Quartermaster Sergeant (Warrant Officer Class 2) Orderly Room Staff Sergeant (Warrant Officer Class 2)

Unit	Composition	Commander
Brigade or Regiment	3–5 Battalions Transport company and others as needed 3 Batteries (one battery = between 2 & 6 guns): Indian army mountain battery contained 3 sections each of 2 guns = 6 guns South African battery = 4 guns No 1 Light Battery, later No 6 Battery (Loyal North Lancashires) = 2 guns	Brigadier General
Division	3 Brigades Own artillery – 3 or 4 batteries Communication unit; Transport; Cavalry Squadron; Field Ambulance	Major General
Corps (not in EA)	2–4 Divisions	Lieutenant General
Armies (not in EA)	2+ Corps	General

Main Players in the war in East and southern Africa, 1914–1919 (for others, see name index)

	Pre-War	War (8.1914)	1915	1916	1917	1918	1919
Great Britain							
Prime Minister	HH Asquith (1909–7.12.16)		Asquith (Coalition 7.6.15)		D Lloyd George (7.12.16–1922)		
SoS War	Lord Haldane	HH Asquith/ HH Kitchener (6.8.14–5.6.16)	HH Asquith (Nov)	Asquith 5.6.16–7.7.16; D Lloyd George (7.7.16–10.12.16)	Lord Derby (11.12.16–19.4.18)	A Milner (20.4.18)	WS Churchill
First Lord	WS Churchill (24.10.11–27.5.15)		AJ Balfour		E Carson	A Geddes	
First Sea Lord	H Jackson						
SoS Colonies	L Harcourt (1910–1915)		A Bonar Law (31.5.15–12.1916)		W Long (12.1916–1919)		A Milner (1918–1920)
SoS FO	E Grey (1905–12.16)			Lord Crewe (Acting)	AJ Balfour (11.12.16–1.19)		
SoS India	Lord Crewe (5.11–5.15)		A Chamberlain (5.15–7.17)		Lord Montagu (7.17–3.22)		
Viceroy	C Hardinge (10.10–4.16)			Lord Chelmsford (4.16–4.21)			
War Office							
CIGS	CWH Douglas (6.4.14–25.10.14)	J Murray (26.10.14–26.9.15)	AJ Murray (27.9.15–22.12.15)	W Robertson (23.12.15–18.2.18)		H Wilson (18.2.18)	

	Pre-War	War (8.1914)	1915	1916	1917	1918	1919
DMO/I	C Callwell (1914–1916)			Macdonough (DMI) (1916–1918) Maurice (DMO) (1915–1918)		W T Fuse (1918–)	
Sec to CID	MPA Hankey						
Foreign Office							
Under SoS FA			R Cecil (30.5.15–10.1.19)				
Under SoS FO	E Crowe (11.1.12–1919)						
Permt Under SoS	A Nicholson			C Hardinge (20.6.16–1920)			
Sec for overseas trade					A Steel Maitland (20.10.17–1919)		
Amb to France	Lord Bertie (19.5–19.4.18)					Lord Derby (20.4.18–1920)	
Envoy to Belgium	FH Villiers (1911–1919)						
Amb to Portugal	L Carnegie (1913–1928)						
Consul in LM	EN MacDonell (~1900–1919)						

	Pre-War	War (8.1914)	1915	1916	1917	1918	1919
Colonial Office							
Private Secretary	JCC Davidson (1910–12.16)			HF Batterbee (1916–1919)			
Permt Under SoS	P Anderson (1911–2.16)			GV Fiddes (2.16–1921)			
Asst Und Sec	G Fiddes (CO) (1909–1916) HW Just (Dominions) (1909–1916)			G Grindle (1916–1925)			
Parl Und Sec	A Emmott (10.11–1915)		A Steel Maitland (1915–1917)				LS Amery
Governor BEA	HC Belfield (1912–4.17)				CC Bowring (Act 4.17–31.12.18)		E Northey (1.1.19–)
Governor Nyasaland	G Smith (23.9.13–12.4.23)						
Governor Uganda	F Jackson (1911–1918)						R Coryndon (1918–1922)
South Africa & BSA Co territories							
Governor General	H Gladstone/H De Villiers (31.5.10–14.7.14)(Act)		S Buxton (9.9.14–1924)				

	Pre-War	War (8.1914)	1915	1916	1917	1918	1919
Prime Minister	L Bctha (31.5.1?–19.8.19)		FS Malan (Act 4.15–7.15)	FS Malan (Act 6.16–9.16)			JC Smuts (8.19–1924)
Deputy PM	JC Smuts (31.5.10–19.8.19)						
Min of Defence	JC Smuts (31.5.1?–19.8.19)			L Botha (Act 2.1916–1919)			
UnderSec Def	HRM Bourne C Thompson						
Min of Lands	FS Malan						
Min of Finance	JC Srruts			JX Merriman			
GiC SA	W Murray		C Thompson			Martyn (2.3.18–)	
SA HC to UK	De Villiers						
SA HC	H Gladstone W Murray (31.5.10–4.7.14) (Act)	S Buxton (9.9.14–1924)	W Schreiner				
Administrator		D Chaplin (24.12.14–)					
Commanders							
British East Africa		AE Aitken (–22.11.14) R Wapshare (22.11.14–3.4.15)	MJ Tighe (4.4.15–26.11.15) A Smith-Dorrien (27.11.15–3.2.16)	JC Smuts (19.2.16–20.1.17)	RA Hoskins (20.1.17–1.6.17)	J v Deventer (1.6.17–1919)	

	Pre-War	War (8.1914)	1915	1916	1917	1918	1919
Northern Rhodesia/Nyasaland			E Northey (1915–1918)				
Cape Squadron	HG King-Hall (11.15–)						
EA Squadron		FW Caufeild (11.15–)					
India							
Military Sec to IO	E Barrow (1914–1917)						
Belgium							
King	Albert						
Prime Minister			C De Broqueville (1.16–)				
Foreign Minister	J Davignon/ NE Beyens (Act 7.15–)		NE Beyens (1.16–8.17)	C De Broqueville (8.17–1.18)		P Hymans (1.18–)	
Colonial Minister	J Renkin						
Dipl Counsellor	P Orts					Baron Moncheur (18.9.18–)	

	Pre-War	War (8.1914)	1915	1916	1917	1918	1919
Acting Sec Gen Min to London		P Hymans (5.15–17.1.16)				P Orts	
Min without Port			P Hymans (18.1.16–)				
Supreme Military Commander	C Torrbeur						
Commanders			AC Huyghé Josué Henry G Stinghlamber	F Olsen G Moulaert			
Portugal President					S Pais		J do Cento e Castro (12.18–10.19)
Min Foreign Affairs	D'Andrade					Monitz	
Gov Gen PEA	AX de Castro						
Expeditionary Force		PF de Amorim	M Mendes (8.15)	JCF Gil	PF de Amorim TS Rosa		
Governor Angola	N de Matos (1913–1915)		P d'Eca				
Angola Commander		A Rocadas	P d'Eca				

	Pre-War	War (8.1914)	1915	1916	1917	1918	1919
France							
President	G Clemenceau						
Prime Minister				Ribot (9.16–)			
Sec Gen Quay d'Orsay	J Cambon (–1917)						
United States of America							
President	W Wilson						
President emissary	House						

Main events of the war in East and southern Africa, 1914–1918

Date	Southern Africa	Central Africa	East Africa	On the water
29 Jul 1914		Precautionary measures	Precautionary measures	
31 Jul 1914				*Königsberg* leaves Dar-es-Salaam
5 Aug 1914	At war	At war	At war; EAMR form CID meet re colonies	
8 Aug 1914				*Astrea* shells Dar-es-Salaam
10 Aug 1914	Germans raid Cape from SWA SA agrees to occupy Swakopmund and Luderitzbucht			
13 Aug 1914				*Gwendolin* disables *Hermann von Wissmann* on Lake Nyasa
14 Aug 1914				*Hedwig von Wissmann* attacks Congo *Percy Anderson* captures German dhow on Lake Victoria
15 Aug 1914	De la Rey at Treurfontein		Germans capture Tavera	
17 Aug 1914				*Pegasus* raids Tanga
21 Aug 1914	Germans cross Orange River			
24 Aug 1914			Germans invade PEA (Mazimbwa)	
1 Sep 1914			IEF C arrives at Mombasa	

Date	Southern Africa	Central Africa	East Africa	On the water
5 Sep 1914		Germans repulsed at Abercorn		*Guendolin* captures Old Langenburg on Lake Nyasa
8 Sep 1914	Buxton becomes Governor General	Buxton becomes High Commissioner		
13 Sep 1914				*Kavirondo* action on Lake Victoria
15 Sep 1914	Rebellion breaks out	1st Rhodesian Regiment recruiting opens		Germans leave Mwanza on Lake Victoria
17 Sep 1914	Germans cross at Nakob			
18 Sep 1914	Beves occupies Luderitzbucht			
20 Sep 1914				*Königsberg* sinks *Pegasus* in Zanzibar harbour
21 Sep 1914		Schuckmannsburg in Caprivi Strip occupied		
22 Sep 1914	Botha becomes CiC			
24 Sep 1914				Germans seize Belgian island on Lake Kivu
26 Sep 1914	South Africans defeated at Sandfontein			
12 Oct 1914	Martial law proclaimed			
19 Oct 1914	Germans killed at Naulila (Angola)			
31 Oct 1914			IEF B reaches Mombasa	*Königsberg* located in Rufiji River

Date	Southern Africa	Central Africa	East Africa	On the water
2 Nov 1914			Battle of Tanga	
3 Nov 1914			Stewart repulsed at Longido	
17 Nov 1914			EAMR occupy Longido; Kitchener orders BEA onto defensive; Aitken replaced as CiC	
28 Nov 1914	SA ready to resume SWA campaign			Goliath and Fox attack Dar-es-Salaam
18 Dec 1914	Germans defeat Portuguese at Naulila			
25 Dec 1914	1st Rhodesian Regiment arrive at Walvis Bay		British attack Jasin	
31 Dec 1915	Defence Act permits conscription			
10 Jan 1915			British occupy Mafia Island	
18 Jan 1915			Germans take Jasin	
23 Jan 1915		Chilembwe uprising		
3 Feb 1915	Last rebels surrender			
29 Mar 1915			British beaten at Salaita	
14 Apr 1915				Kronborg cargo salvaged after attack by Hyacinth
15 Apr 1915			Tighe becomes CiC	
6 Jul 1915	Draft surrender terms given to Seitz			Mersey & Severn attack Königsberg
9 Jul 1915	Germans surrender in SWA			

Date	Southern Africa	Central Africa	East Africa	On the water
11 Jul 1915				*Königsberg* disabled
14 Jul 1915			Attack on Mbuyuni	
8 Sep 1915			Settlers vote for conscription	
28 Oct 1915				Spicer-Simson flotillas launched on Lake Tanganyika
1 Nov 1915	SA offers troops for EA			
12 Nov 1915		Northey appointed GOC Rhodesia & Nyasaland forces	CID supports action against GEA	
22 Nov 1915			Smith Dorrien appointed GOC	
6 Jan 1916		Anglo-Belgian conference	Smuts appointed GOC	
12 Feb 1916			Battle of Salaita Hill	
19 Feb 1916			Smuts arrives in BEA	
5 Mar 1916			Kilimanjaro campaign starts	
16 Mar 1916				*Marie* offloads cargo at Sudi Bay
18 Mar 1916			Smuts advance on Usambara railway starts	
6 Apr 1916		Portuguese occupy Kionga		

Date	Southern Africa	Central Africa	East Africa	On the water
18 Apr 1916			South Africans take Kondoa Irangi	
19 Apr 1916			Belgians invade Ruanda	
1 May 1916		1st Native Regt formed for EA		
9 May 1916			Battle of Kondoa Irangi	
1 Jun 1916			Belgians invade Urundi	
7 Jul 1916				Tanga occupied by Royal Navy and Indian Infantry
26 Jul 1916			Gold Coast Regiment arrives	
27 Jul 1916			2nd West Indian Regiment arrives	
26 Aug 1916			Morogoro occupied by British	
4 Sep 1916				Dar-es-Salaam occupied
19 Sep 1916			Belgians occupy Tabora	
26 Nov 1916		Wahle surrenders Lake Nyasa		
10 Dec 1916			Nigerian Brigade arrives	
20 Jan 1917			Hoskins becomes CiC	
1 Mar 1917			Compulsory Service Act in BEA and Uganda	

Date	Southern Africa	Central Africa	East Africa	On the water
21 May 1917			Wingens captured at Tabora; Naumann takes over	
30 May 1917			Van Deventer becomes CiC	
19 Jul 1917			Battle of Narumgombe	
2 Oct 1917			Naumann surrenders	
15 Oct 1917			Battle of Nyangao/Mahiwa	
23 Nov 1917			Zeppelin L-59 leaves Bulgaria	
25 Nov 1917			Germans cross into PEA	
28 Nov 1917			Tafel surrenders; all GEA in British/Allied hands	
20 Jun 1918		Northey appointed Governor and CiC of BEA; Hawthorn replaces him on NRFF		
1 Jul 1918			Battle of Nhamacurra (PEA)	
30 Aug 1918			Battle of Lioma	
28 Sep 1918			Germans re-enter GEA	
2 Nov 1918			Attack on Fife; Germans enter Northern Rhodesia	
12 Nov 1918			Action at Kasama	
14 Nov 1918			Hostilities cease	
25 Nov 1918			Germans surrender	

Adapted from R Gray with C Argyle, *Chronicle of the First World War, vols 1 and 2* (Facts on File, Oxford, 1991)

CHAPTER 1

POSITION ON THE EVE
OF WAR

When the European countries declared war against each other, their dependencies were automatically drawn into the conflict, although some could determine the extent to which they would be involved. This situation was to have advantages and disadvantages for both the motherlands and their dependencies, especially where the dependency saw an opportunity to take advantage of the turmoil in Europe to further local aims. The colonies were meant to support the motherland by supplying natural resources and be an outlet for manufactured goods. During war, people become a natural resource to be exploited, and as the European countries were broadly evenly balanced in military strength, other means had to be found to break the deadlock. As Churchill told parliament in 1921 'the commodities which they [the colonies] produced were in many cases vital to the maintenance of the industries, and particularly the war industries, of Britain and her Allies'.[1] Involving subordinate territories in conflict, though, was not an easy or sudden decision. Britain, for example, had considered defence schemes on a colonial and regional level from before the turn of the century. These schemes covered the importance of the territory in economic terms, how much each territory would cost to defend and if there was any strategic reason why the area should be defended over and above it being British. This chapter looks at the different interests and relationships each of the imperial and colonial countries had in

East and southern Africa prior to the outbreak of war. Understanding the prevailing situation on the eve of war will help determine why the area became involved in the conflict and what each country hoped to achieve.

Although Britain controlled the largest percentage of land in the area under discussion, each British territory was governed differently, with all being administered by the Colonial Office in London. The Union of South Africa was classified as a dominion and had control of its internal policy. It had an elected lower house, an appointed upper house and was led by a prime minister who liaised with Britain through a Governor General. Until July 1914 this was Herbert Gladstone and from 8 September 1914 Sydney Buxton, with Lord Chief Justice Henry de Villiers and Attorney General James Rose Innes acting between. The Governor General was also High Commissioner for the Protectorates of Bechuanaland, Basotholand and Swaziland and for the British South Africa Company territories of Northern and Southern Rhodesia. Between July and September, however, General Wolfe Murray was acting High Commissioner. Of the other territories, Nyasaland was a protectorate overseen by Governor Sir George Smith from 1913, as was British East Africa which had been governed by Sir Henry C Belfield from 1912 when Sir Percy Girouard resigned.

After Britain, Germany was the next largest imperial power in Africa, overseeing nine million square miles and a population totalling 13 million.[2] Initially Germany had no interest in the African continent, but during the scramble for Africa in 1884, Otto von Bismarck, the Chancellor of Germany decided to obtain territory in East and southern Africa. This brought the German empire into potential conflict with Britain, a situation which was averted through negotiation as Britain determined compromise was of greater value at the time than war.[3] Control of the German colonies was managed by the Foreign Office based Kolonialabteilung in Berlin to which the governors reported. In the colonies, the military was subordinate to the political leadership, a situation which was to impact on the campaign in East Africa.[4]

British interest in East Africa dated back to 1884, when Sir Percy Anderson of the Foreign Office and others considered the value of the

territory in preparation for the Berlin Colonial Conference. At that
time, the territory, and, in particular, Zanzibar was valued for trade
potential. However, this interest soon extended to protecting the
Suez Canal and the shorter route to India and the Far East. Initially,
William MacKinnon's Imperial British East Africa Company was
granted permission to develop the area, which included building the
Uganda railway. When the company faltered in 1894, Britain took
over direct control rather than allow another country, particularly
Germany, or company to obtain it. In addition to obtaining the profits
which derived from Indian trading, maintaining control of the territory
would ensure Britain had easier access to Uganda which in turn would
provide access to the source of the Nile, protecting Egypt and the
Suez route to India. Having taken control of the colony Britain completed the Uganda railway, 'sparing no expense' to ensure it, Britain,
remained ahead of its then rival, France.[5]

The railway, opened in December 1901, enabled troops and equipment to be moved inland more quickly and reduced the cost of transporting goods to the coast. The line's construction led to an increase
in Indian immigration as opportunities for work and trade opened.
At this time there were approximately 25,000 Indians involved in
trade, administration and money lending, 5,000 whites farming and
4,083,000 natives. In 1905, the Foreign Office handed over control of
the protectorate to the Colonial Office, and the colony as it was now
designated was overseen by a governor. This change in management
did not affect the territory's geopolitical significance and it remained
an item for discussion in London whenever these took place over the
empire's defence.

Germany too, took an interest in building railways. In East Africa,
between 1893 and 1905, the Usambara railway was built from Tanga to
Korogwe and Mombo and by 1912 the line reached New Moschi, while
the Central line from Dar-es-Salaam to Kigoma on Lake Tanganyika
took from 1904 to 1914 to complete. Whilst these lines were being
built the Germans were dependent on the British Uganda line for
transporting goods which added to the affinity both territories held
for each other.[6] The Portuguese railways were still being constructed
although there was a line going from Southern Rhodesia through to

Beira. In West Africa, the Benguela line was only completed in 1926. The Belgian line extended to Lukuga, twenty-nine kilometres short of Lake Tanganyika.[7] Of all the railways in Africa, the South African railways were the most developed, reaching into Southern Rhodesia.

Development of the area was economically important for the various colonial powers. Therefore, in 1885, Britain, Germany and Belgium agreed to a neutrality clause in what became known as the Congo or Berlin Act which applied to British and German East Africa, the Congo and Uganda. If war broke out in Europe, the territories making up the Free Trade Zone governed by the Act would remain neutral, providing all the relevant European belligerent countries agreed.[8] This stance accorded with the British imperial defence policy determined by the Duke of Devonshire in 1896 which emphasised the role of the British Admiralty. It was only in 1908 that East Africa began to feature in imperial defence discussions when it was acknowledged that Zanzibar was 'one of the finest [ports] in Africa and [...] seen as the centre of commerce between Arabia, India and Africa.'[9]

Despite the area's lack of strategic importance the British government drew up plans in 1897 to conquer German East Africa. This change in relationship between the two colonial powers had been initiated by the threat of war in southern Africa as Germany was believed to be supporting the Boers in the Zuid-Afrikaanse Republiek and Orange Free State by supplying Mausers.[10] At the same time, Germany's navy was beginning to pose a direct threat to British power. However, before Britain was prepared to declare war over the German territory, it had to be guaranteed that it would obtain the German territory afterwards, giving Britain control of a continuous line of territory from Cape Town to Cairo.[11] Although this would ease economic relations between the various British African territories, the defeat of German East Africa was less important than the defence of Egypt in protecting the Suez route to India and the East.

By 1911, the position regarding the defence schemes had altered little, although discussions in London centred on the number of troops needed to protect East Africa and who would pay for them. The clash was between the Colonial Office, which felt internal security issues dominated, and the War Office which feared an attack from neighbouring countries. The outcome was that, if needed, the War Office would supply additional troops to East Africa and that the Imperial government would pay the bill. The need for these additional troops was believed to be minimal providing Britain retained command of the seas as Germany would not be able to send reinforcements to the African continent. Of more specific interest, was the position of Zanzibar where the underwater cables surfaced. The cable ran from Aden to Zanzibar and then onto Durban in South Africa. Lewis Harcourt, Colonial Secretary, felt that if Zanzibar was threatened by another power, the cable should be moved to Mombasa or another British base. In an emergency, the cables could be cut although this seemed unlikely given Germany's interest and need for the cable too. The outcome of the 1911 discussions was a reluctance to declare East Africa neutral given that the British public would not accept the loss of Zanzibar, important to protecting the Indian Ocean trade routes, without obtaining some other territory, and the only territory Britain felt worthwhile was Ruanda.[12]

Although the defence schemes to conquer German East Africa had been completed, by 1908 the 1905 scheme had not been approved by British East African Governor Sir Percy Girouard and in 1911 the authorities in London were still trying to get information on the German East African defences. The then Consul, Norman King, had obtained the information, but due to the pacifist tendencies of individuals within the British colony, these had not been passed onto London. The colonial officials felt they were supported by the Foreign Office position that war 'would endanger the whole civilisation process and be of great detriment to the prestige of the white races.'[13] Added to this was the realisation that in 'both East and West Africa not a year [passed] without at least one small war, [being] undertaken to restore order'.[14] That the fear of uprisings was of particular concern to all colonial governments in Africa was evidenced by the fact that the two local governments, British and German East Africa, agreed that they would support each other in case of this eventuality.[15]

Having designed plans to conquer German East Africa, the idea of declaring the territory neutral under the terms of the Berlin Act was reviewed annually in Britain by the Colonial Defence Committee reporting to the Committee of Imperial Defence. Similarly, the German General Staff was sufficiently open-minded to recognise that Britain would not necessarily adhere to keeping its territories neutral and this led to a contingency being worked out on the basis that supplies from Germany would be limited, if not non-existent. As with the British plan, the Germans took into account both the external threat from another country and the possibility of an internal native uprising. However, given the need for troops in Europe, the German colony would have to become self-sufficient.[16] Two dominant arguments influenced the debates in both countries and presumably in the others too: neutrality would enable the colonies to develop economically, yet if natives saw white men killing each other, this would damage their prestige and undermine their authority. War, however, would enable the empires to expand. The solution, therefore, was to leave the situation as it was until the actions of another country forced the issue, particularly as the balance of power was changing and Britain was indecisive as to whether France or Germany was the biggest threat to its interests.

The position of neutrality had been further reinforced when Britain acknowledged that of the German colonies, German East Africa was the most important but during a war it was unlikely reinforcements would be sent out.[17] Of all the German colonies, the only one likely to become belligerent would be German South West Africa in the hope of initiating a rebellion among the Boers in South Africa. Given the choice, the Kaiser had decided that German South West Africa could be sacrificed to maintain German East Africa: 'There was a secret memorandum, dated 1891, that the Director of the Colonial Department kept in a sealed envelope: "The Emperor is prepared to give up South-West Africa if necessary, so that all energies may be focused on East Africa."'[18] At this time, Dar-es-Salaam, in German East Africa, was an important coaling and telegraphic station which made it a threat to British shipping in the Indian Ocean and Persian Gulf. It also 'formed the missing link in Britain possessing territory across the length of Africa, while ensuring for Germany a continuous line of possessions across the African continent, provided that it gained part of the Belgian Congo.'[19]

It was inevitable, therefore, that the two imperial countries would eventually clash over their territorial desires, yet they were prepared to work together against other imperial powers to further their own goals. Germany and Britain agreed in 1898, and reaffirmed in 1913 but did not ratify, that if Portugal defaulted on its loans to the two countries they would divide Portuguese East Africa and Angola between themselves.[20] Given that the initial agreement was made the year after plans were determined to defeat German East Africa, it seems that Britain's desire for African territory was greater than its concern with Germany supporting the Boers in South Africa. Despite this agreement with Germany, in 1906 the British Liberals reaffirmed the 1386 treaty and the 1898 Treaty of Windsor to protect Portugal against losing its colonies. The Treaty of Windsor in effect nullified the Anglo-German agreement as it was concluded after the latter.[21] To complicate matters, there were questions over the validity of the 1906/1898 treaty as Portugal became a republic in 1910 and Britain was not quite clear in itself whether it acknowledged the new government. Until that decision was made, all agreements were in limbo despite the Portuguese government's attitude that legislation passed by the monarchy still held unless changed.[22]

Portugal had two main colonies in Africa – Angola in the west and Portuguese East Africa, now Moçambique. Although the country could ill-afford to retain its colonial empire, it would not part with any territory due to the loss of prestige this would entail and the political outcry there would be in Portugal. The colonies were regarded as integral parts of the motherland. However, the men sent out to colonise the territory and administer it were not expected to return to the mother country as they were often undesirables which Portugal was keen to get rid of.[23] This resulted in little attention being given to what was happening and unlike British, German and French colonies, there was much mixing between the races and mistreatment of the indigenous peoples. However, the tensions between the local administrators, military, company directors and the home government were no different to those experienced by the other colonial powers, except perhaps that the Portuguese government was too weak and fragile to actually maintain any semblance of order. In addition to the uncoordinated management style within and across each region, the Portuguese army was poorly regarded. The senior military officers were appointed based on their political standing and as Portugal was going through a stage of changing governments every six months or so, military officers changed regularly. This meant that invariably the commander had very little military experience, there was no cohesive military policy and the troops were often adjusting to new leaders.[24]

Portugal had few desires in Africa. Initially, the country had hoped to 'join Angola and Moçambique through austral Africa potentially to form a second Brazil'. However, as its power deteriorated so did this idea.[25] As a result, Portugal became more dogmatic about retaining the territory it had and preventing Britain and Germany from acquiring it. Yet if the opportunity arose, Portugal wanted to obtain what was called the Kionga Triangle – a piece of land around the Rovuma River that it believed Germany had stolen in the carving up of Africa.[26] Apart from this, the country was to some extent reliant on Britain as to how involved it could get in time of war as Britain would have to supply most of the military equipment and finances. In addition, there were concerns that if Britain, Portugal's ally attacked a country which Spain supported, Portugal would need to be protected against its age-old enemy.

Another country Portugal needed protecting against was the Union of South Africa.[27] Following the Union's formation, Portugal became more wary of South Africa's intentions regarding its East African territory. Agreements existed between the two countries, renewed shortly before Union in 1909, whereby the Transvaal would receive 'volunteer' labour for the mines and South Africa would send goods over the Lorenço Marques railway.[28] South Africa wanted this railway, of which, Portugal was fully aware. British Foreign Secretary, Edward Grey, was conscious of this fact too. He wrote to the British Ambassador in Berlin, Sir William Goshen, on 29 December 1911 that 'the Union of South Africa will never rest so long as she (Portugal) has Delagoa Bay: on every ground, material, moral and even Portuguese, it would be better that Portugal should at once sell her colonies. *But* how can we of all people put pressure on Portugal to sell: we who are bound by an alliance to protect and preserve her colonies for Portugal – an alliance renewed secretly for value received during the Boer War?'[29]

Another country which had concerns about South African intentions was Belgium. Belgium assumed control of the Congo from King Leopold in 1908 following pressure from Britain and the United States of America. This had been due to the king's mismanagement of the territory and poor human rights record, even for that time.[30] Belgium, having recently assumed control of the territory, was therefore keen to keep the Congo neutral as the mother country was so small it would be unable to send troops to support the colony in time of war, even though it already had the largest number of troops present in Africa. The Force Publique consisted of around 15,000 troops spread over twenty-six districts. Transport difficulties abounded with the troops being reliant on the Congo River and a railway which ended short of Lukuga on Lake Tanganyika.[31] However, once war was declared and Belgium became involved, the capture of territory to use at the negotiation table became an attractive option, especially when Germany occupied Belgian territory in Europe.

Further south, in Africa, each of the occupied territories had its own views, sometimes contrary to the home government, on how it should be managed and what it wanted in the future. When war broke out in 1914, these territories, although drawn into the conflict as subordinate to those in Europe, saw an opportunity to further their own aims. Therefore, understanding what their motivations were and the territory's relationships with neighbouring countries should prove useful.

Starting in the north, Uganda was of particular interest to the colonial powers for its access to the source of the Nile. At the close of the nineteenth century, it was believed that whoever controlled the Nile had control over Egypt. In April 1894, Britain declared Uganda a protectorate overcoming the protests of Germany, France and Belgium which had all been interested in the territory.[32] Uganda had a small settler community, a white volunteer reserve, and 4KAR (King's African Rifles) to deal with problems along the Sudanese border.[33]

Moving clockwise, bordering on Uganda was British East Africa. The colony was mainly settled by pseudo-aristocracy who had moved there for the adventure. As a result the colonials had access to influences in the House of Lords enabling them to by-pass the Colonial Office when it suited them, and which the Colonial Office found most annoying as the governors tended to support the colonials rather than their imperial employers.[34] Most of the colonials were settled in what was called the White Highlands and amongst those settlers from England there were Boers who had moved north following the 1899–1901 war in southern Africa. Some of these Boers had initially settled in German East Africa as they objected to British rule. However, after experiencing German colonial rule felt that they were better off under the British. Others had moved straight to the British East African colony as they had been sympathetic to Britain and had been ostracised by their fellow Boers.[35] The British East Africa colony had a battalion of King's African Rifles, 3KAR, but also funded 1KAR recruited in Nyasaland to garrison the British East Africa frontier.[36]

Before war erupted, there were only three King's African Rifle battalions in East Africa, spread across Uganda, British East Africa and Nyasaland. A fourth in Nyasaland, 2KAR, had recently been disbanded with its troops joining the German schutztruppe.[37] The British East African territories were therefore unable to defend themselves against an external attack. A position realised when war broke out in 1914 with the officer commanding, Lieutenant-Colonel LES Ward stating that 'never was there a dependency of the English Crown so entirely unprepared for war.'[38] The situation was exacerbated with the Inspector General of the King's African Rifles, General AR Hoskins, being on leave in England from where he was sent to the Western Front. As Ward followed the news of events in Europe he predicted war would soon be declared and despite having retired from the regular forces, arranged to move down to Nairobi to assist as necessary before his replacement arrived. The governor claimed he had arranged this.[39] On the declaration of war, Ward assumed 'command of all the armed forces of the Crown in East Africa, Uganda and Zanzibar' as he was still on the active list and the most senior officer in the area.[40]

South of the British territory was German East Africa which Heinrich von Schnee, the governor since 1912, wanted to keep out of the war in order to continue developing it economically. Within the German system, the governor was in complete control of the colony, both administration and military, reporting into the Kolonialamt in Berlin. Although decisions had been made in Berlin to change this situation, the outbreak of war put paid to any implementation. This meant that when General Paul von Lettow-Vorbeck, commander of the German forces, arrived in German East Africa in January 1914, he was subordinate to the governor. With very different remits, the two men were bound to clash, as they did in preparing the colony for the eminent outbreak of war in Europe. In 1913 there were 5,336 white settlers in German East Africa of which 4,107 were German and 882 were planters and settlers of Afrikaner, Greek and Italian origin.[41] Of these, there were almost 2,700 white males of military age in the colony and 'a great number of retired military'.[42] The German colony, despite what Lettow-Vorbeck felt, would be able to hold its own for a while in the event of war.

Having arrived in the colony in January 1914, Lettow-Vorbeck set out to reconnoitre the territory and to prepare it for supporting the motherland when and if war in Europe erupted. He believed that Britain would disregard the neutrality act and set about making his plans accordingly,[43] but he 'did not succeed in arousing sufficient interest in the matter on the part of the authorities'. He had to fight against the 'ruling opinion [which] was that [the Germans] were on exceptionally good terms with the English, and that a war, if it came at all, was still in the distant future.'[44] His second tour, in April 1914, included a friendly visit to the Belgian Congo and following further trips around the country he discovered that 'A telegram could only reach [Neu] Langenburg from Dar-es-Salaam by the English line through South Africa',[45] showing how interlinked the whole of East, Central and Southern Africa was.

In addition to sharing communication channels, the two colonial powers seemed to accept askari or troops who had fought for the other side. This was notable when a battalion of King's African Rifles was disbanded in Nyasaland on the southern border of the German colony. With the Germans offering better pay than the British, it was inevitable that the askari would seek employment across the border. The German askari were employed for longer periods than their British counterparts and were also better known by their white officers who seemed to have a longer term of duty than the British officers. Another difference was that the British tended to move their troops around as needed, whereas the German troops were generally used to maintain order in a specific area. During the war, these relationships did not seem to make a marked difference between the strengths of the two sides, except that the German askari did remain rather surprisingly loyal as they moved further away from their traditional areas. So long as they were fed, clothed and paid, the askari would remain loyal.[46]

Moving further south, the German territory was bordered by Portuguese East Africa on the coast. Much of the country had not been explored and the 1,680 troops in the area were widely spread over the large territory. As mentioned earlier, there was little central command over these troops resulting in lax discipline. The Portuguese East African colony was split into regions, each managed differently depending on how the area had been obtained and subjugated. Moçambique province to the north of the Zambezi River was governed by a government-appointed governor. South of the Zambezi River was governed by the Moçambique Company while the territory in the far north between the Lurio River, bordering Moçambique Province and the Rovuma River was controlled, from 1912, by the Niassa Company. This territory in the north, bordering on the German colony was the most vulnerable and that least controlled by Portugal.[47]

Bordering on the west of the Portuguese territory and totally land-locked, was the British protectorate of Nyasaland. Its eastern neighbour was the chartered company territory of Northern Rhodesia.[48] Nyasaland had previously been administered by the Central Africa Company until 1907 when control moved to the Colonial Office. That same year, 1907, a defence scheme to protect the British territory against incursions from Germany and Portugal was put into place. The Governor, Sir George Smith, was newly appointed in 1913 and controlled the territory, consisting of approximately 800 whites and 300 Asians, with the support of various administrators. Although the country was relatively peaceful, there was an underlying discontent amongst the followers of John Chilembwe, an independent missionary, who was promoting 'Africa for the Africans'.[49] However, this discontent was not enough to elicit any concern amongst the leading settlers or the home government as noted by an official in the Colonial Office in response to Smith's actions on the declaration of war: 'Nyasaland would be the last community in Africa where there is likely to be any native trouble: the natives are peacefully disposed and very well content with British administration.'[50] There was only one battalion of King's African Rifles to help maintain order in what seemed to be a missionary-dominated environment; another battalion having been decommissioned in 1911.[51] In addition to the King's African Rifles, there was the Nyasaland Volunteer Reserve which consisted of 150 men and the 350 Native Police.[52]

At the most southern end of the continent was the Union of South Africa – a major player in the war in East and southern Africa and the home of Jan Smuts. One of the reasons that South Africa had been colonised was to provide a 'half way point to India'.[53] But by 1914, the importance of South Africa to world trade and military significance had deteriorated despite the claim in the official history of the German South West Africa campaign that South Africa was 'indispensible to any scheme of Empire defence'.[54] The opening of the Suez Canal and the discovery of gold and diamonds inland was the cause. Expansion to the interior of the continent meant that the cost of protecting the territory had outweighed its value, although this did not stop Britain from trying to obtain the goldfields of the Transvaal. Following the formation of Union on 31 May 1910, Britain was confident that there was no major threat from South Africa's neighbouring territories given the Union's strength and the fact that it was within the British Empire.[55]

The major threat to South Africa and Britain's empire in southern Africa was the internal disunity amongst the white population. By 1914, the country was into its second government. Louis Botha, the Prime Minister and leader of the South Africa Party, had called an election in 1912, two years into his first government, in order to rid his cabinet of James Barry Munich Hertzog who refused to resign following anti government outbursts on the position of empire. Hertzog had been the Attorney General of the Orange Free State during the 1899–1901 war and refused to reconcile with Britain. Early in 1914, he formed the National Party which became the Afrikaans anti-British voice in South Africa and quickly gained popularity. The white South African population was clearly divided into a loyal English speaking pro-Britain party, the Unionists led by Thomas Smartt, the pro-Empire South African party which contained both English and Afrikaans speakers and the National Party. Until the outbreak of war, the National Party was linked with the pro-British but anti-capitalist Labour Party which refused to support Botha's South Africa Party as they were too close to the mine-owners. However, on the outbreak of war, Thomas Creswell's Labour Party severed its relations with the Nationalists and sided with the South Africa Party.

Both parties, the National Party and South Africa Party, were nationalist, a position President Steyn of the Orange Free State distinguished by the terms 'high' nationalism which was that preferred by Hertzog and his followers and 'general' nationalism which was followed by Smuts and Botha.[56] The latter were prepared to support, and remain in, the British Empire so long as it worked in South Africa's favour. Of the parties in South Africa, the only genuinely national party in the country was Botha's South Africa Party while the others were all localised within one or two provinces. The South Africa Party had worked hard under its leaders, Louis Botha and his deputy Jan Smuts, to resolve the existing race problem at that time which was between the white English and Afrikaans (Boer) speakers. With the support of the mine-owners and leading politicians such as JX Merriman and Sir Percy Fitzpatrick who wanted to see the Union succeed within the British Empire, Botha and Smuts were able to win the 1910 and 1912 elections.[57]

When war broke out in 1914, South Africa's military and government systems were still in their infancy. Herbert Gladstone, Governor General from 17 May 1910 to July 1914 had tried to convince Botha to implement some order into the government of the country, but these attempts were ignored. Botha tended to run his government as he had before Union. He had a small cabinet of no more than ten members who met shortly before parliament was convened and on special occasions, although Spender claims Botha met his cabinet colleagues daily in Pretoria, and as they were in the same building, they 'frequently all had lunch together'.[58] Function was important: The role of the cabinet was to administer and that of parliament to pass legislation. Parliamentary success was determined by the speed with which parliamentary business was concluded, and as noted by the Round Table in

1914 it required 'strong leadership [...] to keep the House from frittering away its time,' which was not good for democracy as debate was curtailed.[59] Government of the country was split between two centres, Cape Town and Pretoria which were over one thousand kilometres apart. When the politicians were not in Cape Town for the parliamentary season or in Pretoria, they were touring their constituency or overseeing their farms. The result was that decisions were often taken by a small group of available politicians (over lunch) and mainly by Prime Minister Botha and his deputy Smuts who were more often in Pretoria. This arrangement meant that administrative functions had hardly developed and were unable to support the government as effectively as they should have done.

Although military systems were not fully developed by 1914, a cabinet post for defence had been created in 1910. Smuts filled the role and was provided with an undersecretary as his deputy. This position was filled by HRM Bourne who was based in the Department of the Interior. Bourne's role was 'central to all correspondence and communication among the War Office and its local commander, the Colonial Office and its local representatives, Smuts, and other interested parties.'[60] The situation was complicated by the fact that Bourne had no military background and that all support from Britain was oriented towards supporting the empire during a war so as to reduce the impact on the motherland. Additional complications within the Union revolved around the merging of two military systems, namely the dominant British system and the Boer commando system which after the 1899–1901 war had morphed into shooting clubs.[61]

The South Africa Defence Act brought the South African Defence Force into being in 1912. '[I]t was in essence a thorny fusion of Boer and Colonial forces with British instructors, representing in many ways three military traditions.' According to van der Waag, in 1913 there were six arms of the Defence Force 'placed under a divided command to protect sectarian interests and diminish the possibility of a coup; [Brigadier-General HT] Lukin the former Commandant of the Cape Colonial Forces, became Inspector-General of the Permanent Force, while [the] former Boer general, [Brigadier-General] CF Beyers, became Commandant General of the Citizen Force.' Various posts were then filled 'with friends and supporters' by some of the officers such as Beyers. This led to 'stunted development and war planning; and created distrust, even fission, in the new structures', especially when Beyers suggested that the Defence Force leadership was 'trying to make British soldiers of the people'.[62]

The formal creation of the Union Defence Force in 1912 meant an increase in personnel and improvisation when war broke out.[63] Bourne retained his position taking over the secretariat, whilst a general staff section was introduced for military organisation and an administrative section for logistics. The total South African military personnel numbered around 25,000.[64] Their task was to protect the country against external attacks with the police taking responsibility for internal control. Of the four possible identified threats against the Union, three concerned internal uprisings by the natives whilst only one was a fear of an attack by neighbouring German South West Africa. As an attack by the German colony would only likely happen in the event of Germany going to war with Britain, Botha had made it known to Britain that, if war was to break out, South Africa would be keen to use the opportunity to incorporate German South West Africa.[65] The fact that the borders of the Union had not been clearly defined in the 1910 Act, pending Rhodesia's incorporation, was to feature significantly in the early days of the Union's deliberations about declaring war on the German territory.[66] Interestingly, but not surprisingly, given the internal politics within the Union, whenever it came to military matters, both defensive and expansionist, the least of the concerns, internal native uprisings, was most promoted, even leading to those anti-empire citizens retaining their weapons during the war, a similar policy enacted in the German territories.[67]

Moving up the west coast of Africa and bordering on the Union, was German South West Africa. Germany had been given control over the South West Africa territory in 1888 by Britain, much to the disgust of various leading politicians in what became the Union. In response to their outcry, Britain conceded and retained the port of Walfish Bay which later became part of the Union territory and was to play an instrumental role in the naval campaign of German South West Africa.

German rule in South West Africa was piecemeal. A north-south divide had been introduced in the colony with the central and southern areas being known as the 'Police-Zone' following the Herero uprising of 1904/5 which Lettow-Vorbeck had been involved in quelling. Both halves were overseen by a governor, who from 1910 was Dr Theodore von Seitz. The Caprivi Strip (now part of Namibia) which extended a finger into the continent giving the Germans access to the Zambezi River, was owned by the British from Bechuanaland, but managed by the Germans. It only formally became part of the ex-German colony in 1931.[68] Communications within the German colony were good with the railway having been completed in 1910 and wireless stations being used extensively although not always securely. The problem was that the troops were split into small contingents to protect pockets of white settlers. They were thus prevented from forming a force to be reckoned with when attacked. To fool the South Africans into thinking there were more German troops than what there were, the Germans called their battalions, regiments. This seemed to have worked as the South Africans maintained the Germans had a force of around 7,000 troops as opposed to the official estimate of 5,000.[69]

North of the German colony, was the Portuguese colony of Angola. It had been a Portuguese colony for longer than Portuguese East Africa, yet its infrastructure was similar if not worse. It consisted of four provinces: Moçamedes, Huila, Cunene and Cuando Cubango. By the time the 1914 war broke out, the Benguela railway was still incomplete and the colony still undeveloped as it proved to be the most difficult of the African territories to subjugate.[70] Germany had desires over the territory and in November 1913 had determined to open a consul-general in Luanda which provided the German mission with an opportunity to research the area and identify weaknesses. They soon discovered that Governor General Norton de Matos (appointed in 1913) had few troops with which to defend the colony and that the Angolans were 'on edge' about the intentions of the Germans with whom they had formed an *Angolan Bund* in 1912. Unbeknown to the Angolans the German aim was to 'possess the south of Angola!' thereby enabling German South West 'to be [...] a country, a nation.' This unease was exacerbated by the Germans giving lip-service to the border between the two territories and that before war broke out, the German vice-consul at Moçamedes was known to be distributing supplies for an eventual German invasion.[71]

Neighbouring Angola, inland and north of South West Africa, was the British protectorate of Bechuanaland, now Botswana. This territory does not feature in our story except as part of the British Empire and a source of porters and railway workers, although it had its own police force, the Bechuanaland Police Force, which was mobilised on the outbreak of war.[72] It was overseen by the High Commissioner in South Africa who was also the Union Governor General and a resident agent who supplied him with information on the internal affairs of the territory.[73]

Moving further east, lying between Bechuanaland and Nyasaland and north of the Union was the territory of the British South Africa Company which had been formed by Cecil John Rhodes in 1889. Between 1890 and 1894 various treaties were agreed defining the boundaries in Africa.[74] The company was granted two charters over Northern and Southern Rhodesia respectively which enabled it to govern the territories under the watchful eye of the High Commissioner in South Africa. When South Africa became a Union in 1910, it was expected that Southern Rhodesia, at least, would join when the charter expired.[75] The company was therefore present during all Union discussions. However, when the opportunity came to join the Union shortly before war broke out in 1914, the settlers chose to wait until the 1920s before making their final decision and the charter was appropriately extended. Under the terms of the charter, the company was not permitted to maintain an army but after pleading with the Colonial Office, was granted permission to have an armed police force to maintain internal order and to allow settlers to form and join shooting clubs. The latter could be used as a volunteer military force if required and sanctioned by the High Commissioner. At the outbreak of war, there were approximately 2,000 whites and 850,000 blacks in Northern Rhodesia and 30,000 whites and 750,000 blacks in Southern Rhodesia.[76]

Finally, although not having a territorial presence on the African continent, but with a long associated history reaching from the south along the east coast, was India. When Britain was developing the East African colony, Indians went across to help build the railways and to trade. The territory was also seen as a possible outlet for Indian settlement. For example, Sir Harry Johnston in 1894 was promoting the Kenyan highlands as being suitable for Indian immigration, saying it should become 'the America of the Hindu'.[77] This idea was followed by suggestions that the territory be offered as a home for the Jews who were being displaced in Europe and in 1903, Chamberlain suggested it be colonised by the Finns.[78] Before 1907 the territory clearly was not of major importance to the British Empire. Further south, Indians had been indentured in the colony of Natal to work on the sugar plantations as Zulu men refused to, believing manual labour to be woman's work.[79] Indians soon saw opportunities inland and started to move which brought them into conflict with the Boers, who in turn, limited immigration into the Transvaal or Zuid-Afrikanse Republiek and banned them from the Orange Free State. When MK Gandhi took up the challenge of Indian rights, shortly after the turn of the century, the issue moved onto the empire agenda and was still unresolved at the outbreak of the war.[80]

The First World War, therefore, provided the catalyst for age-old frustrations to come to the fore and be resolved. It gave an opportunity not only for the physical settling of scores through conquest but also psychologically through a battle of wits fought out by the Foreign Offices of the different countries and the soldiers on the ground. As a result, the consequences were far-reaching, impacting on the men who fought and the local communities of both the invaded and invading countries.

CHAPTER 2

TO WAR, 1914

Following the assassination of the Austrian Archduke Ferdinand and his wife on 14 July 1914, Europe braced itself for war. As different groups attempted to mediate, preparations for military action continued and by the end of the month it was apparent war would not be averted. Eventually on 5 August 1914, Britain declared war on Germany, France having done so on 4 August 1914 in support of its ally Russia which had entered the fray on Germany's invasion of Serbia.[1] These decisions, not taken lightly, were to have a huge impact on the African continent as the European dependencies there were drawn into Europe's struggle. Europe was thrown into chaos, a situation which resonated to Africa and other areas impacted by the declaration of war. This chapter aims to shed some light on the decisions and actions taken in, and about, East and southern Africa on the outbreak of war.

As rumours of war started to filter into Africa from the end of July 1914, the governors of the African territories were faced with difficult decisions. Both British and German East Africa saw their priority as helping each other maintain the idea of white supremacy and to support the other if needed against potential native uprisings. 'German East Africa was too near to be dangerous. Just a handful of comrades who spoke German, over the border as it were ... So nobody worried. There was nothing to worry about.'[2] This was the attitude of most settlers and their respective governors. However, the military felt otherwise. In German East Africa, it was the local military commander, Lettow-Vorbeck, who refused to acknowledge his subordinate position to that of the governor, whereas in British East Africa, it was the military powers in London that caused the governor difficulties. Further south, in central Africa, the governors were not expecting to go to war given the small number of white settlers in the area and the fact that their territories were so far removed from the main theatre. Maintaining peace and the status quo would be their main focus. In South Africa, the Governor General was faced with how to reconcile split views where the government supported the war and saw opportunities for further developing the country whilst significant sections of the population felt otherwise and were prepared to rebel.

East Africa, Uganda and London

The outbreak of war in Europe led to a confrontation of the military and administrative powers in the colonies. Feelings of patriotism came to the fore resulting in some colonists leaving on the first available ship to join friends in Europe. It was during a meeting of the British East Africa legislative council on whether 'there should be a close season on duck shooting on Lake Naivasha', that the news of war was received. The British colony, unlike its German counterpart, was caught off-guard, although foreigners in Dar-es-Salaam did not know what was happening.[3] Martial law was declared and the sale of ammunition banned, whilst German nationals were arrested.[4] Rash decisions were made without the long-term implications being thought through and with little infrastructure in place to support the rush of 1,800 volunteers, including some Somali residents, signing up to protect the British colony, chaos was inevitable.[5] On the day war was declared, most of the Boers travelled through to Nairobi to enlist, those from Uasin Gishu forming a regiment known as the Plateau South Africans. Mombasa, being undefended, the locals took matters into their own hands and made floating mines out of empty kerosene tins.[6] On 6 August 1914, the military authorities in Nairobi ordered whites in Magadi and Kijiado to form the Magadi Defence Force to defend against a possible German attack from Longido. It was a motley arrangement of men consisting of 'a railway guard, one a chemist, one an accountant, another a builder, with farmers and game hunters making up the number. The force was mounted on mules and armed with every kind of rifle except the service .303.'[7] Enthusiasm was such that Trzebinski claims British East Africa had 'the only army which fought first and trained afterwards'.[8]

In British East Africa, the governor was at odds with the settlers. This was aptly expressed by Lord Cranworth, a settler, who explained that activity took place at Nairobi House whilst 'Government House remained in dignified aloofness and desertion. No-one thought of asking His Excellency what he thought about the war. Nobody knew whether he was or was not thinking about it.'[9] Thornhill's claim that the Governor of East Africa was instructed by the War Office to 'Defend your country, if you think it worthwhile!' seems typical of Kitchener, rather than the general War Office, who felt the war would best be won in Europe.[10] Kitchener's sentiment, suiting Belfield's pacifist nature, perhaps drove him to the aloofness that annoyed settlers, yet, when he left the colony in 1917, the settlers complained about his removal.[11] The East African press, too, believed the war was a hindrance to Africa and published commentaries calling for neutrality at various points in response to the position taken by Belfield who openly stated it was 'Business as usual' and 'deliberately discouraged settlers from volunteering'.[12]

There were also questions over the loyalty of some inhabitants. The Boers, for example, were to cause both British and German East Africa concern. In British East Africa, a Boer loyal to Britain, Captain Frans Arnoldi, wrote an open letter to his fellow Afrikaners imploring them and those in South Africa to support Britain in its fight against Germany. He drew on the fact that numerous Boers had experienced German government and it was not something they wanted to experience again. This, for him, was sufficient reason not to support the Germans, and that the good treatment he had been afforded by the British in East Africa warranted giving them the support they needed in their struggle. Of the estimated one thousand Boers in the protectorate, only seven faced trial in 1917 for not responding when conscription was introduced in 1916.[13]

The Boers in German East Africa were to cause some concern too. The Germans though, took a different approach to the British, especially as many of the Boers were technically British citizens following the incorporation of the Boer republics into the Union of South Africa and the British Empire. According to a Mrs Pienaar, 'The German authorities do not trust the Boers. ... The great majority of Afrikaners in Tanganyika are definitely neutral. ... There are a few who are going to cast their fate with the Germans and fight'.[14] The Boers were, therefore, given a choice – either pledge an oath of loyalty to Germany and be allowed to retain your weapons or be interred. For this latter purpose, an internment or 'safe' camp had been set up at Kondoa Irangi. Thornhill notes that the Germans treated their prisoners quite brutally at the start of the war with the result that many eventually took the oath for practical reasons. The hunter, Piet Pretorius, later to become chief scout for the British in East Africa and hunt down the *Königsberg*, recalled his first experiences of the war. He learnt of the outbreak of war on 14 August 1914 and within a few days was aware of a German column descending on his camp in the south-east of the German colony. Despite being shot in both legs, he was able to get away taking twenty-six days to reach medical attention. It had been a close call, but for the support of local natives, he would not have made it.[15] As Mrs Pienaar pointed out, though, there were a number of Boers who chose to support the Germans, such as Piet Nieuwenhuizen and a poacher van Rooyen, who became scouts for Lettow-Vorbeck during the war. Others, such as Gert Pretorius, moved to British East Africa before the war and became scouts for the British, whilst others moved to Portuguese East Africa for the duration of the war before formally settling in British East Africa.[16]

On hearing about the outbreak of war, Belfield updated the British Colonial Office. He 'had declared emergency measures and begun mobilization of the 3,000 European military age males who were living in Uganda and British East Africa.' As the majority of the King's African Rifles were involved in operations against Somali tribesmen in the north and in the west suppressing native revolts, only two companies were available to defend the German East African frontier and 440 miles of the Uganda railway.[17] Lloyd-Jones notes that at the outbreak of war: most of 3KAR, half of 1KAR and half of 4KAR were in Jubaland; the rest of 3 and 4KAR were in Northern Frontier District and Turkana; one company in Zanzibar; and three weak companies of

1KAR at Zomba.[18] The defence of the Uganda railway was slightly eased by the presence of the Uganda Railway Volunteer Reserve which had been formed before the outbreak of war and mobilised on 9 August 1914. Under Captain HV Kershaw, sixty men and a King's African Rifles patrol defended the line between Voi and Sultan Hamud, a distance of 147 miles. They took the first German prisoners on 24 August 1914 and were relieved of duty when the Indian Expeditionary forces arrived shortly after 1 September 1914.[19] Yet, for all his apparent compliance, Belfield remained resistant to war planning and instructions. His passive attitude no doubt added to the confusion in London where numerous ministries were responsible for different aspects of the same campaign. Not long into the war, following discussions between the War and Colonial Offices, instructions went out from the Colonial Office on 11 August 1914 that Belfield support the military.[20]

In Uganda there were four companies of volunteers. Apart from the 1st Company, the other three were formed in June, August and October respectively, the 3rd being an Indian company. On the outbreak of war, 4KAR and two hundred men of the Uganda Police Active Service Unit were deployed to protect the Kagera River bordering German East Africa as were the Baganda Rifles.[21] Although Uganda was not felt to be under great threat, precautionary measures were taken.[22]

In London, as the likelihood of war increased, the Colonial Office asked the India Office to hold an infantry brigade ready for service in East Africa.[23] On the outbreak of war, the request for the Indian brigade to be sent to East Africa was passed onto the Joint Naval and Military Sub-Committee of the Overseas Defence (Attack) Committee, responsible for '[deciding] on objectives with a view to producing a *definite effect* upon the result of the war, and to submit the broad lines of its proposals to the Cabinet.' This was to meet the requirement that 'All operations were to be regarded primarily as designed for the defence of trade and not for territorial conquest [... and] the troops used for the purpose should be such as would not in any case be available for the main theatre.'[24] Given the scale and nature of the war, the Western Front had priority call on troops. However, when the committee met on 5 and 6 August 1914, it recommended that the 'Admiralty arrangement for the protection of commerce would be facilitated' by an attack on Dar-es-Salaam. An offensive would also 'best guarantee' British East Africa.[25]

This decision accorded with previous British deliberations about the territory. In 1898 when Britain drew up plans to conquer German East Africa if war broke out in Europe, EA Altham recommended that Indian troops be used to capture and hold Dar-es-Salaam. Other schemes had also acknowledged that the terrain was not suitable for white soldiers and suggested that Indians be used.[26] The capture of the territory, however, was of secondary importance given that the outcome of the war would be determined in Europe; although its capture would provide Britain with a bargaining tool if needed. This latter position was reinforced by Altham in 1907, although his position on the use of Indians had changed – he now 'deprecated' their use in East Africa and felt they should not be relied on.[27] Despite Altham's recent assessment of the Indian troops, the sub-Committee decided to ask India to send three battalions to Zanzibar and East Africa rather than the Committee of Imperial Defence (CID) request for two.[28]

The situation, however, soon got messy. Having decided that three battalions be sent to East Africa, Sir Edward Barrow, the Military Secretary at the India Office, who was in London on leave pending retirement, questioned this believing that only two were necessary, but, let the matter rest on learning that a War Office battalion consisted of four companies rather than the usual eight found in an Indian battalion. The decision was again deliberated with the outcome that troops for East Africa would not be drawn from those identified for Egypt, as that area was strategically more important. The Viceroy, Lord Hardinge, was sent a telegram setting out the situation and told that the purpose of the expedition, to be run in the same way as the 1900 Boxer Rebellion, was to put the German ports out of action. Further complications set in when Turkey entered the war as Germany's ally.[29]

Turkey's involvement was of such concern to the British government that the India Office and East Africa were pushed to the background. This sidelining of India's involvement was exacerbated by the fact that Barrow was in London and that Lord Kitchener, who had reformed the Indian Army in the previous decade before moving to Egypt, had just been made Secretary of State for War. London, therefore, believed that it knew what support India could offer, resulting in the government in India feeling isolated and that those in London making the decisions were out of touch with what was happening in India and Africa. In general, Kitchener and the Viceroy were in accord regarding the use of Indian troops – Kitchener seeing India as a 'supply depot', whilst Hardinge promised to give 'India's last man and last gun to the British government'.[30] The issue was over the detail and feel in India, which only those on the ground could address. In his post-war memoirs, Hardinge abrogated all responsibility for the troops sent to East Africa. These had been chosen by Barrow and were 'worthless' in Hardinge's eyes.[31]

German East Africa

To protect his colony Governor Schnee decided that the floating dock at Dar-es-Salaam would be sunk. He did this following the departure of SMS *Königsberg* from Dar-es-Salaam on 31 July 1914 to avoid capture and in the knowledge that the German declaration of war did not extend to the German 'overseas possessions'.[32] Keeping the territory neutral was in accordance with the German General Staff plan of 1912 which acknowledged that the best plan for the German colony would be neutrality providing all the other colonies adhered to the neutrality clauses of the 1885 Berlin Act. On 23 July 1914, the Reichskolonialamt confirmed its position, noting that the 'Imperial Navy [did] not intend to protect places on the coast of the German Protectorates', and that the governor was to declare all ports 'open'.[33] Having sunk the floating dock on 5 August, Schnee failed to disconnect the wireless station and following the *Königsberg*'s commandeering of a British merchant vessel (the first of the war), HMS *Astrea* attacked Dar-es-Salaam on 8 August 1914, firing the first shot in anger in the war. Nine days later, HMS *Pegasus* attacked Tanga. Both moves were in accordance with the war book and had been supported by the CID decision on 5 August that wireless stations were to be disabled and control gained of harbours, providing local forces only were able to do so.[34] The attack on Dar-es-Salaam led Schnee to force complete compliance with the Hague conventions of an open port. He ordered the wireless stations destroyed, an action Lettow-Vorbeck put down to 'excessive fear of its falling into enemy hands', and the sinking of the *Möwe* on 9 August 1914 to prevent the port being used for military purposes.[35] This released the crew to serve under Lettow-Vorbeck and its captain, Zimmer, joined the *Hedwig von Wissmann* on Lake Tanganyika to command the water forces there.[36] The other ships in the port, *Tabora*, *Feldmarschall* and *Koenig* were disabled – the *Tabora* causing some discomfort. The British believing that the Germans had disguised the *Tabora* as a hospital ship boarded her and found the only patient in bed with his trousers on. Understandably, the Germans felt the investigation of the ship an affront. In the subsequent confusion, EC Holtom the British doctor sent to investigate the *Tabora*, was taken prisoner.[37] To avoid further confusion, Schnee then signed a neutrality agreement with HMS *Astrea* and later with HMS *Pegasus* following the attack on Tanga.[38] Lettow-Vorbeck, however, felt the naval attacks on the colony were a declaration of war and that he was now responsible for the safety of the colony.

Schnee's actions brought the conflict between the military and administration to a head, to the extent that Lettow-Vorbeck's outbursts earned him the nickname 'Mad Mullah'[39] – a name which was probably reinforced by his having a weak left eye which needed a spectacle, and which should not be confused with the Mad Mullah, a Muslim leader, who was operating in Somaliland and after whom Lettow-Vorbeck most likely got his nickname.[40] Lettow-Vorbeck believed that it was 'our military objective to detain the enemy, that is English, forces, if it could by any means be accomplished. This, however, was impossible if we remained neutral'.[41] On 15 August 1914 the Reichskolonialamt confirmed that Schnee was still Lettow-Vorbeck's superior, but this did not stop Lettow-Vorbeck. He 'authorised the armed steamer *Hedwig von Wissmann* to act aggressively on Lake Tanganyika' and an attack on the Portuguese in the south despite their being neutral. The Germans had raided the forts, killing all within including the doctors and Schnee had to work hard to convince the Portuguese that the military attack on 24 August 1914 had been a mistake.[42] His task was possibly made more difficult by the German attack on Angola the next day. Launching attacks on the Portuguese had been a double-edged sword. On the one hand, it would bring Portugal into the war and give Germany the pretext it needed to claim the Portuguese territory it wanted. On the other hand, it would close off access to coaling ports where supplies could be landed. However, it was Britain's desire that Portugal remain neutral at this early stage of the war which carried the day and enabled Schnee to reduce the tensions in the south.[43]

Lettow-Vorbeck had started recruiting as soon as he could. He returned to Dar-es-Salaam on 3 August following Schnee's message and, as many of the settlers were in the capital for the opening of the Tanganyika railway, it would have been relatively easy to organise for the colony's defence. However, as Lettow-Vorbeck was subordinate to Schnee who wanted to keep the country out of war, recruitment and preparations were made more difficult. Eventually, Lettow-Vorbeck was able to concentrate the existing forces in the colony at Pugu, one day's march or twelve miles away from Dar-es-Salaam. The police were placed at his disposal, askaris were called up and reservists were mobilised. In Pugu, stores were issued, training organised and road building planned to aid communication and supplies as the traditional route of using the ocean was no longer available. Retired Major-General Wahle who had arrived on 2 August 1914 to visit his son took control of arrangements. Here, at Pugu, on 8 August, they heard the bombardment of Dar-es-Salaam. In response to reports of a landing north of Dar-es-Salaam Lettow-Vorbeck, with the agreement of Schnee who was on his way to Morogoro, was permitted to travel to Konduchi. Before leaving Pugu, Lettow-Vorbeck saw two officials carrying surrender documents, but it was only on arrival at Konduchi that he realised Schnee had agreed the surrender of Dar-es-Salaam and despite his attempts to supersede the governor, he had to remain subordinate.[44]

Lettow-Vorbeck became concerned at the slow rate of recruitment when he heard a rumour that 2,000 British (Indian) troops were to land at Tanga. He overreacted and ordered the destruction of the Usambara railway despite the difficulties such an action could cause him later. Schnee saved him this embarrassment by forcing him to countermand the instruction.[45] Meanwhile, Lettow-Vorbeck continued to take the initiative to protect the German colony and on 14 and 15 August 1914, the Germans under Major Georg Kraut captured Taveta in British East Africa; an action which marked the start of attacks on the Uganda railway. However, before the attacks started in earnest on 8 September 1914, there was a lull in activity as both sides took stock of the situation and organised their new troops. Despite having the initiative in the Kilimanjaro area, Lettow-Vorbeck continued to build up his forces there and when challenged by Schnee on 11 October 1914, explained that he was hoping to entice the British to attack him and was purely on the defensive. The pending attack was important, as his troops were feeling rather disillusioned following a few defeats they had suffered around the country and the ensuing lack of action; Portuguese East Africa on 24 August, Mwanza on 11 September and the loss of ships. The implication of further defeats was that his askari could start defecting to the British as soon as the latter were perceived to be the stronger force.[46]

In contrast to Lettow-Vorbeck's usual practice of troop placement and despite German naval superiority on Lake Victoria, the local German troops decided to concentrate their various forces at Mwanza to reduce feelings of isolation. This left the Uganda border relatively undefended as the few British troops in the area were not at strength and for a while this area, too, experienced no military engagements. The situation changed in September 1914, when Lettow-Vorbeck ordered an attack. The Germans were repelled on 11 September when the British managed to deploy an additional 300 troops. Following a reorganisation of the troops along the German border and the replacement of the commander, a state of calm returned for the next few months.[47]

The tension between the governor and his military commander must have been reflected back in Germany. Schnee had been encouraged to give up the coastal regions because the German navy did not see fit to defend them given the strength of the British navy and that the German navy was concentrated around Europe. This was contrasted by the Reichskolonialamt under Wilhelm Solf who, when asked about Germany's colonial aims, set out the desire for a 'German *Mittelafrika*'. *Mittelafrika* would consist of French, Belgian and Portuguese territory, but not British, as Germany did not see its way to defeating that country in the early days of the war.[48] This led the German government to ask that the African colonies remain neutral. Forwarding their request through the neutral United States of America, it only reached the British towards the end of September 1914. Given the hostile actions which had already taken place on all sides by the end of August, it did not seem feasible to declare the zone neutral. The position was reinforced by France and Britain in October and November respectively. On 13 October, Belgium reluctantly declared war on Germany in Africa despite all its earlier plans to keep the territory neutral and its failed attack on 4 October. As with the other neighbouring territories Belgium's hand had been forced by a German attack, on Lake Tanganyika on 22 August 1914.[49]

On Lake Tanganyika, the Germans had a superior force of five vessels compared to one Belgian. Uncertain about Congo neutrality, the Germans allowed the Belgian vessel *Alexandre del Commune* to leave Kigoma on 6 August 1914. However, they decided on 15 August that the Congo was not neutral and proceeded to cut telephone cables and destroy canoes on Congo territory. Finally, on 22 August, the Germans attacked the Belgian base, damaging the *Alexandre del Commune* which was withdrawn into the Lukuga River.[50] It would remain there until 1916 when the allies regained control of the lake. The Belgians retaliated by moving sufficient troops of the Force Publique into the area and attacking the Germans on 4 October 1914. The Germans repelled the attack and an uneasy calm between the two sides ensued for the remainder of 1914, aided as Britain, Belgium's ally had little direct interest in the area at the time.[51] This calm provided Belgium with an opportunity to rethink its position in Africa. A large part of mainland Belgium had been occupied by the Germans and victory in Africa would enable Belgium to retain some pride. It would also provide the country with tangible gains to use at the bargaining table, if needed to reclaim territory in Europe. Yet, in reality, Belgium's African aims could only be strengthened by working closely with Britain.[52]

Britain, Belgium and Northern Rhodesia

The relationship between the two allies was not problem-free and the Belgians became frustrated as the authorities on the ground were

receiving different messages from the British to those they were getting from the Belgian government. Part of the confusion resulted
from the involvement of various departments in London. Each department was responsible for a slightly different aspect of the war in East
and Central Africa with the result that each obtained slightly different information from their sources in Africa which they then had to
combine to see what was really happening. Instructions then had to
be given in a coherent manner ensuring that each department's individual interests were protected. The situation was potentially made
more complicated by General Wolfe Murray's dual role of Acting
High Commissioner of the chartered territories and Commander of
the Imperial Troops in South Africa. In accordance with the charter he assumed command of the military affairs and liaison with
the Commandant General of Northern Rhodesia. All communications for the High Commissioner still went through the Governor
General of South Africa as the Colonial and War Offices had failed
to register that between Gladstone's departure and Buxton's arrival,
the roles were split. This was particularly noticeable when Harcourt
responded to the British South Africa Company letter of 6 August
1914 that all necessary instructions had been communicated to the
High Commissioner.[53] Wolfe Murray therefore had to rely on his
counterpart to forward relevant communications to him before he
could relay them onto the various residents. This situation was made
more complex, albeit for a few days, when de Villiers died.

   This breakdown in communication channels may well have led to
one of the early 'international incidents' of the campaign. The British
government had decided not to involve the Belgians in the campaign
as far as they could, but, this decision had not been communicated
to the outlying areas which were relatively unprotected, having only
two companies of King's African Rifles to oversee the border. The two
Rhodesias, controlled by the British South Africa Company, had not
been permitted to recruit an armed force before the war with the result
that in Northern Rhodesia there was a small black police force, the
Northern Rhodesian Police, to protect the territory against a slightly
larger German force.[54] In Southern Rhodesia there was the white British
South Africa Police, some of whom were sent to Northern Rhodesia as

required. Unbeknownst to the powers in London, and presumably to Wolfe Murray, in early August 1914, the Belgian Congo administration agreed to co-operate defensively with the Rhodesias. As the threat of a German attack on Abercorn in Northern Rhodesia became more likely, a local magistrate and District Commissioner, CP Chesnaye, realising that the British troops were not able to help, appealed directly to the local Belgian force under Major Olsen. Without consulting the Belgian authorities, Olsen agreed to help and sent a battalion which arrived on 22 August 1914 with instructions to remain strictly on the defensive and not to cross the border. Given that a German attack was ordered on 24 August at Abercorn and another on Karonga in Nyasaland on 9 September, the arrival of the Belgian troops at various points along the border was timely. A British force also arrived on 9 September 1914. The British, using long-term prisoners to carry the machine guns, resisted the Germans and a lull ensued with the Germans settling at Bismarckburg. Under the temporary command of Major HM Stennett, further attacks were repelled with 'considerable loss to the enemy'.[55]

Diplomatic relations remained strained when the Northern Rhodesia Resident felt that sufficient troops were available for defence purposes and that the Belgian 2nd Battalion would no longer be needed. The Belgians felt snubbed and withdrew their troops from the Abercorn area. Whilst discussions between the British and Belgian governments were taking place to resolve the 'crisis', the Belgian Vice-Consul General in the Katanga Province Congo, C Tombeur, and the Administrator for Northern Rhodesia together with Commandant-General Colonel AHM Edwards, were independently arranging for Belgian troops in Northern Rhodesia to operate under the orders of the senior British Officer.[56] That the incident was amicably resolved was down to the respective Foreign Offices and the realisation that both countries ultimately needed the other to contain the Germans in East Africa.

Given the size and spread of the British South Africa Company territories in central and southern Africa, the confusion and mixed responses should not be surprising. From as early as July, when the possibility of war appeared more likely, Colonel AHM Edwards made preparations to defend the Northern Rhodesian territory by gathering information on the northern border of the chartered territory and to occupy the German town of Schuckmannsburg in the Caprivi Strip (*Zipfel*) to the south of the territory. When war was declared, the British South Africa Police Force was mobilised and within weeks the civil defence groups which had been permitted for protection against native uprisings had been brought into active service. Volunteers were welcomed. However, as the Army Council determined that they should protect Northern Rhodesia before going to Europe, around one tenth of the male population left the country of their own accord or signed up for the 1st Rhodesian Regiment.[57] As a result, the forces available in Northern Rhodesia were not enough to provide sufficient defence for the territory and this led to the request for Belgian assistance, despite the Colonial Office discouraging this.[58]

Apart from attracting volunteers who could have better defended the territory's borders, the British South Africa Company's offer in October to raise 500 men for active service in German South West Africa as the 1st Rhodesian Regiment caused little difficulty. The company had offered its services to Britain on 6 August 1914, however. It took twenty-three letters and telegrams until on 1 October 1914 the High Commissioner wired that the Union government would welcome a Rhodesian contingent for operations in German South West Africa. This delay was due to the change in High Commissioner in South Africa and the problems the South African government faced internally. Eight days later the South African rebellion erupted. On 21 November 1914 recruitment began for the 2nd Rhodesian Regiment.[59] However, the raising of further troops proved more problematic and required greater negotiation.[60] Arrangements between the company and the government had to be agreed and contracts drawn up for Rhodesian senior officers to command non-Rhodesians. In the early days of the war, these discussions were just a formality as many of the company directors such as Dr Leander Starr Jameson were patriotic to Britain and ensured that any potential political hiccups were avoided.[61] When it was clear that the war was going to last longer than initially thought, and particularly after Jameson's death in 1917, the company became less co-operative.[62]

Nyasaland

In neighbouring Nyasaland, Governor Smith, on 31 July 1914, asked Captain CW Barton, the senior regular officer then in the protectorate, to prepare the territory in case of war. Three days later and the day before Britain declared war on Germany, the protectorate's Executive Committee determined that Lake Nyasa would likely be the main target when war broke out and so directed the troops to the southern ports. Smith informed the Colonial Office that he had written to all 'Germans to give their parole, under pain of arrest, not to attempt to leave the Protectorate without [his] permission, nor to aid the enemy by information or action directly or indirectly.' He noted that it had 'not been found necessary to make any arrests' and that he had not called out any volunteers on the advice of the Officer Commanding Troops.[63]

By 10 August 1914, the Nyasaland Field Force had come into being consisting of two double companies at Fort Johnstone under the command of Captain Barton.[64] On the lake, the biggest threat was the German steamer, the *Hermann von Wissmann*. Opposing Captain Berndt's *Hermann von Wissmann* was HMS *Guendolen*, captained by Commander Rhoades, the only armed British vessel on the lake. Following discussions by the various military and administrative leaders in the colony, it was determined that Rhoades would try and disable the German steamer so that it could potentially be brought into British use later on. The German vessel had not been expecting war as the message had not been passed on by either the Germans or the British and there was little expectation that the German ship would participate in the war due to repairs it was undergoing. The British attack on the vessel in Sphinxhaven dry-dock was, therefore, seen as unprovoked and out of keeping with Britain's high moral stance. Berndt's exclamation 'Gott for damn, Rhoades, vos you drunk?' on seeing Rhoades was evidence of the two men knowing each other – they used to arrange their annual training cruises to coincide for a rendezvous.[65] The ship was finally put out of action by a company of King's African Rifles in May 1915.

After the ship was first disabled, the British were free to move troops the length of the colony using the lake which saved much time. But, this gave rise to new concerns when it was realised that the Germans might retaliate. Therefore, having moved what troops he had into a defensive position, Smith appealed for Portuguese assistance. He was keen to ensure there were sufficient white troops to protect his territory as he saw the conflict as one between whites and felt that blacks should not be involved. Despite Smith's attempt to not involve blacks in the war, the British Colonial Secretary, Lewis Harcourt, felt he should not accept Portuguese assistance. However, Sir Edward Grey of the Foreign Office and Winston Churchill of the Admiralty, were prepared to end Portugal's neutrality if the British colony was threatened.[66] Before the Portuguese support arrived, Smith's fears were realised when Karonga was attacked on 9 September 1914 especially as the British South Africa Police had returned to Bulawayo due to the threat the South African rebel Maritz posed.[67]

In the lead-up to the attack, the German Imperial Administrator, Steir, actually asked Webb, the administrator of Karonga, whether their two countries were at war. He was getting no response to his queries to the command at Mbeya and was aware that troops were being amassed there. Before the attack took place, the German commander, Captain von Langenn Steinkeller warned Webb to evacuate the whites to 'avert a massacre'. In the event, the Germans were held at bay and the lake was not to be threatened again during the war, although Dr Sanderson, *Guendolen*'s doctor, refers to a total of four operations on the lake. He recalled 'None of [the] expeditions except the first has left me with any clear cut memories – I was present only at the first three. This is probably because the first was pure comedy though it might easily have been tragedy.'[68] The same could not be said of the attack on Karonga, given the loss of life in the subsequent battle. In total 163 men, white and askari, were wounded, killed or captured.[69]

Action in Nyasaland was facilitated when, in mid-August 1914, the Portuguese government had agreed that Britain could send unarmed troops across the East African colony to Nyasaland, the weapons having been sent on earlier. In addition, according to Anderson, when a 'local official offered military support to Britain', it was approved by the authorities in Lisbon.[70] This was despite both Britain and Germany having convinced Portugal to remain neutral and that both countries had agreed to split the Portuguese territories between them. In addition, there was some annoyance with Britain in the early days of the war when Britain sent conflicting messages about the need for Portuguese assistance in Nyasaland.[71] Despite this frustration, the Portuguese continued to support and work with Britain believing that at the end of the day, it stood more to gain by working with Britain than against. Another motivation was that if Britain was successful, Portugal stood a good chance of getting the Kionga Triangle back.

The East Africa coast

On 8 August 1914, Portugal decided to send 1,500 troops to the colony for use if needed and to have troops available to occupy the Kionga Triangle if the opportunity arose.[72] Due to the situation prevalent in Portugal, these troops only set sail on 11 September and arrived in East Africa on 16 October 1914 where they became totally demoralised. Little had been done to prepare them for their task and nothing welcomed them on their arrival. For their ten-month duty, they were led by Lieutenant-Colonel Pedro Francisco Massando de Amorim who was instructed on the one hand to provide a 'mild deterrent presence' and on the other, to defend the colony, suppress any uprisings and co-operate with the British.[73] Working against him was the governor of the northern province of Portuguese East Africa, bordering on the German colony, who was pro-German.[74] This worked in Lettow-Vorbeck's favour, particularly once Schnee convinced the Portuguese Governor General to maintain neutrality after the German attack on 24 August 1914.

Having tested the various forces surrounding the German colony, albeit unwittingly, Lettow-Vorbeck was given a reprieve to deal with the biggest threat to German East Africa – British East Africa and the coast. It will be remembered that on 5 August 1914, the British cabinet was presented with a proposal to send two Indian Expeditionary Forces to East Africa, one to strengthen the defence of the colony and the other to launch an attack on Tanga. This attack on Tanga was finally planned for early November, to be ultimately run by the India Office, and became what has generally been regarded as a 'fiasco'.

The battle for Tanga was fought between 8,000 allied troops (Indian Expeditionary Force 'B' made up of two infantry brigades including one battalion North Lancashires, four regular Indian battalions and Imperial Service Troops) and 1,100 German and native troops. The departure of the Indian troops had been delayed for fear of the SMS *Emden* which was threatening British shipping. The result was that the troops spent nearly thirty days at sea before landing at Tanga. Norman King, previously British Consul at Dar-es-Salaam, felt that the colony did not want to go to war and that the German natives would rebel ensuring an easy British victory. This was in contrast to Intelligence Officer Colonel Richard Meinertzhagen who felt the Germans would put up a strong fight.[75] Major General AE Aitken was therefore faced with conflicting information about the ability and preparedness of the German troops. In the end, Meinertzhagen's assessment proved correct, but it had been ignored.

In addition, Aitken was so confident about defeating the Germans that he turned down the offer of the 3KAR, which meant that he had no troops with bush-fighting experience and even asked the navy not to shell the town so as not to destroy 'our future homes'.[76] Some of his officers commanding India Expeditionary Force B had had very little to do with their men before the battle. There were exceptions such as General MJ Tighe, one of the commanders, who saw his troops a 'few days before embarkation'. The result was that 'nobody knew anybody.'[77] Further, Major FS Keen, or 'Daddy' as he was commonly known, had tried to get some landing practice in before the untrained troops left India, but to no avail.[78] Added to this, 'The voyage was miserable for the Indian troops. Crowded into the troopships, unused to conditions at sea, provisioned by unfamiliar food, with little to no room for physical conditioning, all this, combined with the equatorial heat, took a large toll on the troops both mentally and physically.'[79] Given Corrigan's explanation of how the sepoys on the Western Front were led by British officers who knew their men well, had a strict order of communication and literally led from the front in an attack,[80] it is little wonder that the new and inexperienced Indian troops faltered.

Apart from the issue around the troops, the local naval officer, insisted on informing the Germans that the truce they believed existed following the bombardment on 17 August 1914 did not and also that he sweep for mines before sending his ships in. This delay gave the Germans time to move reinforcements to Tanga and by 4 November seven companies were in the vicinity with another two on their way. Command of the East African coast had passed from Admiral Herbert King-Hall of the Cape Squadron, who on the outbreak of war was responsible for the African coast from Angola around to British East Africa, to Captain FW Caulfeild. As the German cruisers, the *Emden* and *Königsberg* were roaming the Indian Ocean it had been felt more appropriate to move the responsibility for the East African waters to the East Indies Command.[81] However, the exact details of what King-Hall had agreed after the August attacks on Dar-es-Salaam and Tanga do not seem to have been passed onto Caulfeild.

The truce had come about following the British attack on the port on 17 August 1914. This suited both the local governors who did not want their colonies to be destroyed by war. It also met the defence plans determined by the German Colonial authorities as early as 1912, who felt that, in the event of a war in East Africa, the coastal area could be abandoned with the internal areas being defended. When King-Hall asked the Admiralty to ratify the truce following the German demolition of their radio station, the Admiralty refused to do so recognising that they wanted to keep their options open pending future actions. Despite the concerns of the Colonial, India and War Offices, King-Hall was left to let the Germans know the treaty had not been ratified at an appropriate moment.[82] He chose to leave notifying the Germans until just before an attack.

Whilst Caulfeild was insisting on letting the Germans know that the truce had not been ratified and on sweeping the bay for mines, the defence of Tanga was organised; a situation which seemed no less chaotic than the British organisation. Lettow-Vorbeck originally wanted to destroy the railway into Tanga in accordance with the Reichskolonialamt policy of abandoning the coast line as this would slow down any advance by the enemy if they landed. However, Governor Schnee, who was senior to Lettow-Vorbeck, refused to allow him. The struggle for command continued to play out, yet the confusion this could possibly cause seemed to be well managed by those having to interpret the mixed commands they received. The District Commissioner of Tanga, Auracher, first carried out Schnee's orders in keeping the peace until Caulfeild notified him of the imminent attack. He then donned his military uniform and set about defending his town.[83] Troops had been sent by railway to support the defence of Tanga but by the time Lettow-Vorbeck arrived on the night of 3 November, they had been withdrawn. After reconnoitring the deserted town by bicycle, he positioned his troops. Confusion resulted in later reinforcements being sent to the wrong area and as night began to fall, the Germans sounded the recall.[84]

Aitken however, again, refused to listen to Meinertzhagen who gave contrary information to his fellow officers, and ordered the troops to re-embark. The task was completed the next day, but without the equipment which was left on the beach to reinforce the German supplies.[85] Meinertzhagen then negotiated with Captain von Hammerstein to remove the English wounded, which Lettow-Vorbeck sanctioned on condition that those removed would not fight the Germans 'again in this war.'[86] A young naval officer, CJ Charlewood, sent to clear wounded off the beaches, wrote about collecting them. They left four lifeboats with the requisitioned *Helmuth*, now under British control, and gone ashore with a white flag. Having spoken to the German captain in charge of the evacuation, 'several German officers came up and one of them addressed us in English. He astonished us by inviting us to supper.' They declined but when 'he retorted that the work would be easier if we waited for moonrise', they accepted his offer. Six Germans and four British sat down to supper. 'The Germans thought the war would soon be over because they expected the French to give in and then of course it would be useless for Britain to continue the struggle.' Charlewood records that he met an official of the German company which had owned the *Helmuth* who enquired 'how [his] little man-of-war [was] getting on?' He continued, 'I fired at you the other night!'[87]

In essence, the failure at Tanga can be ascribed to the prejudice of the British officers leading the attack, a lack of unity and knowledge of each other and lack of planning in terms of logistics, training and acclimatisation. Other issues were synchronisation and lack of communication, both at strategic and local level.[88] General Arthur Aitken, the Commanding Officer and brother of Lord Beaverbrook, had seen the war in Africa as a side-show which would be completed by Christmas. After this, he would be assigned to the 'real' war in Europe. For all his efforts at Tanga, Aitken was accused of being in 'tragic ignorance of his profession'.[89]

A simultaneous attack from British East Africa into the German colony at Longido also failed. As the plans for the attack on Tanga were being finalised in London, it was thought that an attack from British East Africa into German East Africa inland would help in securing the Usambara railway. This inland attack would be undertaken by Indian Expeditionary Force C from Tsavo towards Moshi. However, the plans for this attack were left too late and too little attention was given to the paucity of communication lines in the area, distances and terrain despite the views of Inspector General AR Hoskins of the King's African Rifles, on leave in England when war broke out, being sought.[90] Instructions went out to General Stewart command-ing Indian Expeditionary Force C and to Aitken to coordinate attacks, which were scheduled for 3 November 1914. However, as a result of the naval truce, the landings took place a day later. When the British failed to take Longido and withdrew on the same day, they allowed Lettow-Vorbeck to concentrate on Tanga.[91] Lettow-Vorbeck took the opportunity of the subsequent reduction in hostilities to organise his communications, build roads and set up weapon and food stores across the country. This move, too, led to a clash between the governor and Lettow-Vorbeck, as the former felt internal stability was of paramount importance whereas the latter felt the colonial officials should support his preparations for war.[92]

The outcome of the failed British attacks on Tanga and Longido was that Aitken was removed as General Officer Commanding and the War Office assumed command of military operations in the area on 22 November 1914, ordering the colony onto the defensive. Brigadier-General Wapshare replaced Aitken as General Officer Commanding. Having been told to put the colony onto the defensive, Wapshare felt this would be detrimental to morale, and was finally given permission by the War Office to 'consider an advance [...] on the Voi-Taveta line while also extending the railway towards Taveta and building the water pipeline.'[93] To do this, Wapshare felt that more troops were needed, but the War Office could only offer a brigade around February 1915. Pending completion of the railway and water pipeline as well as the arrival of the promised brigade, Wapshare decided to launch a campaign at Jasin in an attempt to improve Britain's standing. The Germans eventually withdrew by 27 December 1914 leaving the British troops under Tighe in control of the area until 18 January 1915 when the Germans resumed occupation.[94] The need to launch and win victories was important to both colonies to ensure the support of the local natives. They would tend to support whichever side appeared to be the stronger and in a war which was to be fought in the bush, across unknown land, the loyalty of the local people would prove crucial. For Britain, although the India Office had been removed from the picture, the number of departments involved in managing the campaign in central and south-east Africa was still causing difficulty.

Around the same time that the attacks on Tanga and Longido were taking place, the Admiralty was working to track down the SMS *Königsberg* which had gone into hiding along the Rufiji Delta. The *Königsberg* and *Emden* had been disrupting allied shipping, which in turn was impacting on the war. Before that, HMS *Pegasus* had been sunk by *Königsberg* on 20 September near Zanzibar, which reduced the Cape Squadron's fire-power and was, according to Edward Hoyt, the first naval victory of the Great War between British and German cruisers.[95] The quicker the two cruisers were brought to heel, the better. The *Emden* was eventually sunk on 9 November which meant all resources, a total of twenty-five vessels, could be turned to dealing with the *Königsberg*.[96]

The *Königsberg*'s captain, Max Looff, had seen no reason to be caught in port unexpectedly and the *Königsberg* left Dar-es-Salaam as soon as it became apparent that war was likely. Following the declaration of war, the *Königsberg* sank a merchant navy vessel, the first of the war, which caused great consternation in Britain. However, Looff knew that his time was limited as coal and other necessities would not be forthcoming from German bases or Germany. He would have to raid ships and ports for these. When it was clear that he was running short of commodities and that the *Königsberg* needed some repairs, he hid the cruiser in the Rufiji Delta, knowing the British did not know the delta's layouts or current patterns. Britain, however, obtained knowledge of this move from captured German documents and intercepted codes. On 30 October 1914, the *Königsberg*'s masts were sighted and it was decided that the best way to observe the ship was by plane.[97]

Two Curtiss hydroplanes were sourced in South Africa by King-Hall following Churchill's refusal to send out planes from England.[98] They arrived in East Africa on 15 November 1914, the same day a plane requisitioned by the Germans in July crashed, killing the pilot Lieutenant Henneberger.[99] A week later, H Dennis Cutler, the South African pilot King-Hall had commissioned into the Royal Naval Reserve, spotted the *Königsberg*. Both planes were damaged, the first due to weather and landing conditions whilst the other suffered a crash landing and Cutler's capture on 10 December 1914. Another plane had to be sourced and, while it was, a version of 'cat and mouse' began with Looff moving the *Königsberg* around until he realised he could not hide the vessel.[100] To ease the waiting and in recognition of their situation, King-Hall sent his counterpart Christmas and New Year wishes. 'We wish you a Happy Christmas and a Happy New Year; we hope to see you soon.' Looff replied, 'Thanks, same to you; if you wish to see me, I am always at home.'[101] This was true as every time a vessel was sent to see if it could reach the *Königsberg* it would be fired upon from various look-out posts Looff had set up.

During 1914, the war in East and Central Africa was self-contained. It had not yet made links with the war in the south, apart from troops being raised in Southern Rhodesia for service in South West Africa and the Northern Rhodesian capture of Schuckmannsburg in the Caprivi Strip which Britain had ceded to Germany. On 13 September 1914, two days after he oversaw the Union's decision to invade German South West Africa, Buxton as High Commissioner gave permission for the British South Africa and Northern Rhodesia Police to cross into German territory under the command of Major Capell. The capture of Schuckmannsburg was again evidence of the German approach to protect territory by surrender which the German Resident, Herr von Frankenberg, did on 21 September 1914 after an hour's discussion.[102]

The same though, could not be said about German South West Africa when South Africa declared war on that territory. From November 1914, the town remained garrisoned by the native police of both Northern and Southern Rhodesia while Capell returned to take command of 2nd Rhodesian Regiment when it was being recruited for East Africa.[103]

CHAPTER 3

THE OUTBREAK OF WAR: SOUTHERN AFRICA, 1914

Before war was declared on 4 August 1914, Louis Botha, Prime Minister of the Union of South Africa, was visiting the British South Africa Company territories of Southern and Northern Rhodesia while the other South African politicians were campaigning across South Africa in anticipation of the forthcoming election a year later, in October 1915. On hearing of the likelihood of war, Sir David Graaff, member of the South African cabinet, after meeting Churchill in London telegrammed Botha to let him know the situation. Instead of returning to South Africa on the German ship he had booked from Beira, Botha and his wife returned to the Union overland.[1] At the same time, South Africa was without its Governor General as Herbert Gladstone, Governor General since Union, had terminated his tenure a year early in July 1914 and was on his way back to England. The arrival of his replacement, Sydney Buxton, was delayed due to the outbreak of the war with the result that the Lord Chief Justice, Sir H de Villiers, assumed the role. However, he died two days before Buxton arrived and the Attorney General Sir James Rose Innes assumed the mantle. This posed some difficulty for Botha who had lost a sounding board. Although the Governor General was partial to British interests, he was impartial concerning the South African population. De Villiers and Rose Innes were not and so refrained from offering advice outside of the constitutional boundaries. Buxton arrived on 8 September and on 11 September 1914, before he was up to speed on South African concerns, South Africa had made its decision about supporting Britain and taking on the German South West Africa campaign. The extent of South Africa's participation in the war was to prove contentious with rebellion erupting in October 1914. This chapter examines the internal situation in South Africa at the outbreak of war and the government's decision to send troops to capture German South West Africa.

The British request that South Africa bring the German colony under allied control by subjugating Luderitzbucht and Swakopmund arrived on 4 August and was discussed by the South African cabinet on 7 August 1914.[2] Botha, Smuts, Thomas Watt, de Wet and Henry Burton were in favour of the campaign, whilst FS Malan, HC van Heerden, HS Theron and JAC Graaff were not. They felt the 'loyalty of Afrikaners' would be tested 'beyond what had been proposed in the telegram of 4 August' – namely the removal of the Imperial troops. Asking the Afrikaners not to rise up against Britain was one thing, but asking the people to support a campaign against a group of people, the Germans, which they felt a close affinity to, was something else. Malan was prepared to resign over the issue, but, became unsure when he realised his resignation might not be understood by the country. He was prepared to offer Britain support only, and not invade German South West Africa due to the repercussions this could have throughout the Union.[3] Where Botha and Smuts saw Germany's role during the 1899–1901 war as a betrayal, Hertzog and his followers did not.[4] Other concerns about the campaign revolved around the terrain and the possibility of 'internal black unrest'. If white South Africans left to fight in German South West and there was a native uprising in South Africa, there would be no troops to deal with the rebellion.

Having convinced FS Malan, who was 'the most influential of the dissenters' about the need for the campaign, the others also changed their mind.[5] Botha argued that if South Africa did not take on the campaign there was nothing to stop Britain from asking India or Australia to do so.[6] The implication of another country being involved in the campaign would reduce South Africa's claim to the territory and reflect poorly on the country. Given the relationship between white South Africans and Indians, the threat of Indian troops being used instead of South Africans would have been enough to make the doubters reconsider South African involvement.

Parliament was scheduled to meet as soon as the new Governor General arrived and until then, nothing could be done about invading German South West Africa apart from complete the plans and arrangements for invasion. Smuts as Minister of Defence soon realised that his generals were not all supporting the proposed attack, but, they did not openly object as they were waiting to see whether the invasion would be sanctioned by parliament. In the country, however, rumours had started with talk of rebellion being an option. On 10 August 1914 the decision to destroy the wireless stations at Luderitzbucht and Swakopmund in South West Africa was communicated to London and on 15 August, a meeting was scheduled to take place near Lichtenburg. It is unknown who called for this meeting but Generals Beyers and Maritz were involved, making it clear they were reacting to inside information.[7]

Smuts and Botha had been alerted to the events on 15 August and arranged for their good friend and colleague Koos de la Rey, accompanied by Sir Abe Bailey, a mining magnate and another close friend, to attend and instead of revolution, call for calm. There is some confusion over the purpose of the gathering. HS Webb, Secretary of the National Party, maintained that de la Rey was going to call for the independence of the Boer Republics whereas PH Sampson, a Botha supporter, maintained that de la Rey was going to point out that there was no need to attack the German colony because if Britain won the war, German South West Africa would automatically be incorporated into South Africa. Later accounts record that General de la Rey was to speak at the event as he saw the opportunity of war with Germany for South Africa to obtain its freedom as the *bittereinders* had pledged at the end of the 1899–1901 war. He did not intend for rebellion and asked that burghers attend the meeting unarmed. This was in contrast to the impression given by Beyers and Kemp, who it was believed would manipulate the statement for their own aims. Whatever the message, the crowd, all dressed ready to go on commando, dispersed disappointed, 'dazed and bewildered',[8] and the first phase of the rebellion came to an end.

Smuts was confident, or arrogant, believing that the anger at the invasion of German South West Africa would be forgiven when the colony was brought into the Union.[9] However, the agreement of parliament had to be obtained for mobilising the defence force.[10] This was done between 11 and 14 September during the special session to welcome Lord Buxton as the new Governor General. Although Botha won the vote 92 to 12, the pressure he and his supporters were under was clearly set out by Sir George Farrar, Member of Parliament and owner of the East Rand Proprietary Mines (ERPM):

> I must say that I think that if ever a man has played the game for the British Empire this time it has been Botha, and he has fairly burnt his boats with his own people. They expected the usual opposition from Hertzog, but I really think he had great trouble with his own people. Hertzog's attitude was what we expected – a kind of friendly neutrality, that is, they would be quite prepared to defend their own homes, but why attack the Germans in German S.West, since if the Germans had the better of the Allies they would be in an awkward position. Hertzog argued that the people of England were divided on the question of the War as three Ministers had resigned, and all this rubbish. At the bottom of it all was personal hatred of Botha. What he [Hertzog] wished to convey was if only Botha would consult him all would go well. Anyhow, on the division he only got 12 supporters and it went through.[11]

Hertzog was not the only senior politician to object to the campaign, John X Merriman, leader of the Cape was also against the invasion. However, unlike Hertzog who did not favour the idea of an attack against a German colony, Merriman felt the action would divide the country.[12] In order to overcome the likely resistance of parliament, Minister for War Smuts had arranged a pretext for the invasion. He had realised following the dissent in cabinet, that for the Union to support invading a peaceful country with close affinity to themselves, German South West Africa would need to be seen as having attacked South Africa. On 21 August 1914, the first plan of operations decided upon at Defence Headquarters Pretoria was formulated. Smuts chaired the meeting attended by Beyers, Brigadier-General HG Lukin Inspector General of the Permanent Force, Sir Duncan McKenzie former Commandant-General in Natal, Colonel FS Beves Commander of Cadets, Colonel PCB Skinner on loan from the British Army, and Sir William Hoy General Manager of Railways. After some discussion, it was decided 'to occupy Luderitzbucht while the wireless station and landing equipment at Swakopmund were to be destroyed by naval bombardment.' In addition a force would be landed at Port Nolloth and at Upington. Lukin, Maritz and Beves would each lead a force.[13] The same day, articles began appearing in the press about German troops being seen across the border at Nakob on 19 August and attacks against the local population. However, the Nationalists disputed the position of Nakob on the government's map suggesting that Smuts had moved the border to suit his ulterior motive. Rumours had also been started that the Germans planned to attack Pretoria, and there was growing concern about spies.[14] Piet Pretorius noted that de la Rey's sister was set to follow him as it was feared he was a German spy having come from German East Africa.[15]

'[T]he people are decided on the question; they *prefer* I think to sit tight, but it has not been well managed in this way.' The government had convinced the politicians but not yet the country.[16] Despite this assessment, Farrar felt Botha had '[played] the game [... was] thoroughly sound and doing his best for the Empire.' He continued that 'so long as [Botha] remains on top [...] he will keep the majority of his people together.'[17] However, Botha and Smuts' failure to carry sections of the country with them on the need to invade German South West Africa was obvious soon after the House rose, particularly in the northern Orange Free State and south-western Transvaal – the two areas which had been the last to surrender in 1901. De la Rey had made his point in parliament as part of the debate, but left the House before the vote. He met Louis Botha in the gardens and reiterated that he would not break the law, believing Botha would lead the country to independence when the time was right. He caught the next train to Johannesburg. There he met with Beyers who had resigned his position in the Defence Force and they made plans to go to Lichtenburg and

Potchefstroom. This liaison significantly took place on 15 September, a month after the Treurfontein meeting. The significance of the day of the month, the 15th, although not the month or year, was the day identified by the prophet or *Siener* van Rensburg that something important was to happen. For the die-hards, it was believed to be the day the British government would be overthrown, although Brien suggests it was possibly the day de la Rey would die. It was to be the latter. On their way out of Johannesburg, de la Rey ordered his driver to ignore a roadblock and to continue driving. Unknown to the occupants of the car, the roadblock had been set up to capture the Foster Gang which had recently killed a number of policemen.[18] Not knowing who was in the vehicle, a shot was fired which ricocheted into de la Rey killing him instantly. Initially it was believed that Smuts had arranged for his friend's assassination but these rumours were soon disproved, although not before some damage had been caused. Smuts broke the news to Botha playing golf with the Governor General near Cape Town and the two men immediately left for Pretoria, the Governor General following two days later.[19] Within days, on 20 September, de la Rey's funeral was held in Lichtenburg and it was the last time Botha, Smuts, Beyers, de Wet and Maritz met in peace. After the funeral, Beyers and Kemp remained with the gathering ostensibly to ensure that no damage was caused. However, within a week the rebellion entered its third phase,[20] notwithstanding the publication of a National Party manifesto on the German invasion of Belgium: 'We are prepared to do everything in our power to support the Government and the Imperial Government in order that the cause of right may prevail.'[21]

German South West Africa

Despite the unrest in the country and that various soldiers had resigned their commissions, preparations for the invasion of the German colony continued. Beyers had complained about the unpreparedness of the defence force as well as other technical difficulties whilst Lieutenant-General SG (Manie) Maritz had 'professional difficulties' with the Active Citizens Force under his command. Another significant resignation was that of JCG Kemp, a staff officer.[22] Beyers' point about the lack of preparation was valid. When the cabinet met in early August 1914 it agreed that as a show of loyalty and to return Britain's trust in the country, South Africa would assume its own defence. This resulted in all but one of the Imperial Service Garrisons being recalled to Britain. The remaining garrison was sent to support the defence of Cape Town. At the same time, despite denials in parliament, the defence force was put on alert, pending the decision by parliament to attack South West Africa and to authorise the call-up of reservists, which it had to do within thirty days of the defence force being mobilised.[23] Due to the logistics of launching a campaign, plans had been put in place to go to war as soon as possible after parliament gave its approval, but also to ensure South Africa was in a position to defend itself should the German colony invade South Africa or a native uprising occur. This position was confused when the 'annual domestic service' notifications were sent out shortly before the war started. As a result, given the timing of the notifications, many assumed that they were being called up or conscripted for imperial service in contravention of the Defence Act.[24]

The rebellion officially started on 9 October 1914 when Maritz led 500 troops into German South West Africa, taking a number of his fellow South Africans as prisoner, including Deneys Reitz's brother. Volunteers to counteract the rebellion were called up on 12 October and were personally led by Botha. Once in South West Africa, Maritz arranged a treaty with German Governor Seitz that when Germany won the war, the Transvaal and Orange Free State would be granted freedom and that the Boers would be allowed to annex Delagoa Bay in Portuguese East Africa.[25] Reitz believed that the rebellion for many South Africans was not about the invasion of German South West Africa, but rather to bring about the independence of the two ex-Boer colonies. Others, as with all wars and conflict, joined because their friends did so or for some excitement.[26]

Rather than use volunteers in German South West Africa, Botha and Smuts naturally turned to the defence force, despite being fully aware of the divisions: Beyers, a Boer War die-hard, was responsible for the Active Citizens Force while Lukin was Inspector-General for the Permanent Force. However, for the two senior politicians, the most vexing issue was not the loyalty of their generals, but the possibility of a native uprising. When the Defence Force Act of 1912 was drawn up and presented to parliament, the fear of native uprisings both internally and externally to the country comprised half the case for the armed forces. A police force had been set up in April 1913 to deal with native unrest in the towns but rural policing remained the responsibility of the South African Mounted Rifles who were responsible to the Department of Defence. This latter group could, therefore, not be called up to serve in South West Africa and as they constituted the vast majority of the Permanent Force, the Active Citizens Force had to be called upon. However, only those in the towns were mobilised due to the need to maintain order in the rural areas. This was despite the civil unrest which had erupted in Johannesburg and the East Rand in 1913.[27] The situation was criticised by Farrar, who felt that 'Had they [the government] called at once for Volunteers instead of the Defence Force, they would have got heaps of men and much better material.'[28]

Botha and Smuts had taken a risk and failed. On 22 October 1914, the Boers led by Beyers refused to entrain. Following a request to ex-Free State President Steyn to negotiate with the rebels to prevent a turn to arms, Botha attempted to negotiate with Beyers himself. His arrival supported by a commando was misinterpreted as hostile, shots were fired and armed rebellion ensued.[29] The two men, Botha and Smuts, then took another risk when 'All Burgher Commandos were called out' even though 'the loyalty of many of the Burgher Commandos was doubtful, and it was not known to what extent reliance could be placed upon them in opposition to their countrymen.' However, 'the response was most satisfactory'.[30] Of the 30,000 troops who participated with the government against the rebels, 21,000 were Boers.[31] Botha personally led the troops, refusing an offer by Britain to divert Australian troops to support him, although he did make use of the 1st Rhodesian Regiment which left Salisbury on 14 November for Bloemfontein.[32] By November 1914, only Maritz who had been in contact with the Germans in South West Africa had escaped into Portuguese Angola where, by 9 August 1915, he was captured and interred.[33]

In German South West Africa General Joachim von Heydebreck, to be killed on 12 November 1914 by Boer rebels (the official history claims it was a bomb), led 2,000 German troops and 3,000 reservists. Together with Governor Seitz they refused to support the rebels further than supplying food and equipment. This was to prevent possible problems for Germany and to prevent the South Africans from uniting against the German colony.[34] The colony was reminded by the German Reichskolonialamt to remain on the defensive on 4 August 1914. So, when the rebellion erupted in the Union, the Germans were unable to use the opportunity to surprise and exploit the situation for fear of undermining the rebel cause.[35] Germany felt it better to let the South Africans fight amongst themselves than have them united against the German colony. If the South African government went ahead with the intended attack on the German colony, it would be divided – having to ensure order within its own borders, protect against possible native uprisings and defeat the enemy alongside.

'Practically the whole of the campaign against the Rebels was carried out by Mounted Infantry [ie Boers, although] a few armoured trains were employed early in the operations, and towards the end, for the final rounding up, infantry were rapidly transported great distances across country in motor cars.'[36] Botha maintained a policy of reconciliation in spite of the concerns of the English-speaking population. Only one rebel, Jopie Fourie, was executed as he had not resigned his military commission and Botha was unavailable to caution restraint, while Beyers drowned trying to cross a flooded river.[37] The remainder having spent about a year in prison were released after paying a fine, which invariably the Boer women arranged.[38]

With the rebellion officially over, South Africa could concentrate on invading South West Africa. In anticipation of the pending campaign, the ports of Swakopmund and Luderitzbucht were attacked on 14 and 15 September respectively.[39] However, the subsequent delay caused by the rebellion gave the South African government an unexpected reprieve, time to finalise arrangements and an opportunity for raw recruits to have some experience of campaigning. Buxton's arrival was also to aide in improved preparations for the campaign.[40] Little had been done by Botha to ensure communications between the army and the navy, the latter complaining that Botha was ignoring them. As Botha had never had to conduct a campaign using another service before, it is not surprising that he neglected to include them in his plans. That the campaign lacked organisation is confirmed by Farrar, who was asked by Botha to provide assistance: 'On the Friday [after the September parliamentary session] he asked me to see him and Smuts and they said they were very anxious about the organisation of No. 4 Division in German S.W. under General McKenzie and would I go up with [him ...] Generally speaking, there is no organization – everything has been pushed together without any idea of the magnitude of the job. [...] It is a very difficult job and it almost requires the same organization as Kitchener's expedition to Khartoum as we have in German S.W. also to fight the desert.'[41]

During these months of rebellion and preparation for the campaign in South West Africa, the Germans in the colony took the opportunity to realise one of their long-term goals: occupy the southern part of Portuguese Angola. This would enable Germany to build an African empire across the breadth of Africa. The problem was that Portugal, and hence Angola, was neutral and that the same territories fell into the British Empire realm of interest, specifically that of its dominion, South Africa. However, despite Sir Edward Grey asking the Portuguese government to remain out of the war in Africa, the appeal of action grew stronger and on 11 September 1914, 1,500 troops left for Angola, a decision made before the German attack on 25 August 1914.[42]

On 18 August 1914, the British Ambassador to Portugal, Lancelot Carnegie, wrote to London that the Portuguese government had decided to send 1,000 troops to each of Moçambique and Angola. Those for Angola, as stated in the Portuguese press, were 'to hold in check the natives in the Cuanhama district which has never been effectively occupied.' He continued that 'there is an understanding between the Germans and these natives' and that they 'would join in any German movement against the Portuguese possessions.' The Minister of Foreign Affairs reinforced this move 'as there were practically no white troops in the colonies and the Government had been contemplating this step for some time past and, in order to disarm any opposition to sending men abroad, were taking advantage of the present crisis to carry out their intentions.'[43]

The Angolan Governor General ordered a state of emergency on 12 September 1914 under the pretext of internal control of locals. However, in reality it was meant to stop the Germans accessing the Mossamedes port. Despite being neutral, the Portuguese deported 143 Germans for spying, arms smuggling and stirring the inhabitants.[44] The extra troops which arrived from Portugal on 1 October 1914 meant the Governor General had just under 7,000 troops to protect the west African Portuguese colony. On 19 October 1914, three Germans were shot and 15 arrested at the Naulila border post and fighting ensued. Although this was in line with the Angolan state of emergency, it was portrayed in South West Africa as a hostile attack and with the build-up of Portuguese troops in Angola and no way to communicate with Germany due to the destruction of the wireless stations, Seitz assumed a state of war existed between his colony and his Portuguese neighbour. Fortuitously for him, the Boer rebellion provided the Germans much needed time to deal with the Portuguese.[45]

The Portuguese were concerned about the invasion, as indicated by the Consul General's communication to Buxton on 26 October 1914. In response to the 'serious incident' which had taken place at Naulila, he thought that the newly landed troops at Lourenço Marques would be sent to Angola.[46] That this did not happen must have been regretted when the Germans, commanded by Victor Franke, invaded on 31 October 1914 and defeated a local force. The extent of the defeat led the Angolan commander, Alves Rocadas to believe the German forces were stronger than they were and he withdrew his troops north leaving behind 1,000 rifles and four machine guns which the locals used to revolt.[47] The Germans under Franke launched a successful attack on Naulila on 18 December 1914 in response to Portugal's aggression, but, when it appeared that the South Africans were ready to re-launch the German South West Africa campaign, the Germans withdrew leaving an 'independent' tract of land between the two white nations.[48]

CHAPTER 4

GERMAN SOUTH WEST AFRICA, ANGOLA AND SOUTHERN AFRICA, 1915

The German South West Africa campaign started in earnest in January 1915 after South African troops had landed at Walfish Bay on 25 December 1914. Having announced in the press on 21 September, the day after de la Rey's funeral, that only volunteers would be used in German South West Africa, Botha now insisted on conscription – a move he could legally make following parliament's sanction of the campaign.[1] Those who refused to fight would be imprisoned for the duration of the war, thereby ensuring some measure of peace amongst the white population. As Botha was aware that it was invariably the women who would keep their husbands from enlisting, the threat of imprisonment gave the latter a face-saving alternative.[2] He also decided to personally lead the campaign into South West Africa believing he was the only person able to command the respect of both the English and Boer or Afrikaans speakers, as he 'had a great influence with [the generals], far greater than Smuts, and they would do for Botha what they would not do for Smuts.'[3]

Given the tensions in the country, Botha's decision to lead the campaign was quite a risk. However, it seems to have paid off as the situation proved sufficiently calm for Smuts to get directly involved too, despite being deputy Prime Minister and Minister of Defence. This left Governor General Buxton and the cabinet under FS Malan and

Burton in charge of the country. With no prime minister or deputy to liaise through, Buxton buckled down and did what was needed, especially as the South Africans had no experience of working with the British armed forces. Although generally welcomed by the young government, it did sometimes cause problems as seen by Botha's surmising that the Governor General was 'seriously disturbed about my telegram, but Jannie, however well-intentioned, he pokes his fingers into things which have nothing to do with him. What I feel is wrong is that he goes and talks with my subordinates and not with me […] let him discuss operational matters only with you or with Cabinet Ministers.'[4] This complaint appears a one-off and the relationship between Governor General and his government appears to have been friendly.[5]

The German South West Africa campaign had a significant impact on Britain. It was a short clinical campaign completed within six months with only 266 deaths.[6] It was fought in the second most significant German colony in Africa by soldiers who had fought against Britain less than fifteen years before. However, the desired outcome of the campaign on South Africa did not materialise as the South African Dutch/Afrikaans and English troops ostensibly remained divided, for all the claims of the official history. The divide between the two communities was perpetuated in that the mounted troops were predominantly Boer whilst the English formed the infantry which mopped up after an attack.[7] In addition, whilst conducting the campaign, Botha had to reconcile Boers loyal to himself with British regular troops. When compared to the commando system, the English troops had a very organised approach to battle. This was to be a challenge as Botha had not had to lead English troops in the field before and felt that if he pushed McKenzie to move faster, he would resign. This would then cause difficulties with the Natal commandos and increase existing tensions between English and Afrikaans speakers.[8] In contrast, Collyer maintains that McKenzie's English mounted forces were as good as Botha's Boers as they had learnt to survive in the South African veld in the same way.[9]

The main issues facing the South African troops in German South West Africa were lines of communication, coordination and transport.

Botha, who became commander-in-chief, only really led his northern force and although he met with Smuts, who was coordinating the southern approach on a few occasions during the campaign, the different groups operated independently with their own supplies and strategy. This meant that there was unnecessary wastage and cost when the campaign quietened in the south and became more active in the north. As the campaign moved further north and Botha realised transport and supply strain, he appointed a General Staff. This was overseen by General Skinner, on loan from Britain and the only soldier in the area with any experience of coordinating lines of communications. Skinner worked swiftly to improve matters, but, it still took time given the stage of the campaign and the spread of the forces across inhospitable terrain. Out of the six months' campaign, Botha was only on the move for twenty-four days. The remainder was spent waiting for supplies to catch up. All the communications centred on Pretoria and General Headquarters where the only person in place to coordinate matters at the outbreak of war was HRM Bourne, a civil servant with no military experience. The staff was rapidly increased but systems still had to be put in place and coordinated, and it was in this respect that Buxton felt the need to get directly involved. In addition to what was happening on the ground, the sea and air force needed to be coordinated too, the former being the link between the Union and the forces in the German colony.[10]

The initial plan for attacking German South West Africa had been three-pronged using the existing railways.[11] Botha had not been involved in the initial campaign planning as this was done by the Military Department, namely Smuts. Buxton was aware than both Crewe and Thompson, the Imperial military representatives in South Africa were not happy with the plans and that the three-pronged approach was not what Botha would have planned. The naval bombardment of the coastal towns had taken place in 1914 before the rebellion and this together with Botha's decision to take command of the forces enabled him to make some modifications but not many given the preparations already in place.[12] He organised a five-pronged attack and having instructed his commanders as to their roles, Botha himself joined the campaign on 11 February 1915 assuming command from Swakopmund. Smuts joined the attack coordinating the forces from the south on 14 April 1915.[13]

> 'It is generally conceded that the plan of campaign adopted, ie invasion from five different and widely divergent points and in the face of almost insuperable natural obstacles, was of exceptional merit and conception well worthy of the wonderful genius of Generals Botha and Smuts. South West Africa, in extent 322,446 square miles, is once more coloured red on the map, and great should be our feelings of pride when we contemplate that this huge area of country has been re-gained to the British Empire by the force of arms of a race, now fellow subjects, but fifteen years ago an independent people and at War with the British Empire.' So wrote George Farrar before he died.[14]

It was realised that the railways would play an important role in the German South West Africa campaign given the extreme desert nature of the country and the huge tracts of land that would need to be covered. Although there was an already existing rail network in the territory it did not fully meet the requirements of the South African army, especially as the Germans had destroyed tracks as they vacated certain areas. Sir William Hoy the General Manager of Railways was tasked with remedying this situation, although Smuts and Botha asked Farrar to assist due to his practical knowledge and management of railways. Farrar realised the extent of the task he had been given and was rather grateful for the rebellion which enabled him a head-start in his railway building. The tragedy of the situation was that Farrar was killed on 20 May 1915 before seeing the benefit of his work. Like Lettow-Vorbeck and Smuts later in East Africa, Farrar preferred to do his own intelligence work and this resulted in his death when, in a freak accident, the trolley he was travelling on collided with another.[15]

Comparatively, the German South West Africa campaign claimed few lives despite the poisoning of wells and other atrocity tales of forcing the enemy into waterless areas: 88 South Africans were killed against 103 Germans.[16] This was quite remarkable given the push there was and that motorised transport remained relatively unused. Although he had around six hundred motorised vehicles at his disposal, Botha preferred horsepower as the motor vehicles were unsuited to the sandy conditions of the desert. They were eventually sent to other theatres.[17] South Africa also used planes during the campaign to track down the commandos when they lost contact and to bomb the enemy, in the hopes of forcing them to ask for peace, particularly after they had evacuated Windhoek and moved north.[18] The Germans, too, tried airpower as Farrar wrote to his wife: 'one morning,' a German plane dropped two bombs on the camp – he was fifty yards away. 'One good thing was they put a parachute on, and you could see the bomb drop.' It killed one man and injured another nine. The following day another came and then not again. 'I don't think they will worry us much more, because they have only two aeroplanes and they can't afford to lose one.'[19]

As the South Africans moved forward, the Germans reacted half-heartedly, falling back and laying mines as they did.[20] Their lacklustre effort could partly be explained by Franke being in Angola, but the situation did not improve much once he returned and numerous towns fell to the South Africans without much struggle. According to Strachan, Botha believed this was due to Franke, who had replaced von Heydebreck as commanding officer on 12 November 1914, losing his nerve.[21] On 21 May 1915 Governor Seitz suggested an armistice to Botha to ensure German claims to South West Africa during the peace discussions. Botha refused, despite having achieved the goals set by the British government, namely the destruction of the wireless stations and the occupation of the German ports. The reason was that he now had South Africa's interests at heart and to ensure Pretoria had a claim to the territory, he needed to conquer it. It was for this reason too, that Smuts and Botha rejected the suggestion by Arnold Wienholt, an Australian hunter in Angola in August 1914, that South Africa invade the German colony through Southern Rhodesia. This was despite the proposal being supported by Southern Rhodesian Commander Edwards.[22]

The Germans rethought their strategy and regrouped. Their options were to move into Angola but a famine and lack of order there following the German withdrawal in 1914 made this unattractive.

Botha, though, was concerned that the Germans would look to link up with East Africa, but there does not seem to be any evidence to suggest that Franke considered this. Lettow-Vorbeck in East Africa had. So had a small group of eight Germans, including W Matten-Klodt.[23] Seitz was eventually convinced by Franke to ask for an armistice to prevent unnecessary casualties.[24] This attitude of the military and administrative leaders in German South West Africa was totally opposite to German East Africa where it was the Governor, Schnee, who wanted to keep his country out of the war and the commander, Lettow-Vorbeck, who wanted to continue.[25]

The surrender process began with a letter from Seitz suggesting 'the internment of the German force, with all its arms and war materials, till the end of the war.' Botha rejected this despite the Germans being in the ascendancy in Europe and the advance continued. The next day, Seitz asked Botha for his conditions for surrender and a meeting took place the following day between him and Botha. Before the meeting, Botha agreed a 'local armistice'. To ensure the terms were correctly understood, Botha sent his Chief-of-Staff to verbally explain the situation to the Germans. Botha suggested that the reservists be allowed to return to their pre-war work whilst the regular troops would become prisoners of war. An armistice was agreed for 6 July pending the approval by the Union government of the terms, which they gave.[26]

With final communications taking place between Botha's forces through the German positions, the South Africans resorted to using the Zulu language for confidential messages. The final terms were received by Botha on 8 July at 3am. When Seitz had not accepted them by seven that night and asked for another meeting, Botha threatened a renewal of action. At 2.30am on 9 July, Seitz accepted the terms. At 10am, Seitz, Franke, Lieutenant Bethe commanding the police and some junior officers met Botha. The agreement and arrangements were put in place by Botha on 5 July. They showed his foresight and knowledge of his fellow man when Franke challenged the advance of Brits and Mybergh during the armistice negotiations. Franke accepted Botha's case and occupation of Tsumeb and apologised for a German soldier wounding a Union soldier whilst discussions were taking place. Botha returned to the Union shortly after 15 July.[27]

Botha left the German structures in place but encouraged Boer immigrants who would provide the occupation. Botha's actions had been in spite of the reminder by Colonial Secretary Harcourt on 7 August 1914 'that any territory now occupied must be at the disposal of the Imperial Government for purposes of an ultimate settlement at the conclusion of the war.'[28] In 1918, there were still 12,000 Germans in South West Africa of which half were deported later that year. This approach by Botha enabled him to introduce 'South Africa's own brand of colonialism'.[29] Unlike other occupied German colonies where the Germans were interred or deported to Germany, those in South West Africa before 1918 were disarmed and released. This, for Botha and the South Africans was a political necessity. Interring or deporting Germans would result in the white population being overwhelmingly out-numbered by blacks and if there was a rising by the latter, it would be difficult to contain. Strachan maintains that this speeded up reconciliation between Germans and South Africans, whilst others claim the relationship remained one of ambivalence.[30]

The South African conquest of South West Africa meant a removal of the German threat to Angola. This resulted in a vacuum following Portuguese withdrawal from the area in October 1914. As a result of famine, drought and the effects of war, lawlessness became rife and the Portuguese found it necessary to re-occupy and subjugate the tribes there. This led to a new expeditionary force, under Pereora d'Eca being sent out. On his arrival, stories of brutality arose as he commenced a campaign against the locals, ordering everyone over the age of ten to be killed.[31] By 12 July 1915 all the Portuguese forts previously lost had been reclaimed and military operations were terminated in the area on 4 September 1915.[32] When Maritz was interred in Angola in August 1915 this brought the war to an end in south-west Africa and released the Northern Rhodesian Police from having to guard the Angolan and South West African borders.[33]

Southern Africa

Back in the Union, Smuts hailed the victory over German South West Africa as 'the first achievement of a united South African nation';

a point Mansergh contests.[34] In South Africa, attention turned inwards and to London as there was an election to be fought in October 1915 which Botha would not postpone.[35] The country's voice was important to future South African involvement in the war, and having been out of the country for six months, Botha felt out of touch with the general feel in the Union. Therefore, on his return to the country in July 1915, he focused on preparing for the election.

As early as April 1915, Buxton had suggested that South Africans be sent to East Africa after the German South West Africa campaign, however, Botha cautioned restraint pending the election outcome. The idea of sending South Africans to East Africa had first been raised in August 1914 by JX Merriman, a prominent South African personality and politician, who wrote an eight page letter to Major General Chas Thompson, General Officer Commanding South Africa, and had probably discussed the matter when he met Buxton for dinner, which he did regularly. Merriman suggested that a mounted South African force, meaning Boers, be sent to secure the territory which would ensure the safety of the Suez Canal and hence British shipping. He also felt that 5,000 Indians work with the Boer forces to subdue the territory.[36]

On 14 April 1915, Buxton secretly telegrammed Harcourt, Bonar Law's predecessor, about South Africans going to East Africa, a point he reiterated in a letter twelve days later and then again in May 1915.[37] Buxton's proposal was reinforced by CP Crewe, Director of Recruiting in South Africa and the brother of the then Secretary of State to India. In a letter to Walter Long, Crewe wrote that once the German South West Africa campaign was over, South Africa 'shall be quite ready [...] to help in German East.'[38] He also discussed the idea with Thompson who was in agreement, both believing that the sending of Boers loyal to Britain to fight in East Africa would have a positive political effect in South Africa as they would not openly be supporting Britain as if they were to fight in Europe. They acknowledged that the South Africans fighting in Europe would be mostly English speaking and infantry, whereas the mounted forces would mainly be Boers who would be more suited to East Africa given their lack of training and potential discipline issues.[39] Interestingly, despite the concern in London of South African discipline, no South Africans were court-martialled in any theatre whilst five Australians were. In the whole East Africa campaign a total of 137 courts-martial were held.[40]

In late April 1915, 'Citizen' wrote to the *Transvaal Leader* about sending troops to East Africa. Responses to the letter indicated mixed feelings. Supporting South Africans going to East Africa was the idea of adding territory to the greater South Africa or allowing evicted Belgians to settle there. The argument against was that South Africa had done its bit by sending troops to German South West Africa.[41] Authorship of the letter remains unclear yet the significance of the correspondence for the campaign in East Africa is clear – it opened the debate over South Africa's further involvement in the war. Possible authors include the head of the Transvaal University College who noted that 'our efforts to direct the Government to German East have been successful.'[42] Smuts, too, is a likely candidate having 'meant all along to tackle [German East Africa] only he [kept] his counsel so remarkably well that it was impossible to form that opinion before',[43] although at the time he was on active duty in German South West Africa. In addition, articles began to appear about the value of the German territory for farming, mining and hunting, yet neither the government nor the opposition made use of the press to push their views on the campaign even during the election period.[44] Botha, Smuts and Merriman saw the campaign as an opportunity for South Africa to gain control over Portuguese East African territory the Union had desired for many years. It seems to have been Harcourt, however, who prompted the realisation of the idea to swap German South West Africa for Portuguese East Africa to further the 'Cape to Cairo' railway link. This it would effect by repaying Portugal with captured German East African territory.[45] There was also the concern of having a German neighbour if Southern Rhodesia joined the Union. However, more importantly, participating in the East African campaign would provide the Union with further opportunity to prove that the two white South African races could work together. Having the Boers fight in East Africa was also not contrary to the British war policy of 5 August 1914 as it could be argued that the Boers would not be better used in Europe, although Kitchener's preference was for a 'Division of combined British and Boer brigades as well as a brigade of mounted troops' for Europe.[46]

The Governor General supported the Union ministers in their endeavour. Each time the issue seemed to slip off the radar, he nudged the offending group by sending a gentle reminder as he did with Dr Abdurahman's letter and the future services of South African troops in Africa. Regarding the latter, the letter sent on behalf of the South African government via the Governor General to the Colonial Office proposing that South Africans be used elsewhere in Africa contains almost the identical wording of the Minute received from Buxton a few days' later on the same topic. The letter contains no further explanation or detail on the proposal which suggests that the issue was discussed by the Governor General and his ministers and notification sent to England before formal documentation was completed in the Union.[47] Much of Buxton's business as Governor General was conducted through daily informal meetings with Botha, Smuts and other available cabinet ministers.[48]

In May 1915, while both Botha and Smuts were out of the country, Buxton initiated discussions on sending troops to East Africa.[49] Buxton was uncertain as to the number of Boers who would volunteer for service there given that they had been absent from their farms for six months and that they would not be keen to fight alongside Indians. This fear was reiterated by the Boer delegates, J van Deventer and AM Hughes who went on a fact finding mission to East Africa pending the decision to send South Africans.[50] The two delegates were particularly dismayed to hear that as the Indian troops serving in East Africa were Imperial Service Troops, paid for by wealthy Indians, they would have to consult on all matters.[51] Hughes and van Deventer were misinformed about the nature of the Indian forces. Less than half a unit was Imperial Service, the others were regular Indian troops.[52]

On 21 July 1915, a meeting took place between Thompson, Smuts and David Graaff. Although Smuts and Graaff were keen to send South Africans to East Africa, they did not think, given the tensions in South African between whites and Indians, that South Africans would be welcome especially as India had been given command of the theatre.[53] Smuts questioned Thompson in an attempt to ascertain how far Britain was prepared to go to get South African troops to East Africa without South Africa having to push, as this would have caused difficulties given the political split in the country. To ease tension in South Africa, Smuts wanted to claim that Britain had asked for South Africa's assistance. Thompson's hint that Britain would welcome South Africa's help in East Africa enabled Smuts to openly organise troops for the campaign despite Botha's decision not to commit to East Africa until after the election. South Africa's desire to send troops to East Africa met a number of openly stated aims: supporting the British war effort by providing an outlet for loyal Boers not willing or able to fight in Europe, fulfilling Rhodes' imperial dream and safeguarding South Africa's border if Southern Rhodesia ever joined the Union.[54]

Coloured, black and Indian troops?

A request from Britain for coloured and black troops was rejected by South Africa on 31 July 1915 as the South African ministers felt it would be impossible to raise coloured or black troops to carry arms for service even in East Africa. However, they were prepared to raise contingents to act as drivers, grooms and hands which could be used in Europe, although preferably in Africa.[55] Despite South Africa refusing to raise coloured and black troops and the subsequent proposal being rejected by the Army Council, coloureds and blacks saw service in Europe, and later in East Africa, as support services to the white South African contingents which were sent to the two theatres.[56] In due course, two armed coloured Cape Corps were recruited for service in East Africa and later also served in Palestine.[57]

There was concern about training non-whites to use weapons and follow military discipline. It was generally believed that these men, once trained, would be in a stronger position to rise up against their white masters. Another issue was the length of time it would take to train non-whites to the military standard required, despite the military history amongst certain tribes such as the Zulu. Natives would best be used in roles they were familiar with such as a 'general transport and remounts service corps'.[58] There was further no problem with natives being sent to East Africa 'as white men [could] not be asked to perform work associated with Natives' such as ploughing, hoeing, fetching, carrying and cooking.[59] A number of native South Africans saw service in East Africa although Grundlingh questions the extent to which they volunteered or were coerced. He feels few natives volunteered despite the higher wages as they distrusted whites following the 1913 Land Act which saw many displaced.[60] The difficulty recruiting blacks and coloureds was not helped by news filtering back to South Africa. Fendall noted on 1 June 1917 that there would be trouble over the number of deaths among the natives. Although they were 'of poor physique', they had 'made up their minds to die and did die', many of them on the troopship *Aragon* carrying sick and wounded to Durban. A total of twenty-eight men of the Cape Labour Corps died between 9 and 11 April 1917 on board.[61] The sinking of the troop carrier SS *Mendi* off the Isle of Wight on 21 February 1917 with the loss of 615 South African native lives also did not help recruitment.[62] Despite the negative feelings and distrust of the government, black organisations such as the South African Native National Congress (SANNC), African People's Organisation (APO) and occasional native chief, felt that by supporting the government, they would be rewarded in time as full citizens of the country.[63]

An armed battalion of the coloured Cape Corps under the command of white officers was to see service in East Africa during 1916. The Union government felt justified in raising these troops as the Germans were using armed askaris. In addition, the Cape Corps had 'done admirable service in old South African wars against natives, and would be admirably suited for campaigning under the conditions of hot climates and bush country.'[64] This decision, however, became a contentious issue during the October election as the Nationalists were concerned about the arming of non-white troops and the concessions that coloureds would receive to acknowledge their contribution.

The coloured population, a mixed race group of mainly white male and Malay female, had the vote in the Cape Province. The sensitivity of the vote had been experienced during the 1909 Union discussions when they almost faltered over the granting of non-whites the vote. The Cape Province had been the only territory to permit non-whites the vote, although Natal technically did. The Natal criteria for obtaining the right to vote were so stringent that all non-whites were excluded. The Orange Free State and the Transvaal had constitutionally excluded non-whites from voting rights. This position remained the status quo after Union and could only be changed by a two-third majority of both Houses of Parliament. The Nationalist fear was that voting rights would be extended to coloureds outside of the Cape together with a reduction in the eligibility requirements.[65] Botha circumvented this issue by stating that the contingent was being raised as an Imperial Contingent which meant that Britain was paying for its services and, therefore, there was no financial obligation for the Union.[66] As a result, the Assembly did not have to be consulted. In any event, the arguments posed by the Nationalists for not wanting native troops armed, did not hold for the coloured as the latter had 'superior' white cells and had also proven themselves admirably in earlier wars.[67] The final incentive for raising the Cape Corps was a letter from Dr A Abdurahman to the Governor General on 25 August 1915. He reiterated the African People Organisation's offer of help, listing all the previous offers which had been rejected. Three days after Buxton received the letter, the South African government sent him a Minute proposing the formation of a coloured Cape Corps, which was sanctioned by Britain in September. Buxton, however, only forwarded Abdurahman's letter to his Ministers on 31 August 1915. Given the timing of the correspondence and the relationship between the Governor General and his leading Ministers, it is quite plausible that the topic was discussed and the decision made before the forwarding of letters to allow the South African government an opportunity to demonstrate its open-mindedness.[68]

The only other major constituent group of South Africa not directly involved in the war after the recruitment of the native and coloured contingents for Europe, was the Indian. It was, therefore, decided that the government should 'secure some representation for the Indian community'. They would form Indian Bearer Companies as their 'composition and duties [would be] well understood in India' and they would not carry arms. Raising these companies for service anywhere where Indians were serving would hopefully show India that South Africa was not discriminating against the Indian population.[69] They were eventually sent to East Africa where they had to serve alongside

South Africans despite the concerns raised by the Boer delegation to that theatre.[70] As with the SANNC, APO and other groups, the Natal Indian Association put its struggle on hold to help the country in the hope that after the war, their desires would be realised, if not by South Africa then by Great Britain.[71]

Britain sanctioned the service of the two Indian Bearer Companies and the Cape Corps for East Africa in September 1915. However, when Austen Chamberlain asked in October of that year for coloured troops to serve in India and Mesopotamia, he was emphatically told by Bonar Law that South Africa would not sanction this.[72] The South Africans were frightened that if non-white troops served anywhere other than with white South African troops, they would return to South Africa with ideas of equality which could not be sanctioned.[73] Had Chamberlain requested Indian troops from South Africa, this may well have been sanctioned in the hope that many would have chosen to resettle in India after the conflict rather than return to South Africa.

Election time

The election in South Africa took place during October 1915 amidst the threat of a new uprising in the country. There were four main parties participating: the Unionists and the Labour Party were the smallest, pro-Britain and mainly English-speaking. Many English speakers had left South Africa on the outbreak of war to support Britain under the command of Generals who had progressed in the British army from the 1899–1901 war such as General Creswell. (General Lukin first led troops in German South West Africa before leaving for Europe in 1916 where he led the South Africans at Delville Wood.) However, there was a significant group which felt that leaving the country would only allow the Nationalists a greater say in what was happening due to the lack of opposition.[74] This group was also anti-German and wanted Germans resident in South Africa interred for the duration of the war, particularly after the sinking of the *Lusitania*. Significantly, even the Labour Party leaders, such as Creswell, who had been working with Hertzog prior to the outbreak of war, broke with the Nationalists to support Botha and the war effort.[75] At the other extreme was Hertzog's Nationalist Party which had formed early in 1914. This group was focused mainly in the Orange Free State, was anti-Britain and anti-Empire. The Nationalists also felt that there should be equality between English and Afrikaans and that South Africa's needs should be put before those of Britain. They were pro-German although were prepared to fight Germany if that country invaded South Africa. The centre party was the South Africa Party headed by Louis Botha and Jan Smuts. It was the only true national party representing both English and Afrikaans and was pro-Empire.

Sending troops to East Africa was according to Smuts, indirectly protecting South Africa. Botha, however, felt this was rather tenuous and wanted to feel more certain about the country's reaction.[76] When to hold the election was a delicate matter: Buxton had suggested parliament agree to delay it until after the war, whilst Botha felt it important to go ahead. Even as late as April 1915, they were still discussing which option to go for with Botha informing the Governor General that if the South West Africa campaign was not over by August of that year, he would ask parliament for permission to delay the election. As it was the campaign ended in July 1915 and the election went ahead. This was not before Buxton had done some calculations to ensure there was sufficient South Africa Party support in the country and not on military service.

The extent to which East Africa featured in the election campaign is not easy to estimate as there is very little mentioned in the press. If the campaign did feature, it was in connection with what volunteers would receive, which according to Richard Meinertzhagen were farms.[77] There is no evidence in the South African documents that this was the case. Fiddes, in London, noted on 13 May 1915 that 'when the South West Africa campaign is further advanced it might be well to consider the possibility of getting a South African contingent by the hope of farms.'[78] This idea went no further. The farms the South Africans were talking about were actually in South West Africa, over which South Africa had far greater claim especially as the Union had started investing in the country's railways and postal services.[79]

During the election period, the newspapers carried no manifestos and very little information about the war despite Botha placing such great emphasis on the outcome of the election in determining the extent of South Africa's further involvement in the war. Botha was keen to keep the issue of East Africa out of the elections to prevent a confrontation with the Nationalists over its recruitment and financing.[80] It was only once the election was won, that the South African Party manifesto was published in the press, albeit briefly and it had no mention of East Africa.[81] This was in line with Botha's political view that manifestos should be like 'round pebbles' that one could not get a hold on.[82] Political manifestos were explained at party gatherings where messages were tailored to the audience. So for example, when Botha was questioned in Rustenburg and Potchefstroom about whether the coloureds being raised for service in East Africa were to be given voting rights, he replied in the negative. Yet, he had to acknowledge the coloured contribution to ensure the South Africa Party received their vote in the Cape.[83]

In the main, the election was fought over the position of Afrikaans and the war in general. Other issues on Botha's agenda included Provincial Councils and the desire to incorporate Delagoa Bay into the Union.[84] Buxton felt the outcome would be close, but, was sure Botha would remain Prime Minister. Although this proved to be the case, Buxton had to convince Botha to continue in power. Despite the South African Party having won the election, it could only safely stay in power with the support of the Unionists which Botha felt limited his scope of action.[85] He would have to take the raising of additional troops for Europe and East Africa to parliament, something both he and Smuts were to keen to avoid and Buxton had to remind them of the constitution to ensure they did.[86]

The election result dealt the recruitment effort a severe blow as Botha felt he could not push as hard as he had initially intended. There were advertisements in the English and Dutch press, although the Nationalist Afrikaans press seemed to feel that if they ignored the issue of the campaign, it would disappear. Individuals, including bishops, supported the recruitment effort by attending meetings and pleading for men to volunteer.[87] Recruitment, though, remained slow despite the articles in the press, which led the South African government to delay contacting Britain. Prompted by a 'personal and private' telegram from the Colonial Office regarding the finalising of arrangements and a telegram from the War Office on 9 November 1915 to send the Indian Bearer Companies to East Africa, Botha and Smuts were forced to reconsider the situation.[88] As a result, South Africa did not press to take over complete control of the East Africa campaign thereby leaving the War Office in charge. This dealt a blow to South Africa's desire to eventually take control of the German colony when the war was over.

Despite Botha's caution about recruiting, on 12 November, Buxton wrote to London requesting permission to raise a fourth mounted regiment for service in East Africa, a point he had alluded to in August 1915. This regiment would consist of men from the towns and Natal who were mainly English speaking, and would help reduce the divide between the Boer and English populations so that they could also have 'fun'.[89] The raising of this regiment, sanctioned the following day, would give those loyal to Britain, who had felt the need to stay in South Africa during the election, an opportunity to enlist.[90] It would also reward those who had felt snubbed during the German South West Africa campaign by virtue of their being infantry and having to mop up after the cavalry action. Despite the recruitment drive, South Africa had to rework the contingents it sent over as it had not taken into account the need for reinforcement troops.[91]

A couple of weeks later, on 29 November 1915, Smuts informed the War Office that he would have to 'refuse the military command in German East Africa which the British Government wanted [him] to undertake' due to the difficulties expected in parliament caused by the close election result.[92] This was a week after the War Office had appointed General Sir Horace Smith-Dorrien to the position.[93] The idea that Smuts become General Officer Commanding East Africa was raised in August 1915 by Buxton providing South Africa was able to send 'substantial assistance'.[94] Soon after, Smuts tentatively suggested himself as commander, although a note on the official history suggests Smuts put himself forward as early as June 1915.[95] However, before he could formally make the offer, he was concerned about the situation in South Africa and felt that he would need to remain at home. If the autumn offensive failed, he would reconsider the position.[96]

Given South Africa's internal political situation in November 1915, it was felt inappropriate for Smuts or Botha to leave the country. During December, a recruitment drive was initiated which seemed so successful that Buxton offered the British government additional mounted regiments. The political situation in South Africa was clearly much improved and by January 1916, was such that its leading politicians felt more confident to push their demands, especially as it would now be possible for Smuts to leave the country. Having fancied himself commander of the forces in East Africa from June 1915 and with Smith-Dorrien unwell, an opportunity presented itself and Smuts was not going to let it pass again. Smith-Dorrien's absence from the immediate action provided Smuts and Botha time to reclaim lost ground.

CHAPTER 5

WAR ON THE WATERS AND IN THE AIR, 1915–1917

The middle years of the war, 1915–1917, witnessed a change in strategy in the main European and the subsidiary African theatres. During 1915 German South West Africa and Cameroon were removed from German control leaving German East Africa to be subjugated and uprisings in Egypt to be contained. In Europe, 1915 saw the battle of Vimy Ridge and the failed attempt in the Dardanelles. Nineteen-sixteen became the year of the Somme. During this battle, following the arrival of the South African forces under Lukin which had detoured via Egypt to bring the Senussi under control, the South Africans made what is regarded as a heroic stand at Delville Wood. The attack at Delville Wood, where two-thirds of the South African Division was lost within five days of battle has been etched into the memory of South Africa's First World War involvement. The following year, 1917 saw the battles of Arras and Passchendaele or Third Ypres. This year, too, proved significant with the withdrawal of Russia as an ally in February following the Bolshevik Revolution and Vladimir Lenin replacing the Tzar as supreme ruler. The United States of America in turn entered the war on the side of the allies in April, not to replace Russia, but, as a result of the Germans sinking the passenger liner the *Lusitania*. In Europe as in East Africa, the Germans were fighting on more than one front and needing to become self-reliant as blockades were imposed, although not always effectively.[1] This chapter and the following two explore the different aspects of the war in east and central Africa. The wider international scene and political decisions in London will be discussed in a later chapter.

Whilst the land war in German South West Africa was racing on and that in East Africa was plodding along, the lakes were seeing action. At Bukoba on Lake Victoria Nyanza in northern German East Africa, an important signal station needed destroying. Kitchener finally sanctioned action against it after pressure by General MJ Tighe, Wapshare's replacement as Commander-in-Chief. Tighe pressed for the action in order to boost Indian morale[2] following the arrival of the 25th Royal Fusiliers (Frontiersmen), the attack was launched under the command of General Stewart. The forces were landed on the coast and by the end of the day Stewart's men overlooked the town. On 22 June 1915 the signal station was destroyed and on 23 June they occupied the town, whilst the Germans under von Steumer withdrew. The victory was 'the first undisputable success we have achieved in the country' – a loss of thirty British soldiers to 350 Germans. The British burnt down some houses and raided others before leaving – an action not accepted but understood given the extent of the victory.[3]

On 10 January 1915 Mafia Island was brought under British control in an operation overseen by Colonel LES Ward. This gave the British a base close to the Rufiji Delta from where action could be coordinated against the *Königsberg*.[4] The need to rid the area of the *Königsberg* and for the British to strengthen their hold over the Indian Ocean was reinforced by the success of the *Kronborg* (previously known as the *Rubens*) in getting supplies through to the Germans. Around 14 April 1915, *Hyacinth* attacked the ship in Manza Bay having intercepted the ship's code. Despite the ship being damaged by *Hyacinth*, the British were chased off and the contents salvaged. Most of the *Kronborg's* men remained to fight with Lettow-Vorbeck, however, Captain Carl Christiansen wanted to continue with the navy. Annoyingly for the British, he was able to return to Germany through Portuguese East Africa after meeting and sharing news with Lettow-Vorbeck and Schnee. Lettow-Vorbeck claimed later that allowing the salvage of the *Kronborg's* cargo 'was the greatest mistake of the entire campaign' and clear evidence that the *Königsberg* was the major threat in the area.[5]

Sometime after the capture of Mafia Island, the Germans captured a dhow at Kisija carrying propaganda material for the natives, confirming that the island was being used as a base for operations, most likely against the *Königsberg*.[6]

In the search for *Königsberg*, King-Hall, leading the search, lost two seaplanes, an armed whaler and another boat to the Rufiji Delta. A request was, therefore, sent to South Africa to ascertain the whereabouts of the hunter Piet Pretorius to help track down the ship, especially as he knew the area having had a farm in the vicinity. The request was received with shock by the South African government which was of the belief that Pretorius was a German spy. However, as he had been specifically asked for, the South African government arranged his transport north.[7]

On his arrival in East Africa, Pretorius found that the coastal area had been cleared by the Germans so that the natives would not talk and disclose what was happening. Working with some trusted locals, eventually two natives were captured along the main road the Germans had built from Dar-es-Salaam to the Rufiji and they took Pretorius to the ship. Who actually found the *Königsberg* is a little unclear. Hatchell claims it was three villagers who helped the British while others credit Pretorius with the find.[8] Whichever it was, Pretorius was instrumental in ascertaining how deep the water around the *Königsberg* was and also that the ship's torpedoes had been removed by disguising himself as an Arab trader visiting his son.[9] In addition to all the shipping power to contain and destroy the *Königsberg*, a total of eight planes were used. The first two, as previously mentioned, were Curtises bought in South Africa in 1914 and destroyed in action during November 1914 with the pilot taken prisoner. Following this, Churchill sent out two Sopworths which arrived on 20 February 1915 under the command of Flight Lieutenant John Tullock Cull and when they succumbed, four landplanes were found. All four were later put out of service. One of the planes, sent out especially from Britain under the command of JA Fullerton, and which arrived on 3 June 1915, guided the two flat-bottomed monitors, *Severn* and *Mersey* in their attack on the *Königsberg* on 6 and 7 July. The *Königsberg* was finally put out of action and sunk on 11 July 1915.[10]

However, the British had to wait six days for a thick fog to lift to ascertain that it was a 'vast disorder of tortured steel, made the more unlovely by broken bodies strewn at every angle.'[11] This, though, was not the end of the *Königsberg*. Captain Max Looff had salvaged all he could off the ship before sinking her, sending the ten big guns initially to Dar-es-Salaam where they were used for the defence of the capital and other strategic areas. The result was that the *Königsberg* guns were to feature regularly in the remaining war in eastern and central Africa, as were those of the British *Pegasus* which had been sunk on 20 April by the *Königsberg* in Zanzibar harbour.[12]

The sinking of the *Königsberg* was a mixed blessing for both sides. For the British, it released thirty-five vessels for service elsewhere: two battleships, ten cruisers, six additional ships, colliers and other auxiliaries. King-Hall was relieved by Rear Admiral EB Charlton to resume his focus on the South African coast.[13] The German sailors, in accordance with the *Königsberg* motto, 'To be strong before the enemy, to be the upholder of your country, and to remain faithful until death and through battle and all that will always be the supreme rule of your crew', joined Lettow-Vorbeck's forces as infantry. Looff and his men, due to the insistence of Governor Schnee, moved north and took responsibility for the defence of Dar-es-Salaam. Lieutenant Jeb Rosenthal was sent to Lake Tanganyika to captain the *Kingani*. This, in turn, enabled Commander Zimmer to take over the *Graf von Gotzen* which, unbeknown to the British and the Belgians, had been smuggled onto the lake on 8 June.[14]

Lake Tanganyika

On Lake Tanganyika, the Germans had complete control which was affecting the movement of troops from the Congo and in itself posed a threat to that country. The Germans had two steamers, the *Hedwig von Wissmann* and the *Kingani* as well as two motor boats and other small vessels of which the *Peter*, *Dix Tonne* and *Netta* were included. This was compared to the Belgian *Alexandre del Commune*, put out of action in November 1914, and the *Baron Dhanis* which still needed to be assembled. The Belgians, therefore, turned to Britain for assistance.[15]

In April 1915, a force under the command of Lieutenant-Commander Geoffrey Basil Spicer-Simson was organised to take control of the lake. This force had been the brainchild of hunter John Lee who submitted a paper to the Admiralty on 21 April 1915 suggesting that two boats be sent overland from Cape Town to Lake Tanganyika to take on the Germans. With Churchill in the Admiralty and supported by Sir Henry Jackson, who had met Lee, this seemingly impossible idea was adopted and set in motion. Jackson based his decision on it being 'both the duty and the tradition of the Royal Navy to engage the enemy whenever there is water to float a ship'.[16] Spicer-Simson was chosen to command the force as he was the only person available, a factor which indicates that the theatre was not of great strategic importance but enough of a niggle to take a chance on. If Spicer-Simson failed, it would not be a problem and nothing much would have been lost. In what is regarded as true Spicer-Simson fashion, the trip was dogged from the start with various mishaps including Spicer-Simson forgetting to order food for the base at Lukuga. On 2 July, Spicer-Simson and his crew arrived at Cape Town to start their epic overland journey to Lukuga, opposite the German base at Kigoma. They left on 16 July, five days after the *Königsberg* was sunk.[17]

Having arrived at Lukuga, Spicer-Simson set about arranging a harbour for his boats. This was to bring him into conflict with the Belgians as from November, Spicer-Simson began to show his true colours. He had in the march to Lake Tanganyika already exhibited some peculiarities, but once at base, he transferred into a kilt, becoming known as *commandant a la jupe*. He took umbrage at the Belgians who regarded him as having a lower rank than Commander Stinghlamber and frequently lost his temper. Following various disagreements between the Belgian armed forces and Spicer-Simson, it was agreed by both home governments that command of the water rested with Spicer-Simson and of the land forces with Stinghlamber.[18]

The Germans had heard about the boats, *Mimi* and *Toutou*, from their spy network but did not fully believe the story. Rosenthal and a colleague tried to ascertain what was happening. However, they were more concerned about the *Baron Dhanis* than *Mimi* and *Toutou*. Unable to find anything out when their disguises failed, Rosenthal tried another twice, eventually being taken prisoner on 1 December 1915 when he was abandoned having taken longer than expected to get back to the ship. Spicer-Simson was only informed of the capture on 7 December and was refused permission to question Rosenthal which increased tensions between the two forces. The two boats, *Toutou* and *Mimi* were eventually launched onto Lake Tanganyika on 22 and 23 December respectively. On Christmas Day, to his surprise, Spicer-Simson discovered the *Graf von Gotzen* which was bigger than the two ships he already knew about. The British, however, soon obtained control of the lake, the first victim being *Kingani* on Boxing Day. The *Kingani* was damaged, but not sufficiently to sink it, and a number of its crew killed. It was taken over by the British, repaired and became known as HMS *Fifi*, becoming the first German ship to be captured and taken over by the British navy during the war. At the same time, the *Del Commune* had been repaired and was ready to return to action under the new name of *Vengeur*. It too came under Spicer-Simson's command as part of the agreement over land and water commands. Also added to the resources of the allies at Lake Tanganyika were two airplanes built by the British but piloted by Belgians.[19]

Following huge storms in January 1916 on Lake Tanganyika, the *Hedwig von Wissmann* set out in February to follow up rumours it had heard about the *Kingani*. The captain of the *Hedwig*, Job Odebrecht, soon became confused as the boat approaching him looked like the *Kingani* but was flying the British flag. The detail is confused, except that the *Hedwig* was hit in the ensuing chase, was abandoned and destroyed by explosives set by the Germans to prevent the allies taking her. The only part of the ship left intact was the ensign which Spicer-Simson added to his collection, making it the first complete ensign of the war to be taken. The local German military commander, Walhe, who could not work out why the *Kingani* and *Hedwig* had disappeared asked for replacements – the *Adjutant* and the *Wami* which at that time were on the coast. Lettow-Vorbeck agreed as the lake posed a threat to the German western border and arrangements were put in place to transport the boats from the coast inland on the Central railway. *Wami* arrived at the lake in April 1916, whilst the *Adjutant* was sent across in pieces to be ready for action in May. This left the recently built *Graf von Gotzen* as the strongest and only remaining German vessel on the lake.[20]

Spicer-Simson, however, refused to engage the *Graf von Gotzen* and soon left for Stanleyville and Leopoldville, in the Belgian Congo. In doing so, he rejected General Edward Northey's request to attack the *Gotzen* and disobeyed Bonar Law's instructions not to commandeer the *St George* at Banana at the mouth of the Congo River. In any event, the boat arrived too late. Spicer-Simson returned to Lake Tanganyika on 12 May 1916 just as the Belgians were looking to attack Kigoma. The British were planning to attack Bismarckburg with the latter supported by the British flotilla. At the last moment, however, Spicer-Simson refused to risk his ships, following which he then refused to transport Belgian troops across the lake. The Germans under Lieutenant Hasslacher escaped, but, were killed by the Belgians when they got to Ujiji.[21] Unsurprisingly, this caused conflict between the two commanders and their governments, leading to discussions in Europe. Using the seaplanes which had arrived in late December 1915, the Belgians bombed the *Gotzen* on 10 June, but, as their troops closed on Kigoma, Gustav Zimmer decided to scuttle the ship as well as the *Adjutant*, before it was destroyed or captured. On 18 July 1916, Charles Tombeur captured Kigoma following which the British decided to recall Spicer-Simson. Dr Hanschell, the force's doctor, however, decided to invalid Spicer-Simson out and he arrived back in London in September 1916 to resume his job at the Admiralty. The Belgians also recalled their commander, replacing him in February 1916 with Lieutenant-Colonel Moulaert, and assumed control of the lake, adding the *Baron Dhanis*, the refurbished *Del Commune*, to their force.[22]

Back on the coast

As General Horace Smith-Dorrien the new commander of the British East Africa forces was making his plans for East Africa at the end of 1915, a request made by Governor Schnee to the German government was being fulfilled. The Reichskolonialamt, having received a request from Schnee for supplies, sent these to East Africa aboard the *Marie* which left Germany on 16 January 1916. In addition to military equipment which had been the main feature of the earlier *Kronborg* (*Rubens*) cargo, the *Marie* carried 'pre-packed loads suitable for porters [with] much-needed food, medicine, clothing and equipment'.[23] *Marie*'s cargo, including an Iron Cross for Lettow-Vorbeck and awards for others, under the watchful eye of Captain Sorensen, was off-loaded on 27 March 1916 in Sudi Bay. In early April, on leaving the bay the *Marie* escaped, though slightly damaged by HMS *Hyacinth*, with a message from Schnee to the Reichskolonialamt.[24]

Schnee's communication would only arrive at the Reichskolonialamt in January 1917. It included a suggestion by Looff that a submarine and supply ship sent to the north of Madagascar would be able to disrupt British blockade shipping to enable the supply ship through. German bureaucracy, however, meant that the request was only dealt with in April. Despite Colonial Secretary Solf's plea that the assistance was needed to give Germany chips for bargaining with at the peace table, General Ludendorff rejected it and nothing further was done at that time.[25]

On 19 June 1916, the British navy finally occupied Tanga and by 20 September the remainder of the German East African coastline. The task had been undertaken by 'eight armed whalers, tugs and other small craft'.[26] The occupation of Tanga which should have eased the supply lines did not as General Smuts, who had replaced Smith-Dorrien as commander of East Africa, did not believe its occupation would substantially make any difference to the campaign. This was despite the town being the start of the Usambara railway which ran across the north of the German colony to Moshi. In addition, when the railway and communication lines needed additional protection, Smuts instructed General Hannynton, in charge of the Imperial General Staff, to undertake this himself. The outcome was the diversion of two companies of railway builders to fight the Germans before they could return to their task of completing the railway, thereby delaying and hindering much needed supplies getting through as quickly as possible.[27] An attack on Bagamoyo was undertaken at the request of Smuts who could not provide any land support. Admiral Charlton agreed and executed a planned attack using his naval forces including the *Severn* and *Mersey*. Once the naval troops were landed they

forced the Germans out of the trenches. A seaplane attacked the fleeing Germans and on 15 August 1916 the Germans handed over their
town.[28]

In the air

The use of the air to wage war was relatively new, the first flights
having been made in the late 1800s.[29] Flight had not long been possible and passengers were yet to use this as a means of transport. The
war, though, provided an opportunity for experimentation. South
Africa had made arrangements in the 1912 Defence Act for a South
African flying corps and in 1913 a flying school, under the command
of Brigadier-General CF Beyers, had been started in Kimberley. In
May 1914, the first six potential pilots were sent to the Royal Flying
Corps training school in Upavon on Salisbury Plain and on the outbreak of war some returned to South Africa, whilst others joined the
Royal Flying Corps voluntarily. On 26 January 1915, four of the pilots
were appointed officers and tasked with supporting the campaign
in German South West Africa which they did as part of the flying
unit of the Active Citizen's Force; under the command of Captain GP
Wallace. They eventually had a total of six Henry Farman F27 and
two BE2C for the campaign although the BE2Cs proved useless due to
their wooden frames which were unsuited to the desert climate.[30]

The Germans had two pilots, who arrived in 1914, in South West
Africa who dropped bombs as recorded by Farrar, but, withdrew
them to reconnoitre other areas and to repair them.[31] By the time the
Germans surrendered, the two planes had made fifty flights dropping
bombs and taking photographs before crashing and being put out of
action.

Following the German surrender in South West Africa, the South
African Air Force was demobilised to allow the men to volunteer for
the Royal Flying Corps. There they were formed into 26 South Africa
Squadron (RFC) and on 25 December 1915 were ordered to German
East Africa. They were recalled in June 1918 having had a tough
role reconnoitring, bombing and assisting communications.[32] In East
Africa, the Germans had a biplane which crashed on its second flight

killing the pilot, Lieutenant Henneberger, on 15 November 1915.[33] The plane was rescued and repaired by its owner Bruno Büchner who then flew goods to Morogoro where he and his wife were later interned by the British.[34]

Four seaplanes and four landplanes were used with trial and error in tracking down the *Königsberg* in September 1915. One of the problems facing pilots in East Africa, irrespective of whether they were flying land or sea planes, was the weather and altitude. This was of particular concern for the seaplane pilot where the lakes were often at an altitude the planes were designed to fly. This meant pilots had to find new strategies to get the planes in the air, a situation made more complicated when they were to carry bombs and other weights.[35]

The Naval Air Service Detachment arrived at the end of September 1915 at Maktau and made its first flight on 12 October.[36] Two British planes were used to bomb Neu Moschi and then Handeni towards the end of 1915. On 18 December 1915, Capell based at Maktau recorded 'another plane fallen and come to grief, pilot uninjured; this leaves us five out of the eight we started with, it would appear they are most unreliable.'[37] Another crashed on 30 December 1915 and again the pilot was unhurt.[38] On 27 January 1916, a plane returning from Oldorobo was brought down by the German infantry whilst another successfully bombed Taveta. After this, they were used to track the Germans when the ground forces lost contact and in 1917 they dropped propaganda leaflets amongst the German askari and porters.[39] Similarly, they were used to boost morale as seen by the first South African bi-planes which 'buzzed' the troops at Kondoa Irangi on Union Day 31 May 1916 and delivered additional cigarettes on Christmas Day.[40] Later in 1917, when Smuts handed over command to General Hoskins, the latter flew from Kilwa to Nairobi to confer over the change.[41] The detachment left for Egypt in January 1918 after Lettow-Vorbeck entered Portuguese East Africa.[42]

It was commonly believed that the plane filled the native with awe. Thornhill records that an old man, *mzee*, believed that the King of England directed his men from the 'four-winged bird' which flew over 'making a loud noise' and which, when it 'lays [eggs] on the German camp, [. . .] they explode and kill people.' He continued, 'Yes, I always had my thoughts that it was only a king who could manage so formidable a bird.[43] As the war progressed, however, and natives became more familiar with the plane, or *ndege* (Kiswahili for bird), they learnt to avoid its 'iron eggs' by hiding. Every time a plane crashed, its prestige diminished and not just amongst the black population as recorded by Capell.[44]

Following Schnee's communication which went back on the *Marie*, the German government arranged for materials to be sent to German East Africa by air as opposed to sea given Britain's dominance of the latter. The only means available to them for this purpose was the zeppelin or air ship of which they only had a limited number. The decision, therefore. to send supplies to East Africa by this means shows how the German colony was regarded at home. Solf had issued a paper setting out why Germany should retain the colony and this decision was a clear indication that his arguments had been accepted.[45]

On 21 November 1917, zeppelin L-59, the largest ever, took off from Bulgaria under Lieutenant Captain Ludwig Bockholt for the Makonde Plateau in East Africa. This was the second zeppelin, the first L-57 having caught fire during a test flight. The zeppelin had been designed so that the whole ship could be recycled by Lettow-Vorbeck and his men as the expectation was that it would not get back to Germany. The flight is recorded as being uneventful, but when it was over Egypt it received a message to turn back. Myth has it that the British intercepted the flight, having broken the German code, and told them to turn back as Lettow-Vorbeck had surrendered. In fact, Lettow-Vorbeck had managed to get a signal through neutral wireless stations that he did not hold the plateau and had been forced to retreat. There would, therefore, be no safe place to land the zeppelin and so on 23 November, it turned back.[46] According to Lloyd-Jones and Paice, Lettow-Vorbeck denied any knowledge of the zeppelin except for having heard rumours from the natives at Lindi.[47] As it turned out, the ship could have landed in German controlled territory but that was the nature of the campaign, nothing was guaranteed. King claims, based on 'authentic, inside (unofficially supported) information and statements [...] that VonLettow (sic) was stated to take over relatively high command on the Western Front.' The purpose of L-59 was, therefore, to fetch Lettow-Vorbeck back to Europe.[48] Although the existing records suggest this was not the purpose of the zeppelin flight, the 'inside information' suggests it was discussed and indicates a level of concern about German progress in Europe.

For the remainder of the war, the British navy continued to support the East Africa campaign by delivering supplies and transporting wounded to South Africa and elsewhere as required.[49] On 23 July 1917 the War Cabinet determined to clear up East Africa which was seen as a nuisance. Thirty-five ships were needed for the theatre, so to speed up the defeat of the Germans in East Africa all reinforcements that could be released from the Western Front and other theatres were to be sent to East Africa.[50]

CHAPTER 6

EAST AFRICA, 1915–1917

As will be seen in later chapters, the continuation of the war in East Africa proved to be a contentious issue in London. Decisions there impacted directly on the war in Africa insofar as reinforcements and supplies had to be sourced and although the general principal that reinforcements sent to East Africa would not detract from the forces needed in Europe, the time spent discussing the theatre must surely have had an impact on the European theatre. The development of the campaign from relatively static in 1915 through to active in 1916 and then what has been regarded as guerrilla or bush-warfare in 1917 can be traced back to the decisions made in London although some, such as KP Adgie, credit Lettow-Vorbeck with the changes in approach.[1] This chapter charts the progress of the war on the ground in East Africa setting the scene for the later political discussions in chapters 9 and 10.

In 1915, despite the lull in set battles, there were still regular skirmishes between the opposing forces. This made the need for locally recruited volunteers imperative, particularly along the Uganda railway where the Germans attacked regularly in the hope of disrupting supplies.[2] In a two-month period, thirty-two trains and nine bridges were recorded as destroyed.[3] Although there had been a mad rush of volunteers when war was declared, the lack of action and arrival of Indian Expeditionary Force C in September 1914 and then in March 1915 the 2nd Rhodesian Regiment led many, with permission, to slip back to their farms as the need to harvest their crops seemed more important:[4] 'I would not mind letting my shamba go to hell if we were only doing something; but sitting here twiddling my thumbs while my coffee berries are falling off the trees and rotting is a little more than I can bear.'[5] This complaint was not unique and at this stage of the war, there was no consideration of leaving it completely to the women as it was believed that the war was not going to last that long.[6] Later in the war, women would oversee neighbouring farms as well as their own, especially as many farmers were single.[7]

For those who remained at the front, some semblance of normality set in with the men being relieved at regular intervals, having access to mail and the conveniences of life as much as they existed.[8] That there was an expectation of another life whilst war was being waged is evident in Smith-Dorrien's letter to Asquith shortly before he left England in December 1915. He asked the Prime Minister for a generous expenses allowance as he had heard Nairobi was expensive and he would be expected to entertain.[9] The difficulty for the British commanders was keeping morale up and the men in a fit state for battle. The Germans were in a better position as Lettow-Vorbeck used the opportunity to prepare his forces for being self-sufficient. This foresight of the German commander was rewarded when, at the end of June 1915, rumours started to circulate that Louis Botha would be leading 15,000 South Africans to East Africa once the campaign in German South West Africa was over.[10]

In January 1915, Lettow-Vorbeck decided to reoccupy Jasin and following a siege of the British forces under Tighe, Lettow-Vorbeck succeeded despite suffering a shot through his hat and arm. It was to prove an expensive victory causing Lettow-Vorbeck to realise that he would only be able to fight 'three more actions of this nature' due to the shortage of Non-Commissioned Officers (NCOs) and Officers.[11]

In the west, Ewart Grogan had arrived in the Congo to link up with the Belgians, the Belgian Commander Josué Henry being a friend. A meeting at Lake Kivu between Henry, Grogan and Colonel Malleson agreed operational terms and connected a telegraph to Nairobi to assist with communication. With the lakes in allied control, and supplies coming in, the Belgians successfully protected their borders against German attacks. This led to such an increase in confidence that they felt it possible to attack Ruanda and Urundi. However, the proposal had to stay a plan until sufficient carriers could be found.[12] Soon after the meeting, Henry was instructed to report into Tombeur, Vice-Governor of Katanga Province, who had been appointed supreme military commander of the Belgian Congo forces.

Over June and July 1915, Kurt Wahle on instruction from Lettow-Vorbeck attacked the British at Saisi in Northern Rhodesia. Here, the Belgians were unable to break through to support their allies but Major JJ O'Sullevan of the Northern Rhodesia Police refused to surrender despite being short of water. Finally, on 2 and 3 August, the Germans gave up and withdrew.[13] The attack on Saisi undermined the German intention as the natives were so impressed with the British defence that they refused to change their allegiance. The net result was that the Germans became demoralised and the area remained relatively quiet until Lettow-Vorbeck moved the focus of activity south.[14]

The end of 1915 saw preparations being made by Britain to make the East African campaign more active and bring about the defeat of the German colony. At the end of November 1915, General Sir Horace Smith-Dorrien was appointed Commander-in-Chief East Africa. On 23 December 1915, he received approval for his operations and set sail for South Africa to confer with colleagues there before going north to East Africa in February 1916. However, during the trip to South Africa, Smith-Dorrien fell ill, eventually requiring an operation, and whilst his staff were meeting the South Africans in Pretoria, he remained in Cape Town. From his base at the Mount Nelson Hotel, he instructed Tighe in East Africa on the actions he needed to take. As a result, Longido was captured on 21 January 1916, Mbuyuni on 22 January and Serengeti on 25 January bringing Salaita and Taveta into striking range.[15]

By the end of January 1916, Smith-Dorrien felt sufficiently well to believe he would be in the field in March, by which time the newly arrived South Africans would be ready for an offensive. However, Botha, Smuts and Buxton felt that to delay action would be 'a serious mistake and fraught with grave disadvantages'.[16] Buxton also did not believe Smith-Dorrien would be well enough to take command of an early offensive. The British government, therefore, decided to replace Smith-Dorrien with Smuts, a decision Asquith later recalled was made purely for 'political reasons'. It could only have been, as Smuts had no military training and his sole military experience consisted of leading a commando of three hundred men through the Cape during the 1899–1901 war and coordinating the southern attack in the 1915 South West Africa campaign, which by the time of his arrival had quietened down. He had no experience of leading large numbers of men, planning attacks or working with a staff to ensure equipment and food were available for the troops. He was used to living off the land as he went along and doing his own reconnaissance. Nevertheless, Smuts' position as commander of the East African forces responsible to the War Office was confirmed, including Kitchener's approval, on 3 February 1916 and accepted by Smuts on 5 February.[17]

A week after Smuts' appointment and before he arrived in the country, the South Africans saw their first action in East Africa. This was at Salaita Hill on 12 February 1916. During the battle, the battle-raw South Africans turned and fled whilst, unlike Tanga, the Indians held their ground.[18] On the one hand, this proved Smith-Dorrien's claim that 'the South Africans would not be sufficiently trained by then'.[19] On the other, it highlighted the race issue foreseen by van Deventer and Hughes before they arrived and by Stewart who noted in his diary how the South Africans spoke in a derogatory fashion to and about the Indians.[20] Although for those South Africans involved at Salaita, there was some change in their relationship with their fellow Indian comrades as noted by Francis Brett Young, a doctor serving in East Africa, who commended the working relationships of the soldiers.[21]

Smuts arrived in East Africa on 19 February 1916 and four days later on 23 February announced he wanted to launch an offensive despite it being the start of the rainy season.[22] His instructions were those of Smith-Dorrien: 'to undertake an offensive defensive with the object of expelling the enemy from British territory and safeguarding it from further incursions.' Any other action against German East Africa 'should be postponed until General Sir Horace Smith-Dorrien has reported in light of the experience gained before the rainy season.'[23] Smuts, however, was too impatient to wait.

By 8 March 1916 the first actions under Smuts' command were taking place in the Taveta-Salaita Hill area. Smuts had rearranged his forces, reducing the size of the two British Divisions under Stewart and Tighe in favour of the Boer commander Jaap van Deventer. By the middle of the month, the Germans had been cleared from (or had moved out of) the area around Kilimanjaro. Smuts took the opportunity to make further radical changes to his forces, having Stewart and Malleson sent back to India and Tighe retired. Smuts claimed Stewart had moved too slowly around Kilimanjaro resulting in the Germans escaping. In reality, Stewart had had the more difficult task and his instructions changed whilst on the move.[24] Smuts replaced them with South African commanders, as he did the Chief of his General Staff. JJ Collyer became Chief of the General Staff, van Deventer and Coen Brits commanders of 2nd and 3rd Divisions respectively whilst the displaced British Reginald Hoskins, previously Chief of the General Staff, was given command of 1st Division.[25] Smuts' reorganisation of the divisions may well have been further impacted by the introduction of conscription in British East Africa during March, having been approved in 1915, and the Boers who refused to serve under British commanders.[26]

Portuguese East and Central Africa

Further south, Portugal, still officially neutral in 1915, decided to take advantage of the uncertainty around its position to occupy the Kionga Triangle on the German East African border. Lisbon issued the order in June and arranged for an expeditionary force of 1,543 men to leave for Africa in August 1915. This second expeditionary force arrived on 7 November 1915 under the command of Major Moura Mendes, but had no resources or colonial experience. The force was further constrained by the local Governor of Niassa who was pro-German. That the situation was beyond the men was expressed by one soldier who noted that personal survival was priority and that 'every hour of our miserable days passed with the hope that the true whereabouts of the enemy would be overlooked.'[27]

On 9 March 1916, Portugal declared war on Germany. This had been pre-empted by a change in British policy. Initially, Britain did 'not want Portugal to establish too great a claim on [its] gratitude or to be under obligation to protect their Colonies or divide up German territory with them'. Now in 1916, Britain wanted access to the German ships interred in Portuguese waters.[28] This suited the Portuguese, who informed Britain on 3 April 1916 that it wanted to 'occupy a piece of territory to the south of the River Rovuma', which the Germans had 'stolen' from them when the border was initially defined.[29] A week later, they informed Britain that they hoped to do this 'without affecting any co-operation with British forces north of Lake Nyasa.' This was so they would not have to be indebted to Britain.[30] The next day, on 10 April 1916, under the command of Major da Silveira, Portugal occupied Kionga after the Germans evacuated the area.[31] Within the week, they asked that this section of land be excluded from Britain's sphere of control for the duration of the war.[32]

To launch his offensive into German territory from Central Africa, General E Northey needed the Portuguese to protect his eastern flank. Frustratingly for Northey, this would not be possible as the Portuguese, in April 1916, were preparing their move into the Rovuma River delta. The Portuguese were also keen to prevent incursions by the British into what they saw as their territory and so resisted working with the British. In typical East African fashion, Northey's planned offensive failed to achieve its goal as the Germans had started to withdraw before the advancing troops. Although Northey's force was unable to contain the Germans, they were able to occupy various towns in the German colony. Following this advance, Northey liaised with Smuts, who suggested he continue moving north to push the Germans into a contained area. By the end of June 1916, the territory between Lakes Tanganyika and Nyasa had been cleared of Germans.[33]

On 16 April, the Belgians started their advance on Ruanda, initially instigating revolts among the local tribes against the Germans. The result was the German evacuation of Kigali and Nyanza by mid-May 1916. The shortage of porters meant the Belgians could not advance further until Belgian commander Tombeur realised using the lake would ease his transport problems. He was supported by Ugandan transport units as agreed at the Lutobo Conference on 6 February 1916.[34] Moving troops across, Tombeur continued his advance on

Ruanda and Urundi, only to clash with Smuts, who towards the end of May 1916, had decided it was time to advance once more, and, again, restructured his forces. He instructed Crewe to march on Tabora from Lake Victoria and by July 1916, most of Ruanda and Urundi was occupied.[35] However, achieving this goal had been marked by friction between Tombeur and Crewe over supplies and administration. Wahle, the German commander in the area, took advantage of this disunity and escaped. Meanwhile, Kraut, who was the target of Smuts' own advance, had withdrawn. The allied troops and the march took its toll through the extreme heat and lack of water. Finally, at the end of May, the two opposing forces clashed and, again, the Germans retired. Before moving on, the allies were forced to consolidate, rest and await rations and other supplies, a task which took approximately two weeks.[36] Lettow-Vorbeck's plan of distracting Germany's allies from the main theatre was working, albeit not in the exact way he envisaged.

Whilst Kraut was withdrawing, Lettow-Vorbeck fought one of his last battles of the campaign in German East African territory. This was at Kondoa Irangi at the end of April. Misjudging the situation, Lettow-Vorbeck stumbled into a South African trap and suffered one hundred casualties to thirty-one South Africans. This encounter had been a chance one as van Deventer had left his previous base earlier than he should have which meant he missed the rain and was in Kondoa to face Lettow-Vorbeck. Following the battle at Kondoa Irangi, Lettow-Vorbeck had his base at Tuliani. Here, they were bombed quite regularly losing valuable documents but only one person was injured as everyone had learnt how to hide themselves.[37]

Feeling confident, Governor General Alvaro Xavier de Castro naively suggested that Portugal invade German East Africa as a means to protect the Portuguese territory and to support Smuts' advance. As a result, the third Portuguese East Africa Expeditionary Force arrived on 27 June 1916 commanded by General José Cesar Ferreira Gil and received the same welcome as the previous two forces – no supplies and low morale.[38] Gil had no colonial experience but was felt to be more appropriate than Colonel Garcia Rosado who thought his task impossible.[39] Shortly before Gil's arrival, a Portuguese attack on the German border was defeated at Narimanga on 27 May 1916 by a lightly held German garrison. That this German garrison was there was due to Schnee's insistence back in August 1914.[40]

A change in strategy

During July 1916, a formal change in strategy was determined. However, the reality was nothing had changed, except that there were soon fewer troops available to defeat Lettow-Vorbeck. The War Office needed a decisive victory in the East African theatre, but this did not work for Smuts who still wanted to prevent bloodshed. He, therefore, looked for alternatives. At this strategic time, Botha visited East Africa at Smuts' request, travelling as Colonel Campbell, which led to rumours that peace would soon be declared. During Botha's visit from June to August, Smuts announced that the war in East Africa was likely to become a guerrilla conflict. The set battles there had been would no longer feature, however, wit and cunning would. On 6 July, Smuts wrote to the War Office that 'When our forces are thus transformed no useful purpose will be served any longer by my continuing in command, and I hope that I shall be permitted to return to my duties in the Union Government.'[41] He had been in East Africa for five months and unlike the German South West campaign, which was virtually over within the same time, there was no seeming end to the one he was leading in East Africa. He had also suffered from bouts of malaria and although he did not let these affect him, they must have taken their toll, as did the knowledge that Botha's health was ailing.[42]

Smuts, though, still had work to do despite being ready to leave. When it was pointed out to him that there was no replacement for him, he felt it best to continue the campaign south of the railway. During this time, in the lead up to the battle at Wami in late August, Smuts and Lettow-Vorbeck 'oppose[d] each other' as 'this move was under the orders of General Smuts in person' and 'Lettow-Vorbeck was in charge of the enemy column' at Ruhungu.[43] His new target became the Ruaha River, despite steps being put in place to replace the white and Indian troops in the theatre. For political and other reasons, Smuts believed that the mounted troops could be released and that the infantry would be able to end the campaign in two months. He, therefore, asked for 6,000 Belgian troops without their officers to assist him. But, by November 1916, he no longer felt the need for Belgian assistance as the King's African Rifles would suffice.[44] The reasons for his optimism remain scarce, although the recent raising of the 1st Rhodesian Native Regiment consisting of Matabele tribesmen commanded by Lieutenant-Colonel AJ Tomlinson, albeit for service in the south of the German colony, may well have played a part – he could leave the remainder of the fighting to native or non-white troops.[45]

Having captured the Central railway it was thought, or rather hoped, that the Germans would capitulate. The railway was seen as a lifeline across the developed part of the German colony and with it gone there was, in effect, no German infrastructure remaining especially as many farmers and officials had moved south with the troops. Smuts, therefore, thought it would be worthwhile offering the Germans surrender terms, but the War Committee rejected this idea on 18 August. Despite this rejection, at the end of September Smuts offered the Germans terms, which Schnee rejected under pressure from Lettow-Vorbeck. As the War Committee predicted, the offer was seen as evidence that Smuts 'had reached the end of his resources'.[46]

Central Africa

Having captured Urundi and Ruanda, the Belgians moved on Tabora, the provisional capital of German East Africa, at the request of the British. The idea was that once the town was in allied hands, the Belgians would vacate it in favour of British administration. However, on 2 September 1916, Tombeur ordered Tabora's capture, regardless of Crewe's intentions. Using the lakes and railways for their advance, even though the latter needed repairs, the Belgians moved in and occupied Tabora. Once again, Wahle accompanied by Schnee slipped away, vacating Tabora on 18 September.[47] Having reached Tabora before the South Africans, and due to British indecision, the Belgians changed their mind about vacating the area and introduced their own administration and showed generosity in allowing Ada Schnee, the

governor's wife, to remain in the governor's house.[48] This occupation of Tabora under the civil control of Colonel Malfeyt did not suit
Smuts, who harboured a belief the Belgians were being unco-opera-
tive. The British War Office, therefore, offered a compromise which
the Belgians declined, claiming that their communication lines would
be threatened, even if maintained and supplied by the British. In addition, the natives would regard the Belgians as weak if they withdrew
after defeating the Germans and this would lead to a reduction in the
fighting morale of the troops.[49]

Turning points

September 1916 marked a turning point for Smuts in the campaign.
His latest attempt to force the Germans to fight or surrender failed
as he had again misjudged, or ignored, the weather conditions and
health of his forces. He had also left a gap through which Lettow-
Vorbeck's troops would be able to break free. To aide their escape, as
the Germans withdrew from Morogoro, they laid landmines towards
the railway station using shells they could not fire.[50] Smuts' men could
go no further, needing rest and rations, and at the end of September he
was offered a welcome respite by the rains. Although the rains brought
their own problems, they enabled a time for reflection and consolida-
tion. Smuts took the opportunity to inform London of his plans.[51]

Realising how unfit his fighting force was due to disease, Smuts
decided to send the worst affected South Africans home to recuperate.
Sending them in small groups would prevent him being accused of
'butchering' the youth of the Union. But, Smuts issued the order without ensuring that the necessary procedures and systems were in place
with the result that chaos ensued. The news filtered through and when
a formal complaint was received from Colonel Kirkpatrick, the Officer
Commanding 9/SAI, regarding negligence, Smuts was forced to set up
a court of enquiry to investigate.[52] Later, in 1918, the *African Herald*
called for an Imperial enquiry into East Africa as the campaign was 'a
monument of meddle and muddle, [...] arising from gross neglect
and incapacity in the non-combatant services.' Smuts' defence was that
sacrifices had to be made and Lettow-Vorbeck said the same thing at

the peace treaty when the Germans were accused of committing atrocities: 'No doubt, in a long war cases of brutality and inhumanity do occur. But that happens on both sides.' The Army Council defended Smuts by claiming that he 'materially shortened the campaign'.[53]

Following the earlier capture of Tanga by the British forces, Smuts failed to use the harbour to shorten supply lines despite being prompted to. However, he was persuaded to use Kilwa, a port further south, which had been brought under British control following the destruction of the *Königsberg*. He visited Kilwa during October to finalise arrangements for the push which would start in November. On 7 November 1916, Smuts requested General Northey, Commander of the Rhodesian and Nyasaland forces, be placed under his command for operations. This was affected a week later and the northern and southern commands of East Africa were united for the first time during the war.[54] In reality, this was just a formal process as Smuts and Northey had been coordinating their actions as far as was possible. The move would, however, ease communications between the two groups, and as Smuts' forces had moved so far south, would make coordination easier.[55] Reinforcements started to arrive from Nigeria and once transport was found to move them from Dar-es-Salaam south, they could participate in the offensive. As in September, Smuts believed this action would result in Lettow-Vorbeck's surrender.

The Germans were forced further south as Smuts and Northey's forces, together with Belgian support, converged on them. Towards the middle of 1916, Lettow-Vorbeck was faced with the option of either surrendering or breaking into Nyasaland or Portuguese East Africa. Surrender was not an option as this would defeat the object of attracting allied resources to the theatre. Nyasaland, although not as strongly protected as Northern Rhodesia, would still prove a challenge given British control of Lake Nyasa and Northey's command.[56]

The increasing pressure south of the Rovuma led Lettow-Vorbeck to order attacks in October. However, the Germans had unknowingly moved into territory which was anti-German with the result that the local inhabitants provided the British with information to the detriment of Lettow-Vorbeck's forces. Wahle's forces, in the west of the colony, struggled too after they had evacuated Tabora.

Carriers deserted and ammunition had to be destroyed due to lack
of transport. For a group who were totally operationally isolated with
no back-up available, this was disaster. In addition, with the rains
and being in areas at times unsuitable for harvesting, the Germans
needed to obtain food from other sources. They were therefore forced
to attack possible bases to acquire food and ammunition.[57] Lettow-
Vorbeck's only viable option appeared to be an invasion of Portuguese
East Africa. To ascertain whether an invasion of Portuguese East Africa
would be feasible, he sent Captain Steumer on a food-collection mission and on 9 May 1917 he and his men entered Nyasaland. They were
held just inside by Northey's men.[58]

Portuguese East Africa

In the south, Portuguese Commander Gil was trying to find ways to
fulfil his remit with the troops available. His work was cut out for
him as Lisbon continued to apply pressure: 'Our prestige as a belligerent nation will be considerably diminished and our interests as a
colonial nation prejudiced if an offensive against the Germans be not
at once undertaken by the decided invasion of the territory beyond
the Rovuma.'[59] To fulfil this desire, Gil had to work with Smuts and
the allied forces. However, when Smuts presented him with a plan to
attack through Newala to Liwale, Gil took fright as his troops had no
training, although he could not say this openly. Following discussions,
they agreed a closer target on the Lukuledi River.[60] The relationship
with the Portuguese became tense when Gil realised that Smuts was
trying to contain Portuguese action to the Rovuma Valley. To add
to Gil's frustrations, when he was ready and able to move, a native
uprising broke out in the Zambezi area. Despite having to send troops
south to deal with the uprising, Gil decided to go ahead with Smuts'
plan.[61]

Smuts' plans coincided with Lettow-Vorbeck's decision to tackle the
Portuguese straight on as his forces were desperate for whatever food
they could obtain. Max Looff, having surrendered control of Dar-es-
Salaam to the British, was instructed to move south and 'eliminate
the Portuguese'.[62] Schnee had been behind Lettow-Vorbeck's decision.

By finding employment for Looff away from Lettow-Vorbeck, Schnee would further reduce the tension between the two commanders as Looff, in his naval capacity, was senior to Lettow-Vorbeck. Sending Looff south meant that he could also remain in command of the men he had commanded on the *Königsberg* and later in Dar-es-Salaam.[63] Within two days, Looff had re-occupied the territory captured by the Portuguese definitively defeating Gil's forces and pushing them back across the Rovuma. Despite this defeat, the Portuguese government reported Gil's actions as positive and the withdrawal from Newala in December 1916 was described as a 'brilliant' retirement.[64] However, in reality, Gil, who was unwell with dysentery, was recalled to Lisbon and Governor General Alvaro de Castro took over command until a fourth expeditionary force under Colonel Thomas Souza Rosa arrived in September 1917.[65] In the interim, Smuts sought permission to bring British vessels into Portuguese waters 'in case of future emergencies.'[66]

Skirmishes and engagements took place during December 1916, when for the first time Mills bombs were used in East Africa. The night attack on Picquet Hill at Kibata, overseen by General O'Grady commander of the British brigade, was a success for the allies. Lettow-Vorbeck having positioned his force on the other side of the hill, lost his first set battle since Kondoa Irangi, whereas his troops on the other side were successful.[67] Despite this loss, he was able to withdraw south. On Christmas day, the Germans thought they had been given a Christmas present when they noticed bombs being dropped on the allied troops by their own. The 'bombs', however, were extra cigarettes. Action again took place in the days after Christmas but as usual, after holding their own for a while, the Germans withdrew to fight another day.[68]

Early in 1917, Smuts was instructed to capture the Portuguese-desired German territory of Kionga before the Portuguese could recapture it. The Colonial Office was still trying to expand its empire despite the Foreign Office having proved that the only thing the Kionga was good for was to support German smuggling.[69] On 2 January 1917, van Deventer withdrew from the chase due to lack of supplies and a week later he was unexpectedly withdrawn to Dodoma in preparation for a return to South Africa. In line with Smuts' decision in July to withdraw wounded troops from the battle field, van Deventer and his men were the first to be repatriated with others following close behind. The British and Indian troops who had been in the field almost since the outbreak of war were left to continue the fight. Even though van Deventer's forces had been withdrawn, the Germans were still being dislodged but not defeated. Not long after, an opportunity to engage the German commander presented itself along the Rufiji River if the crossing at Kimbambawe could be destroyed. For reasons unknown, the commander tasked with the destruction of the bridge, General Beves, failed to do so and the Germans were able to escape. Follow-up action ordered by Smuts also failed, this time due to a shortage of porters and in desperation, the King's African Rifles were tasked with introducing the old-Boer War tactic of crop-burning.[70]

On 8 January 1917, Smuts was informed that his forces had 'received less than 10% of its essential supplies in the preceding two weeks' and that starvation was likely to occur in the forward lines. The same day, he was told to hand over command to General Hoskins so that he, Smuts, could return to South Africa before going to London to represent the Union at the forthcoming Imperial meetings scheduled for February.[71] This move seems to have taken Smuts by surprise as he was writing to his wife on 27 December about possibly being home in March and spending an extended period of time with her on their farm before he did any more travelling when the request from Botha came for him to go to London.[72] Smuts used the opportunity to explain the situation:

> The military situation in East Africa, is fortunately, such as to make a change in command, and some reorganisation comparatively simple, and indeed the steps that are now contemplated in consequence of the sudden demand for General Smuts' services elsewhere are those which would have been taken in any case very shortly ... His [enemy] forces in consequence of casualties and desertion are much reduced in strength and morale.[73]

By 18 January, the Rufiji was in full-flood with the area to the north clear of German troops. And, on 20 January, Hoskins took over command of the East African forces whilst in the middle of battle. Smuts' press release and upbeat reports led to Hoskins being instructed by the War Office, three days after he assumed command, to release as many white and Indian troops for Europe as possible, a factor which would further reduce the demand on shipping. When Hoskins explained that the removal of these troops would make him ineffective, General W Robertson, Chief of the Imperial General Staff, agreed to let him keep what he needed. But, Hoskins could do no more until the rains abated in mid-February.[74]

On 25 January 1917, on his way to South Africa, Smuts met Portuguese East African Governor General Alvaros de Castro to plan operations on behalf of Hoskins who could not get away. Smuts asked for territory to be cleared of food and other material, but de Castro was in the process of organising replacements and men and it would prove difficult. The two men agreed an exchange of liaison officers would ease communications and Errol MacDonell, previously British Consul to Portuguese East Africa, was appointed to Portuguese Headquarters as liaison officer in mid-March. This greatly helped improve relations with the Portuguese. A short while later, Major Azumjuju Martins was sent to British Headquarters.[75] MacDonell was aware of the difficulties he would face:

A very large number of Portuguese Officers and men are fully alive to the fact that they have up to the present made a hopeless fiasco of the German East campaign, and though this has been stated to me in private, if any foreigner were to make a similar statement he would incur the obloquy of the Military, Press and public ... I shall be looked upon with suspicion by the military authorities.[76]

Both Hoskins and Lettow-Vorbeck were needing to re-organise their forces. Hoskins' lines of communications needed to be overhauled and the divisions restructured given a net reduction of 8,000 troops. Hoskins needed reinforcements and asked that South African troops return to East Africa. This was rejected by Botha who felt it would be difficult politically, especially as he was recruiting for Europe. In addition, there was 'a "strong feeling" of reluctance to serve in East Africa' due to the stories and rumours of those returned from the theatre. Hoskins had a manpower shortage and had to fight to retain the forces the War Office thought he should return to Europe.[77] As an officer of the 40th Pathans noted: 'I do wish to goodness that they would not say that the show is all but over. It is not. It is easy enough to advance through a country where the enemy do not intend to stand. The real difficulty is when he has got down to an area he has decided to stand in, and where he knows every inch of the ground and you know none ... Do believe me when I say that all *our* difficulties are ahead of us.'[78]

In March 1917, Robertson informed Hoskins that following a War Cabinet meeting, if the Germans fled into Portuguese East Africa, they were to be pursued until defeated.[79] The shortage of porters due to paucity of pay and poor working conditions had caused a number of offensive actions to be prematurely halted or not followed up. This led to the Compulsory Service Act being passed by Britain in March which enabled the conscription of carriers and labour as required. The Belgians too had difficulty recruiting carriers in the Congo despite its size. They felt further restricted in recruiting labour in occupied German territory as this contravened the Hague Convention. They were concerned that if they did recruit German natives, the Germans could retaliate. The Belgians were also wary of South African intentions given Smuts' earlier attempts to use Belgian troops.[80]

Lettow-Vorbeck realised he needed to reduce the size of his force if he was to fulfil his aim of distracting allied troops away from Europe. With the increasing shortage of food in the areas he was moving around in, he reduced the number of carriers and personal servants to ease food requirements. Instructions were to live off the land. In addition, the appeal of moving into Portuguese East African territory was growing: Lettow-Vorbeck would no longer be subordinate to Schnee, with the weak Portuguese defence, food would be more easily obtainable and with the native residents being more pro-German, he would be in a better position.[81] The difficulty would be the section between the Rovuma and Rufiji Rivers which was little known and where food was scarce.

Meanwhile, further north, on 4 May 1917, Hauptmann Max Wintgens, who was operating outside of Lettow-Vorbeck's wishes, called a halt on occupying the Kitunda Mission so he and his fellow Germans could recuperate from typhus. Two weeks later, Wintgens surrendered to Belgian Major Bataille three days' walk away from Tabora. His officers decided to continue the struggle under the command of Captain Heinrich Naumann who went onto defeat the Belgians at Ikoma, east of Mwanza on 29 June 1917 – the worst defeat they had during the war. Having heard about a native uprising in the north, Naumann decided to head in that direction and cause further trouble for the British. However, on reaching the British East Africa border, he realised the uprising was in Somaliland and would have no immediate impact on the struggle in East Africa. He therefore turned round and marched south reaching Kondoa in July.[82] On 2 October 1917 Naumann surrendered to the Cape Corps at Wanyoki when his ammunition ran out. He became the only German to stand trial for murder in East Africa – that of Lieutenant Sutherland – and for 'cruelty to native women.' He was released in 1919.[83]

Changes in command

Back in the south, Hoskins looked for operations to begin in May when the rains came to an end. In preparation, he met with de Castro on 9 April to plan for the German entry into Portuguese East Africa. De Castro offered to send troops into Northey's operational area through Nyasaland. Despite Hoskins' attempts to change his mind and to get the Portuguese to defend their side of the border, de Castro refused. When Hoskins requested even more troops to meet the requirements of his proposed plan, Robertson lost confidence in Hoskins' judgement. Anderson maintains it was poor staff-work and badly phrased telegrams which were the cause of Hoskins' recall.[84] When Smuts, in London, turned against Hoskins' command in mid-April, his fate was sealed. With Robertson already feeling uncertain about Hoskins' command based on uncoordinated requests and the need for War Office support, it was decided on 23 April to replace him:[85]

The Chief of the Imperial General Staff stated that for some time he had not felt that the British operations in East Africa were being carried out as satisfactorily as could be desired. He had discussed the matter on more than one occasion with General Smuts, who, while holding a high opinion of the officer in command, Major-General AR Hoskins, had agreed that apparently he had lost grip of the operations and had perhaps become tired.[86]

Van Deventer arrived back in East Africa on 29 May 1917 and was instructed to bring about an 'early termination of [the] campaign'. In doing so, he was to '[limit] demands for tonnage to [a] minimum' as it 'is essential to release at earliest possible moment vessels absorbed by supply and maintenance of your force'.[87] Once van Deventer arrived back in East Africa, he was able to convince Botha of the need to return some South Africans to East Africa. He argued that as the Indian troops were not up to strength, the campaign would suffer if additional troops were not made available. Defeat and failure would cause greater political problems in South Africa than not sending the troops and so some units were returned albeit with new recruits.[88]

Unlike Smuts, van Deventer worked with his General Staff especially with Brigadier General SH Sheppard. He also realised the need for direct engagement with the enemy and the need for careful planning and preparation. With fewer South Africans in the theatre and van Deventer not being involved in politics in South Africa, he was able to make decisions about engaging the enemy which Smuts had not been able to do. On 10 June 1917, van Deventer had worked out his plan of attack and notified the War Office. On 18 June, he met with the Belgian commander Huyghé at Dodoma to finalise their working relations. Given transport difficulties Huyghé was prepared to be flexible over the command of Belgian troops to prevent a German breakthrough. Offensive action would begin on 27 June with new South African battalions arriving to support van Deventer.[89]

During July 1917, various skirmishes took place between Lettow-Vorbeck's troops and the allies at Narungombe. Van Deventer ordered the attack to protect his men at Kilwa so that they could get to the high ground away from malaria. German Captain von Liebeman held back the newly arrived South African forces, but was eventually forced to retreat when he ran out of ammunition, his men failing to use those of the opposing force which were lying around. Despite this success, van Deventer had to wait until October before he could move. Once again supplies and health were working against the allied commander.[90]

Minor actions continued to take place as Lettow-Vorbeck's forces started to converge from around the country. Lettow-Vorbeck was slowly starting to get a more complete overview on the state of his troops as communication channels had been erratic given their spread and the dominance of the allies. The allies were trying to pre-empt Lettow-Vorbeck's next move and ensure their supply lines would be able to support any possibility. Van Deventer had also decided that the best way to deal with Lettow-Vorbeck was to harass him in the same way Lettow-Vorbeck had attacked the Uganda railway in 1915.

In Portuguese East Africa, Colonel Thomas de Sousa Rosa arrived with the fourth Portuguese Expeditionary Force on 12 September 1917. He, too, was appointed more for political reasons than for his experience of colonial warfare. MacDonell, the British liaison officer described him as 'most impulsive', 'unrestrained in his language' and having a 'distressing peculiarity of changing his mind at least three times before arriving at a decision.'[91] He was also regarded as pro-British. None of the issues, lack of equipment and organisation, encountered by the first three expeditionary forces had been resolved, although of all the commanders sent to Portuguese East Africa, Rosa did manage to restore some discipline. He did so by imprisoning a number of officers who had been released on parole by Lettow-Vorbeck.[92] In addition, he had to contend with the Makonde uprising which had started whilst Gil was still commander, and other hostile groups. Difficulties continued with the relationship between the two countries. Van Deventer wanted the Portuguese to stay on the defensive whilst Rosa wanted to go on the offensive. Having been instructed by his government that he was subordinate to the British, he had no choice but to stay on the defensive. This was despite his concerns about the morale of his troops.[93]

On 10 October 1917, Lettow-Vorbeck moved to support Wahle at Mahiwa. On the 16th he found the enemy entrenched opposite his own men and decided that a surprise attack was needed. Captain Goering would lead the attack. Shortly after moving off, his men changed direction having been surprised by the newly arrived Nigerian brigade which, in turn, was surprised by having unexpectedly stumbled across the Germans.[94] On 18 October 1917, a full-on battle took place between the British troops and Germans at Mahiwa. Both sides lost substantial numbers and material. As a result of various errors, General Beves was removed from his command of allied troops. The outcome of the battle was inconclusive, but it would take van Deventer's forces three weeks to recover.[95] Not far away, Major Kraut's German troops were holding back the Gold Coast troops,[96] but were eventually forced to retire to protect the German supplies. With the pressure on his forces, Lettow-Vorbeck decided the best option was to attack Lukuledi which was held by the King's African Rifles. Again, neither side gained any significant success. Following this, Lettow-Vorbeck decided that the only way to continue the war was to move into Portuguese East Africa.[97] On 24 October 1917, Schnee and Lettow-Vorbeck met officially at the request of the latter. Lettow-Vorbeck announced that the war 'could and must be carried on', and that it was also time for the forces to move into Portuguese East Africa.[98]

This was the start of what Looff called 'the battle against the wolves', when Lettow-Vorbeck ordered him to surrender with a group of wounded. In effect, Lettow-Vorbeck decided to sacrifice a group of loyal soldiers in order to save rest.[99] He had some difficulty getting men to surrender as they feared the British justice system following a few significant instances, such as Naumann.[100] Whilst sorting out who was to go and who was to remain, on 7 November 1917, van Deventer started encircling Lettow-Vorbeck and asked the Portuguese to protect the border. Lettow-Vorbeck decided to withdraw from Chiwala rather than fight in order to preserve supplies, especially ammunition and quinine. Once safe, on 17 November 1917, he had all his men undergo a medical to determine who would stay behind.[101]

Into Portuguese East Africa

On 25 November, the Germans under Lettow-Vorbeck left their colony. The same day the Portuguese at Negomano were warned by Major Cohen, MacDonell's Intelligence Officer that the Germans would attack imminently. Despite this warning, the Germans overran the Portuguese. However, Tafel, still in German East Africa but trying to meet up with Lettow-Vorbeck, surrendered on 28 November 1917. He had been chased and distracted by Piet Pretorius and his scouting company. By the end of the month, the German colony was clear of German troops.[102]

Almost immediately, the British War Office ordered the removal of as many troops as possible. All Indian troops were withdrawn for service in other theatres while the West African troops were to go home. Van Deventer was, however, able to negotiate his forces and the troops from the Gold Coast together with their carrier corps from Sierra Leone remained, although he lost the Nigerian troops. Van Deventer took the opportunity of the Germans being evicted from their own country to offer them the opportunity to surrender. His note, sent on 4 December was only received by the Germans on 8 January 1918 as Lettow-Vorbeck had marched so rapidly south into Portuguese territory. Despite receiving 'a severe and unexpected blow',[103] on being told of Tafel's surrender, Lettow-Vorbeck ignored the offer to surrender.[104] Once again, he took the terms as an indication that van Deventer had been taken by surprise and that he was 'at [his] wits' end'.[105] The expectation that Lettow-Vorbeck would surrender was so strong that there were celebrations in Durban.[106]

On 17 December 1917, Lettow-Vorbeck moved his headquarters into Chirumba (Mtarika) which had been vacated by weak Portuguese forces. As the place was well stocked having been a base for the Portuguese Niassa Company, he decided to stay for a while.[107] For the next stage of the campaign, Lettow-Vorbeck split his force into three companies, each a few days' march apart. This would enable the troops to feed off the land more easily. Each group had its own field hospital, carriers, boys and followers. Each group was spread out, marching at least twenty miles a day, some women followers giving birth whilst on the march. Having made 'an important capture [including cloth], the whole convoy stretching several miles [looked] like a carnival procession.'[108] Yet, they were able to elude their enemy, helped by the latter not pursuing them for the first three months.

CHAPTER 7

PERSONAL, PERSONNEL AND MATERIAL

One could be forgiven for assuming that because a soldier holds a specific rank, they will behave in a given manner based on their training. However, personality and experience determine how that training is applied. Before and during World War One, not all officers were systematically trained as the British army had been restructured in 1907 following various enquiries into the management of the 1899–1901 war in southern Africa.[1] These reforms were still being embedded in 1914. In addition, India and each dominion had its own military traditions and these too impacted on the way the war was conducted. East Africa, perhaps more than any other theatre, suffered from the diversity of its leadership. This chapter discusses various issues such as leadership, loyalty, intelligence, supply, personal encounters with the enemy, communications, medical aspects, recruitment and life on the front. These issues were present all the way through the campaign and due to their personal nature or impact on the individual, provide an important insight into how and why the campaign progressed the way it did. It is not a complete analysis as new information is constantly coming to light which may change the conclusions drawn to date, but it does provide a starting point.

Leadership

The British disaster at Tanga was clearly down to mismanagement and the attitude of commander Aitken who refused to listen to his

Intelligence Officers and others who had African war experience. Tighe appeared to be well-liked and felt to have energy, however, by the time he was in command of the theatre, he had been so affected by those above him that he reputedly turned to alcohol and became ineffective.[2] The news that Smith-Dorrien was to lead the forces was well-received in East and southern Africa. Despite General French's attempts to undermine Smith-Dorrien and that he was recalled from service on the Western Front for causing a 'blunder', the men in East Africa, especially the Boers, who were to serve under him had no concerns about his leadership ability. The men were 'devastated' when they heard he would no longer proceed to East Africa and that in his stead would be Jan Smuts.[3]

Smuts' appointment was a political one. Unlike the Portuguese political appointments to military positions in East Africa, Smuts was well-liked by a large proportion of the men he was to lead; he was determined to lead an effective campaign and had some knowledge of warfare in Africa. Others including Kitchener and the Indian Officers, however, were uneasy about Smuts' appointment as they were being asked to put their trust in 'an amateur general as well as a Dutchman', who had fought against them not too long before.[4] Smuts was uncomfortable around people unless he knew them and so appeared distant. Yet, many of those who followed him through East Africa referred to him affectionately as he suffered the same deprivations as themselves. Unlike traditional British commanders who stayed behind the lines to direct action, Smuts was in the thick of it, living under the stars and doing his own reconnaissance. The problem with this was that he was too involved and unable to take a step back to review the situation. His eagerness for action was interpreted by some as necessary, as an early victory would build credibility and give his troops confidence in his leadership.[5]

Smuts' leadership style differed slightly, but significantly, to that of his adversary, Lettow-Vorbeck. Lettow-Vorbeck had led his troops from the start of the war, and although he was often in conflict with Governor Schnee, he was regarded as the military leader and respected by his men, Wintgens being the known exception. Lettow-Vorbeck was also known to have a tough side, offering Major Fischer a pistol to shoot himself with after the failure of his attack at Kahe. In contrast, his counterpart in the same encounter, Stewart, was sent back to India.[6] Smuts was also known to have this same tough side as seen in his sanctioning of the execution of Jopie Fourie, the only rebel to receive the death sentence, at the end of the 1914 South African rebellion.

In November 1914, Governor General Buxton noted: 'Smuts is getting overdone, (which I can see) and irritable, and even having tiffs with Botha himself, who is the only one, who can manage him. [...] If Smuts breaks down, it will be a very serious matter, as there is no one competent to replace him. His great constitutional fault is that consultation and discussion are antipathetic to him. He knows his own mind, and likes to take his own way, and is impatient of opposition.'[7] The same could be said about Lettow-Vorbeck – the 'mad mullah' – although Schnee did not have the same influence over Lettow-Vorbeck as Botha had over Smuts.

Lettow-Vorbeck, too, lived in the field with his men, doing his own reconnaissance when appropriate. The difference was that he split his force into separate independent commands which he managed from a central base and which he moved pending the military actions. Unlike the British forces which had no reserve, Lettow-Vorbeck managed the German reserve personally.[8] It was only during the campaign on Portuguese East African soil that he abandoned this practice and in effect 'led from the front'. However, when set-battles were fought as at Jasin and Tanga, he was in the thick of it as noted by the wounds he received at Jasin.[9]

That the two men had different management styles is not too surprising. Although a war of this nature was new to both the allies and Germans, it was fought according to previous experiences. Smuts was used to foraging with his men whilst on the move, whilst Lettow-Vorbeck had a wide range of military experience. He had worked on the General Staff at home during the 1899–1901 Southern Africa war, had been responsible for supplies during the Chinese Boxer Rebellion, a couple of years later had led troops against the native uprisings in German South West Africa and had spent time in the navy.[10] A more rounded experienced officer could not be found to lead the isolated German campaign in East Africa. He too had a gung-ho streak which, unlike Smuts, he had learnt to control despite the frustration it caused him.

Both men were pragmatic in getting the job done. As a result they were seen as ruthless. Maurice Hankey, of the Imperial Secretariat, recalled a comment by his friend Fisher who had seen service in East Africa. 'I thought his observations about Smuts were not discreditable: in order to achieve a coup he had often taken great risks and some of his men had died of hunger, but I suppose generals must do these things sometimes.'[11] The same could be said of Lettow-Vorbeck when von Grawet complained at a time when the Germans were struggling. Lettow-Vorbeck reminded him that 'there is always a way out, even of an apparently hopeless position, if the leader makes up his mind to face the risks.'[12] As a result of this ruthless attitude, personality clashes continued to dog Lettow-Vorbeck. As part of his long-running feud with Looff, in June he demoted him to the command of an *abteilung* reporting into Wahle who had reached the area.[13]

Yet, for all this, both commanders cared for their men. Lettow-Vorbeck ensured before they set off on their long march that there was sufficient quinine for all and made it a disciplinary offense not to take a daily dose. He visited the wounded and kept a close eye on diets, experimenting with alternatives when it became clear that current supplies would run out. Smuts was not as forthcoming in showing his care and it was well known that the condition of the troops in the southern part of the colony under Northey's command fared better than those in the north under Smuts. Although Northey's men suffered from the weather, they had sufficient food and medical supplies.[14] Northey, as a leader would visit men in hospital on Sundays and pick up the stranded and wounded. He 'would see to it that his troops were properly cared for', and in this he was well supported by Lieutenant-Colonels GMP Hawthorne and RE Murray.[15] Medical services in the northern area needed to be reorganised after Smuts left and the Indian brigades exchanged for new ones as they were so depleted by ill-health.[16] Lettow-Vorbeck managed to keep the majority of his officers sufficiently well to see the campaign through whilst Smuts sent his depleted South Africans home as soon as he could.

Politics and the military intertwined. In South Africa, the politician became a soldier and in East Africa, the soldier became a politician. Lettow-Vorbeck felt Smuts was his 'most dangerous and important of [...] opponents', even when the latter had to slow down due to his stretched lines of communications.[17] Lettow-Vorbeck later reflected that what he feared most was Smuts attacking the Taveta-Moshi line, Dar-es-Salaam and Tanga simultaneously. Smuts' failure to do so together with the British failure to sink two supply ships, gave Lettow-Vorbeck the 'luck of the war'.[18] Smuts was tenacious and Lettow-Vorbeck was persistent. Neither was prepared to give up and both continued to lead through bouts of malaria and when injured.[19]

Yet Smuts had a clear lack of understanding of his opponent. Given the supposed links between the two men, Smuts and Lettow-Vorbeck, it is surprising that Smuts, and later van Deventer, ever expected Lettow-Vorbeck to surrender. Although evidence suggests that the two men had never met before, they would have heard about each other and having fought against each other for at least six months, Smuts should have known something about his opponent. So why did he underestimate Lettow-Vorbeck and think he would surrender when the going was tough? Smuts would not have done so if the position was reversed.[20] A possible reason for Smuts to assume Lettow-Vorbeck would surrender was that he was clouded by the German surrender in South West Africa. Fisher, Maurice Hankey's friend, claims it was never Smuts' intention to engage Lettow-Vorbeck but to push him into Portuguese East Africa to further the Union's aims.[21] This could possibly explain van Deventer's actions in offering Lettow-Vorbeck terms. Unfortunately neither man has left a clue to explain his actions. Buxton summed it up after Botha's death when he wrote to Lord Milner that Botha was the mastermind and not Smuts.[22] Botha was a true soldier and leader of men, he had an innate understanding of waging battle despite never undertaking formal training in the field. For example, it was after or during Botha's visit to Smuts in East Africa that the strategy officially changed from 'fixed battles' to 'guerrilla warfare' whilst colleagues noted that Botha used to send Smuts advice on what to do.[23]

Smuts was, however, strong on the political front, pre-empting criticism as much as he could. He did this through reports which were marked with exaggeration most notably about the poor state of the German troops. Although he praised his troops, he neglected to mention how depleted their health really was and the reasons for it.[24] His positive claims about the progress of the campaign caused innumerable problems for those who followed him in command.

Hoskins, who took over from Smuts, never really had the opportunity to prove himself as a commander before being recalled. His men had recognised the mammoth task he had to repair supply lines before any future action could be undertaken. So when news arrived that he was to be replaced by van Deventer on 1 May 1917, there was an automatic backlash and suspicion towards the new commander. The Portuguese were also concerned because once again a South African was in control, and let MacDonell know.[25]

It was commonly believed that Smuts had manoeuvred things for political reasons. The rumours may not have been wrong. On 5 April 1917, Smuts suggested to Robertson that he ask Hoskins 'what he expects to be able to achieve in the next couple of months [as] this may guide you in your decision when we again discuss the matter.'[26] Within the month, Robertson informed Smuts that:

> The War Cabinet decided today that it is necessary to replace General Hoskins. I informed them of your opinion regarding General van Deventer, and in view of it they requested me to ask you to be good enough to ascertain if he would accept the appointment, as they are anxious to make use of his valuable services to bring the campaign to an end.[27]

Smuts enquired through Botha whether van Deventer was prepared to take the command, which he did.[28] At the end of May 1917, van Deventer replaced Hoskins.

Later, having heard that van Deventer had been awarded a KCMG, Sergeant Castle noted in his diary that:

> *Sir* von Splosh – to our great disappointment – stays on ... Thus we again see the evil of Political Influence. Here is a man of no education and no knowledge of up-to-date military matters

commanding a force of all parts of the empire and not being in sympathy or understanding with more than one contingent, his own countrymen from South Africa.[29]

Van Deventer's view of his staff was not much different. He did not trust them but was trusted by the rank and file.[30] The political divide between English and Boer lived on despite all attempts to eradicate the biases.

Boer loyalty

A number of authors have commented on the role of the South African Boers resident in German East Africa during the war and Smuts' ill-found trust in their support of the allied troops.[31] There were a number of Boers who pledged their loyalty to Germany and as discussed in the chapter on the outbreak of war supported Lettow-Vorbeck as scouts. Of the remainder, however, on the outbreak of war in 1914, the Germans had interred and relocated many of these Boers, even if they had sworn an oath to remain neutral and had been settled in the territory for at least ten years. It is, therefore, not surprising that a small group turned to support their fellow country-men. These Boers who had settled in German East Africa were mainly from the Transvaal province of the Union, the territory Smuts spent most of his life in. They were *bittereinders* as opposed to those who went to British East Africa who had supported the British during the 1899–1901 war. By the outbreak of war in 1914, it was believed that the majority of Boers had moved from German to British East Africa as a result of the strict laws imposed on settlers in the German colony.[32] Feeling in both colonies was the same regarding the Boers: mixed and complex. In both colonies, the Boers were given parole and allowed to keep their weapons against possible native unrest. The *Standard*, an East African newspaper, reported in horror that a 'Mr Nause who had been in German East Africa' was given freedom to walk around with his weapons so long as he did not later give information to the Germans. It was also reported that he was not asked to promise 'not to fight at all.'[33] This was quite a contrast to the view of the two colonies being in harmony with each other.

There were similar concerns in British East Africa about the loyalty of the Boers. The claims of South Africans leading Smuts astray may well have had to do with animosity between British English settlers and the South Africans, both English and Afrikaans, as the British colonists did not see them as being any good. Sorrenson maintains that until at least 1912, there were more South Africans in East Africa than British. This had partly been due to a recruitment drive by Lord Delamere in 1904. Sorrenson also maintained that these South Africans were of the 'most volatile and influential element' before World War One. Ewart Grogan was apparently one of these South Africans to move to East Africa, which suggests that Sorrenson is referring to British settlers in South Africa relocating to British East Africa.[34] Lord Cranworth in 1908 wrote of them being 'a solid mass of utterly disloyal colonists'. This was countered in 1912 by Frans Arnoldi, later to lead the Arnoldi Scouts, claiming that 'in the hour of their country's need their services will not be found wanting'.[35] He was proved right. In 1914, all the South Africans, especially in the Uasin Gishu Plateau, signed up such as Russel Bowker, Arnoldi, and others to form scouting troops, all later to be subsumed into the East African Mounted Rifles. This however, did not stop the distrust of the Boers as Fendall noted in his diaries.[36] During the war, Wynn who was with the General Staff, gave his impressions:

> A number of Boers were already with us. I was much impressed by those I met [...] Many of the Boers still harboured hard feelings against the British and only consented to serve on condition they were not placed under British officers. They were ready to fight more for their beloved Africa than for the British Empire. Some confided to me that their dream was of a United States of Africa, stretching from the Cape to Abyssinia and controlled by the Union of South Africa.[37]

Native loyalty

Native loyalty depended on who was seen to be winning the war. In 1915 in East Africa, this was the Germans as Delamere announced to Arthur Steel-Maitland, CE Callwell and HJ Read during his

sojourn to the United Kingdom. If Britain could change this situation, the loyalty of the natives would certainly change.[38] Apart from
native morale, there was concern over native uprisings. This was true
in all colonies and was the reason many whites, even those of dubious
loyalty, were permitted to retain their weapons. The fear of native
uprisings had even determined the armistice arrangements in German
South West Africa when South Africa argued that it was necessary
to keep the Germans in the country and on their farms to reduce
the chance of native trouble. In Britain, Foreign Secretary Grey felt
that as there were more natives than whites in the colonies and that
they had not rebelled before there was no reason why they would do
so in time of war.[39] A Colonial Office official noted in October 1914
that 'Nyasaland would be the last community in Africa where there
is likely to be any native trouble; the natives are peacefully disposed
and very well content with British administration.[40] How wrong they
both were was shown in January 1915.

The loyalty of the native further determined the extent to which they
were utilised in the fighting. Both the German askari and the King's
African Rifles were initially selected from specific tribes such as the
Kamba and Yao.[41] During the war, Lettow-Vorbeck did not seem to
recruit other askari unless they were prisoners who changed sides, or,
after the attack on Nhamacurra in July 1918 were bearers who volunteered to fight.[42] Lettow-Vorbeck maintained the loyalty of his askari by
treating them fairly and having allowed their women to follow the force.
Although loyalty dropped when the forces moved south into Portuguese
East Africa, Lettow-Vorbeck was able to retain a strong core.[43] The
British had more of a dilemma. They did not particularly want to
involve blacks in a white man's war but as the terrain proved unsuitable
for both white and Indian and they desperately needed manpower on the
Western Front, so they started to consider employing more black troops.
Both sides had issues with maintaining carrier or porter loyalty although
the Germans less so as Lettow-Vorbeck employed a relay system where
carriers worked in a limited area, remained close to home and, therefore,
received better care as they had time to recuperate.[44]

Smuts is credited with the policy change in 1916 to using native
troops and expanding the King's African Rifles. However, it was

Major-General R Wapshare who had started putting the steps into place to recruit black troops and train them. From three battalions at the start of 1916, by 1918 there were twenty-two. By 1918, many of these King's African Rifles were ex-German askari who had been taken prisoner and later joined the British forces.[45] As the war dragged on, there was a greater reluctance amongst the local populations to join up although they were more prepared to become soldiers than carriers. This was not surprising given that the former's pay and conditions were better. Volunteering methods have been questioned by authors such as Grundlingh who felt many were coerced into serving, a point supported by Wynn. The latter tells the story of a young man returning home to find his favourite woman missing and on hearing that the Germans had her, he left to join the British forces immediately to get her back.[46]

In Somaliland, directly impacting on the East Africa campaign, due to its proximity, Sayyid Mohammed Abdille Hassan, the real 'Mad Mullah', had been causing problems for the British since the 1890s. The Mullah was said to have 'immense charisma' and be 'a master of desert and guerrilla warfare ... a man of cruel and merciless temperament indifferent to human suffering.' Following the declaration of *jihad* against the British by the Sultan of Turkey on 2 November 1914, the Somali Field Force dislodged his men from three forts. They had to repeat the exercise again in February 1915. The decision was, therefore, taken to contain the Mullah so as to restrict his influence. By 1916 he seemed to be sufficiently contained and what concerns there had been about the loyalty of the Somali Mounted Scouts abated, especially after they were disbanded in August 1915. Further north, trouble brewed in Abyssinia where attempts were made to link with the Mullah in Somaliland, but to little avail as only one shipment of arms was received. However, the political troubles led the War Office to remain cautious and it left troops, badly needed elsewhere, in situ to deal with any potential uprisings.[47]

Closer to home, the Aga Khan, the Muslim religious leader in East Africa, and the Sultan of Zanzibar called on their adherents to be loyal to Britain. This went some way to counter-act the Turkish Sultan's *jihad*. In addition, Norman King, who became an Intelligence Officer after leaving German East Africa as Consul, believed that the raising of the Zanzibar Volunteer Defence Force went some way to increase the loyalty of the Arabs who were felt to be more afraid of the Germans.[48] Overall in East Africa, religious divides did not seem to have had a major influence on the war,[49] despite Schnee's concerns. To pacify the Muslims, Schnee ordered the flying of the crescent moon over some bomas and forts, and to protect against potential uprisings he allowed the Boers resident in the colony to retain their arms provided they pledged the oath of neutrality, or loyalty, to the German government.[50]

Intelligence

Loyalty and knowledge of the local forces played an instrumental part in the success of military intelligence. Captain Dooner, at Lindi, complained about not being able to get any information, whilst Pretorius had no problems using native guides. The latter made a particular point of using German prisoners.[51] Reliance on the friendliness of natives for protection is another point brought out in memoirs such as those by Thornhill. He noted on one trip, which lasted around nineteen days, that had it not been for native friendliness and belief that the Germans would be defeated by the British who would 'establish justice and prosperity', they would not have survived.[52]

Both sides relied heavily upon intelligence they could glean about the other side and a number of scouts have written about their experiences. The most well-known of the intelligence gatherers in East Africa is Richard Meinertzhagen, an Intelligence Officer in the British forces. There were many others including Wienholt and Thornhill, whilst others, Pretorius, went under the title 'scout'. They, too, have recorded their stories.[53] As the 1933 report on the campaign notes: 'Good intelligence was missing in 1914 and 1918 particularly.' This was exacerbated by the fact that 'No pre-war assessments had been undertaken in both German and Portuguese East Africa thus giving the Germans the upper hand.'[54] There had been some independent assessment of the situation in German East Africa by Consul Norman King, but as mentioned earlier, he had been hampered by the pacifist nature of the British East African government.[55]

Throughout most of the campaign in East Africa, the work of small groups of Intelligence Officers and other scouts seemed the most effective. The Germans used such small groups to attack the railways whilst the British used them to track the Germans and also to gather information. Where there was a chance of success, these patrols, often away from the main force for a month or so, would attack the enemy contributing to the overall military effort. Lieutenant Arnold Wienholt was just such an individual. He was eventually captured by the Germans after luring carriers away from the main contingent by speaking German and burning their loads. He was imprisoned and after being moved to another prison as a result of the encroachment of the allies, he and three South Africans who had joined him, managed to escape. Lettow-Vorbeck was able to follow some of Wienholt's work through the remainder of the campaign using captured documents left behind when Wienholt's group was surprised on occasion. For all the seriousness of the war, one cannot help seeing some humour in Wienholt losing a set of keys in a mad dash to escape capture, only to retrieve them some months later from a captured German askari and then to lose them again in another mad dash for freedom.[56] Incidents such as this show the personal nature of the campaign and how interconnected the groups were which passed each other within metres not realising it unless they literally stumbled on each other or were given away by the local native population loyal to the other side. This ability to get close up to the enemy enabled Pretorius to confirm that the *Marie*'s cargo had successfully been offloaded and distributed to the German troops.[57] The hunter-scout Frederick Selous was not so lucky. He was killed in January 1917 guiding an excursion to Behobeho by a sniper in an area unfavourable to the British.[58]

The nature of the country played an instrumental role in intelligence gathering. As far as troops were able to pass each other without being detected, it was also possible to observe large troop movements when the advantage of height was held. Troops on the move created dust clouds which could be followed for miles. Further, as both sides tended to use the same tactics of building fires for cooking a distance from where they eventually spent the night, it was relatively easy to work out what the other side was doing, even if they could not be engaged directly.[59] It was through using this strategy that Lettow-Vorbeck was able to avoid being caught in the encircling movements his enemies kept trying and once in Portuguese East Africa, Lettow-Vorbeck himself started to use the encircling tactic on his opposing forces.

On occasion it was possible to fool the enemy as Wienholt did. Similarly, Lettow-Vorbeck recorded that Germans acted English around Kondoa. This was aided by both sides being similarly dressed and using the same weapons by that time. This mix of uniform also led to troops firing on their own men on occasion as it was difficult to tell whether friend or foe was opposite until it was often too late.[60] They had obviously not heard the advice one elder gave his son about telling the difference between the English and the Germans. The Germans wear long trousers to cover their knees, whereas the English have bare knees.[61]

Supply

The supply of army uniform was virtually non-existent due to the need for ensuring the men were fed. The soldiers were thus reliant on local women to supply them with socks and other necessities.[62] The Germans, too, faced similar issues and when wheat ran out Lettow-Vorbeck experimented with making bread from local products including sweet potatoes. When boots ran out, leather was used to make sandals but although the method was learnt, the Germans never had to succumb to making boots as they were able to replace them and other kit or equipment from captured stores. Some groups even carried their own chickens with them, despite the risk they posed of giving the troops' position away.[63]

The big issue facing all allied troops was shortage of supply. It was experienced in all sectors, but particularly bad in East Africa. A soldier writing to his father on 15 July 1917 from Nigeria, before leaving for East Africa, asked his father for chocolates and things to go into his haversack as 'cooking things' do not always arrive in time to cook. He later noted that conditions in East Africa were the worst he had ever experienced, including West Africa.[64]

The issue of supply lines was crucial to the success of the war. Northey, who was meticulous in his planning, became concerned when he was expected to defend a stretch of territory beyond his means and called a meeting with Sheppard on 18 August 1917 to discuss the issue of his forces – he was becoming increasingly concerned at their dispensation and state of health.[65] The supply of food for the British troops in East Africa was complicated. Unlike the Western Front where the Indians in a battalion or regiment were of the same caste and religion, in East Africa they were mixed.[66] In addition, as divisions consisted of white and black troops too, a whole variety of diets had to be catered for. This had a knock-on effect on supply lines, shipping and the sourcing of food.

A similar issue was experienced with the supply of ammunition for the variety of weapons. Weapons were a hodgepodge of what was available and invariably were out of date, the newer equipment being sent to the Western Front.[67]

> Rifles were old Royal Enfields .303 and they had one machine gun which had "to be dismantled and carried on porter heads in transport." [...] There was no spit and polish after we were in the field, everything had to be carried on porter's heads, the average load was 50lbs. [...] Rations were very scarce at times. [...] We had one Doctor with the Battalion, but his resources were very limited. [...] I do not think I ever saw a Chaplain in the field, I am afraid we lost all count of Sundays.[68]

Mention is made of equipment from France and the Boers in Nairobi were said to be using Portuguese mausers.[69] The latter were possibly obtained on the Boer move from South Africa to East Africa, invariably going through Beira in Portuguese East Africa. These Portuguese weapons were different to the 20,000 rifles and 12 million rounds of ammunition which were used in German South West Africa,[70] the supply of which must have rankled Smuts who wanted as little as possible to do with the Portuguese. The Portuguese had given the rifles as a gift, but, the South Africans insisted on paying for them. In 1916, the Governor of Moçambique asked for 1,000 to be returned with

1,500,000 rounds of ammunition.[71] At the end of the German South West Africa campaign, many of the weapons were reclaimed by the Defence Force to arm later expeditions and so would have ended up in East Africa. Weapons were further sourced by Buxton and the War Office and Admiralty from wherever possible, which resulted in a mix of firepower being used.

Supply was slightly eased in mid-1916 when there was a change from Indian Ordnance under Major Routh to the Army Service Corps under Major Hazelton, Routh having been sent to Mesopotamia.[72] This change made sense given that the India Office was no longer involved in managing the campaign in East Africa. What is surprising is that it took so long to change the arrangements, which seem to have been influenced by the Indian focus on Mesopotamia.

Although the supply of chaplains may have been an issue in the field, they were in the towns and hospitals as noted by ES Thompson who saw at least two during his six-week convalescence in and near Kondoa Irangi.[73] The Bishop of Pretoria visited the theatre, whilst the Bishop of Zanzibar marched with the carrier corps he had raised.[74]

A gentleman's war?

During the campaign, there were a few 'stand-up fights' and other set-piece battles where trench warfare was employed in the initial defence. On a few occasions, sieges had also been affected but did not last long due to the drain on manpower and the lack of water.[75] In these encounters as with the small patrols, it was inevitable that prisoners would be taken. Initially prisoners were sent to camps, the British camps invariably being overseas (e.g. Max Looff ended up in Hull), whilst the German camps were further inland. The German camps consisted of both internees and captured soldiers whose experiences depended on when during the war they were interred.[76]

Accounts in the press suggested that the Germans were cruel to their prisoners, bayoneting or shooting them. This was done on occasions on both sides when men were too injured to move and had to be left behind.[77] Rather than leave them to excruciating or horrid death mauled by animals, they were released from their pain. Some claimed, too, that the Germans were using copper-headed bullets. There is no way to prove this. Given the prevalence of copper in the area and the technology developed by the Germans since the outbreak of war, they may have been able to make copper-heads, but this is speculation. A more plausible reason for the accounts is propaganda. Meinertzhagen mentions writing articles to motivate recruitment and stories of such German atrocities would be the perfect enticement.[78]

Thornhill and others to a degree support the case for German brutality, although, this mainly appears to be during the early days of the war, as experienced by Pretorius, and in isolated patches. As it became apparent that the war was dragging out, so the Germans relied more on British humanity to look after their own sick and wounded, leaving them behind in Arusha and other towns so as to proceed unheeded.[79] This was particularly noticeable from September 1917 when, due to food shortages, prisoners were let out on parole (or left behind) after taking an oath not to fight against Germany again. In January 1917, Flight Lieutenant ER Moon was captured after his plane crashed along the Rufiji. He spoke of the kindness of his captor who provided him with clothing and food. He was also carried along when too ill to walk and his colleague Commander Bridgeman, who had drowned, was given a full military burial.[80] Sergeant Harris of the Motorcycle Corps explained that 'He was released on May 24, but had to promise to remain on the spot for forty-eight hours.'[81] A number of Portuguese camps were overtaken by the German forces. When those captured 'refused to give their word not to fight against' the Germans for the remainder of the war, they were 'sent north to the Rovuma by General Wahle owing to the difficulty of feeding them.'[82] However, Lettow-Vorbeck felt his askari were not treated as well as they should have been.[83]

Communications between the opposing forces happened on occasion.[84] For example, when the commanders felt that the other side was not 'playing fairly', they would write to their counterpart. Wapshare wrote to Lettow-Vorbeck about a woman who was apparently doing 'undesirable things' to prisoners, whilst Lettow-Vorbeck queried an order he had read in a diary to 'take no prisoners'.[85] In similar fashion, Smuts wrote to congratulate Lettow-Vorbeck on the latter being awarded the *Order Pour le Mérite* on 29 October 1916.[86] In addition, as life became more strained for the Germans, Lettow-Vorbeck recalled that 'The English Government issued to us articles of food for the English prisoners which we could not get for ourselves.'[87]

Ceasefires were called all through the campaign when necessary to deal with the wounded, the earliest account being at Tanga in November 1914 and the last in 1918.[88] In May 1915, the British having captured Dr Gothein during a skirmish, allowed him to return to the Germans in Karonga.[89] A month after losing his Portuguese allies, on 7 August 1918, van Deventer sent a letter to Lettow-Vorbeck under truce suggesting an exchange of medical prisoners. This led Lettow-Vorbeck to believe action of some kind was being prepared. He was not wrong as severe fighting took place at Chalau at the end of the month with both sides losing much equipment and many men.[90] The Germans also called ceasefires to remove their wounded and dead. Following severe losses at Lupumbe, Wintgens organised to withdraw his injured and dead under a white flag. This action annoyed Wahle as it brought the full force of the British troops to bear in the area, blocking his route to Mahenge.[91] Captain RWM Langham recalled a case where Dr Harold entered a German camp at Bismarkburg believing the Germans to have surrendered. This was not the case and following a period of gun fire by both sides, the German commandant who happened to be caught with the doctor declared:

> 'We seem to have reached an impasse. I'm your prisoner, but you can't take me away nor get away yourselves. Don't you think we should call it "checkmate", so that you can get your wounded attended to.' [...] Lieutenant Hasslacher then blew his whistle, held up his handkerchief and stood up. By his orders, the garrison brought out lemonade and more bandages for the wounded. Our people brought down stretcher parties and the wounded were carried off.[92]

When ceasefires could not be managed or the troops 'could not get the bodies of our dead, [...] the Germans always bury them in such a case. The 2nd Battn went out four days later to the same place, but found the enemy still in position about there.'[93] Sergeant Harris, too, explains: 'The Colonel [Fairweather] and poor Homan were buried with full military honors. Captain Wintgens of the German forces read the burial service, and a company of Askaris formed the firing party.'[94]

The foresight which Lettow-Vorbeck had of ensuring that each force had its own doctor paid off. He records that after a battle, the allied wounded preferred being treated by a German doctor as they would not have been treated as well by an English one. It is unlikely this was a statement about the medic's ability but rather more about the shortage of them and the distance an injured allied soldier had to travel to access a doctor.[85] Sir Edward Grey's brother, fighting at Kisamu, 'walked 27 miles alone in 9 hours with his arm in ribbons' to get medical attention.[96] Similarly, Lance Dafadar Khan Sahib wounded during a surprise German attack on his patrol walked for six days to receive medical treatment.[97] As the Germans had a doctor attached to each contingent, there was always someone qualified on hand and the wounded could get almost immediate assistance. Although, according to Moon, a prisoner with the Germans, he was told at each camp along the march that he would get better treatment and medication at the next camp.[98] Moon was finally released with others and sick Germans when Lettow-Vorbeck left for Portuguese East Africa.[99]

There were occasions where prisoners were released by their own. On his way to Kondoa Irangi on 12 April 1916, van Deventer's men liberated one hundred Boer farmers and their families from a prisoner camp at Pienaar's Heights.[100] Similarly, when the Belgians occupied Tabora they released thirty-five missionaries, 160 other civilians from the prison and 2,000 prisoners of war. These prisoners and others complained that they had been 'compulsorily employed under a native guard', a situation they felt was degrading.[101]

Hatchell notes that usually in time of war, the civil administration remains in post.[102] However, in German East Africa, they left to fight. During 1916, as Smuts pushed the Germans south and the Belgians together with Northey forced them east, German towns and farms were evacuated. Lettow-Vorbeck 'met many ox-wagons in which

German and Boer farmers, with their families, were driving from the country around Meru Mountain to Kondoa.'[103] The allies, therefore, had to appoint political officers for administrative work. In the south, they came from Northern and Southern Rhodesia, Nyasaland and the Union and were responsible to the Colonial Office with direct control being exercised by Sir Hector Duff of the Nyasaland administration.[104] Smuts, similarly, appointed political officers, his being from British East Africa and elsewhere with the senior officer being Sir Theodore Morrison from India. In addition he arranged for the South African police to be involved in the civil governance of Dar-es-Salaam for the duration of the war thereby ensuring South Africa had additional hold over the territory.[105] On 11 December 1916, both these groups were brought under Colonial Office control when Horace Byatt was appointed to oversee the whole of the German East Africa territory.[106] Byatt, an experienced administrator, wrote to ex-Colonial Secretary Harcourt on his arrival in East Africa about the challenges he faced. He had to set up systems from nothing which was a first for him, and he could not start until it was clear that the Germans would not be returning.[107] This naturally caused problems when the Germans broke back into occupied territory during 1917 and 1918.

Recruitment

Finding replacements for those who were no longer able to fight either through disability or death was another challenge British commanders and their staff had to manage. What is striking about accounts is that replacement troops were sent to join battalions individually and in small groups. Given the nature of the country, the paucity of communications, transport links and the lack of maps it is quite remarkable, to the military outsider, that the troops found their way to where they needed to be, even if they were 'tagged' onto the existing supply lines.[108] Where these could not be drawn from existing sources of supply, they had to be found elsewhere, including in the colonies.

Whilst trying to find a way to activate the campaign in 1915, CE Callwell of the War Office suggested that Captain Martin of the Warwick's put forward his proposal to 'form a corps of bombthrowers from Basutos, Zulus and Swazis who would have no other arms except knobkierries, and implements of that sort.'[109] This would overcome the South African objection to arming blacks as they would be using traditional weapons, and make use of local resources. The proposal seemed to go no further, but is interesting to see how creative individuals were. Given that Lee's proposal of sending boats overland from Cape Town to Lake Tanganyika was accepted, one wonders how Martin's proposal would have fared had Kitchener not been at the War Office.

Having initially supported conscription in British East Africa, by 1917 Lord Delamere had changed his mind about the recruitment of farmers in East Africa. He was concerned about the future economic prosperity of the colony. According to his calculations, the demand for 300 farmers would strip the sector bare. Given that the colony was already suffering under the British ban on coffee imports as well as flax, sisal and wool, depriving the land of farmers would be devastating.[110]

On a broader front, Smuts' announcement in 1916 that the campaign was changing to guerrilla warfare suited the British Army Council which wanted to release all possible troops to fight in Europe. Chief of Imperial General Staff Robertson had already sent Smuts a telegram on 28 June 1916 suggesting that the whites be withdrawn once the Central railway was in allied hands and the rest of the campaign be completed by black troops, as this would free white and Indian troops for Europe. For the War Office, this move would reduce the loss to illness of what it saw as valuable fighting material and release shipping to service Europe. On 29 July 1916 Robertson secretly telegraphed to Smuts stating that '[the] project of today (WO tel 20113) does not emanate from me as I doubt its feasibility and practical value if feasible.' The Army Council, possibly in response to a suggestion by Major Wedgwood who was in East Africa, thought that 'large numbers of native troops could be raised in East Africa for service elsewhere.' Smuts was asked to consult with General Hoskins and others who had experienced the war outside of East Africa before making his recommendations.[111] Robertson's telegram suggests he was against the proposal the Army Council, of which he was a member, was supporting. Smuts responded two weeks later, that 'only [a] very small scheme [was] feasible'.[112]

It was all well and good changing the composition of the fighting forces in Africa, however, given the empire's reluctance to promote non-whites to positions of rank within the military, white officers still needed to be found. Due to the possible trouble recruiting white officers in the Union would cause and as it would be cheaper, the decision was made to recruit volunteers in Britain to become officers of the new battalions of the King's African Rifles which were being raised.[113] WG Hughes explained:

> A circular came from Brigade HQ asking for volunteers, WOs and NCO's to go to Africa to serve with the KAR's. Several NCO's put their names down to go, but they all withdrew before the time came to go. It was quite voluntary: my family were against my going but I thought it a chance to see the world.

> We were promised clothing and equipment but none arrived and we were told it would be on board. We actually went without tropical kit. Our contract was with the Crown Agents and our pay was 2/day above our regimental pay until we passed a Swahili test which I did after about a month and then we came on to Colonial rates of pay.[114]

Others seem to have been lured across by Smuts' belief that the Germans would soon be defeated and they would be required for garrison duty.

> Don't let them worry about me. We are really only going out to a new Training centre. I hear Smuts says he needs 1000 men to garrison EA *when* it is taken and so I daresay we shall be among them. Our hopes are chiefly for Palestine but where we may eventually end up one cannot imagine.[115]

To supplement the forces from South Africa, and particularly from 1917 when the white South Africans were withdrawn, reinforcements were found in West Africa. As the campaigns against the Germans in West Africa concluded, so troops from the Gold Coast and Nigeria were moved to East Africa. The same happened to the West Indian troops, the 2/West India Regiment, who were no longer required for services in West Africa.[116] Carriers were sourced from other countries. Apart from carriers coming from Uganda and the southern African territories, Sierra Leone sent across 5,000 porters and possibly another 6,000 including '1,000 Kroo boys as dock labourers'.[117] The bodies were there to do the work, but as indicated earlier, the diversity brought its own difficulties in terms of victualling.

Life on the African front

Given the nature of the territory, the men had to walk everywhere. The Germans had developed a network of roads and tracks crossing the country whilst Northey had purposely built roads during his preparation phase to enable easy access and delivery of supplies, but the few motorised vehicles there were, were prone to getting stuck in the rainy season.[118] When cars failed or were not suitable bicycles, horses, donkeys or mules were used, depending on what was available. The Motorcycle Corps under Colonel Fairweather, which had motorcycles to patrol the roads, invariably reverted to bicycles as they were quieter and more easily managed on the poor roads.[119] The Germans had a limited number of bicycles, of which Lettow-Vorbeck had one as it allowed him greater freedom of movement for reconnoitring.[120]

There were some mounted troops but these did not last long due to the prevalence of tsetse fly with the result that the cavalry often found themselves infantry. With vast distances having to be covered, during 1915, once troops were in position for defensive action, apart from going on patrol, there was not much for them to do which in itself was stressful.[121] The situation after what was often an arduous journey is illustrated by Capell who noted in May 1915 that:

> This bush work is very trying for troops; rifles must be kept
> loaded, those of the flank and advance guards with safety-catches
> off. It is continual stooping and catching in thorns, listening

to and for sounds; momentarily expecting the crack of rifles at short ranges; for hours hardly speaking in more than the lowest whisper; the continual anxiety that some one may be losing touch; all these combine to make this the most nervy and wearing class of fighting imaginable. No one who has not seen the bush of the Tsavo valley can understand it.[122]

From 1916, camp life was more stringently regulated as the men were never sure when the enemy would appear. Photographs show, and accounts tell of, forces on the march stretching miles across the field and taking all day for the last men to catch up with the first who had left camp before dawn.[123]

With 'time' on their hands, the monotony of the march when it came, and the need to hunt for food, it is not surprising that the myth grew up that the East Africa campaign was one big safari and game hunt. Thornhill in a chapter entitled *On Leave* describes a hunting expedition to shoot a bongo, Richard Meinertzhagen's diary of the campaign has pages on hunting and bird watching, whilst Capell's history of the 2nd Rhodesian Regiment describes 'camera' hunts.[124] What else was there to write about when one could not write anything which would give an indication as to where one was or provide the enemy with useful information? Safety was found in describing the rich fauna they came across to protect mothers and loved ones from the horrors of war and their conditions.[125]

Some, however, did write of the conditions they faced:

Since leaving MURRUPULA on the 16 August [1918] the Regiment had marched continuously every day for 26 days, averaging 15½ miles a day: on three of these days there had been continuous fighting, and on many other days, fighting formations had to be maintained, owing to the proximity of the enemy and the uncertainty of when he would be encountered in the bush covered country. During this period two marches of 28 miles and four others each of over 29 miles in the day had been done. During more than a third of the time all troops had been on short rations.[126]

General Carbutt, author of the above account and of the Rhodesian Native Regiment, lost five officers and his regimental sergeant major due to exhaustion from this constant marching.

Lieutenant Erskine, 1KAR writing from Portuguese East Africa, had a similar story:

> We should reach Battalion HQ about this day week. I could never have imagined a country so wild and desolate as that we have been marching through lately. It is just one huge barren stretch of never-ending forests swamps and jungle. Grass ten feet high and so thick you can see a yard on either side. We go in single file along native tracks twisting and turning. We have advance guards and men out on either side three hundred porters carrying rice and ammo and supplies for the column in the field; then another platoon (the rear guard) behind that again. This is different altogether from France and is very trying because you never know when to expect an attack and the nerves are at high tension all the time. We don't expect to bump up against anything but if we do I think we shall make our presence felt.
>
> I have my bath every afternoon. I get a hole dug in the ground then place an oil sheet inside and fill it with water. I am almost as black as the Askari now.[127]

The only time it appears that the real horrors of the campaign were written about was in letters to parents and wives telling them about the circumstances in which their loved ones died, in memoranda to the War Office explaining defeats or achievements, in memoirs and in diaries. As Capell wrote, 'the whole road stank [...] But it was war – red, savage and infinitely brutal, sparing neither man nor beast.'[128] For many, however, tales of jigger fleas, animals dying from tsetse fever, dysentery and malaria did not make for good writing or for heroic deaths in the same way as being shot on the Western Front did. Many preferred to be on the Western Front as Lord Cranworth noted: 'Ah, I wish to h___ I was in France! There one lives like a gentleman and dies like a man, here one lives like a pig and dies like a dog.'[129]

I freely admit that there was much more metal flying about in France and that there was a lot of gas, which was unknown in East Africa, but then one had good food and a decent supply of it. The climate was more congenial to our natures. One had spells off duty when things were a bit cushy. In France, one was troubled by only one kind of insect, not dozens of different species. And again, France was a civilised country, and East Africa, away from the larger towns was not. I would sooner hear a big shell travelling along like an express train, then hear a lion roar a few yards away. I have heard both very often, but a shell never made my flesh run up my spine until it turned my hair into pin wire.[130]

The following letter to a mother on 26 October 1917 about her son's death on 16 Oct 1917, summed up life behind the fighting.

On Oct 4th, the 1st, 2nd & 4th Battns, under Colonel Mann, began a march across country, hilly, dusty, hot, and covered with thick bush. In most places we could only get water in cupfuls, sometimes having to dig for it. There were 8000 people in the column, far the larger proportion being non-combatants – supply carriers, ammunition, baggage, signal section, field ambulance with all their stores stretchers and personnel. It was seldom that we could walk two abreast, and when in single file the column covered 7 miles of path. This made the marches frightfully slow and tedious.

We kept in touch with the GOC Lindi forces by our portable wireless ... Our casualties, with the Gambia Coy that was with us, were 202, 14 being white.

The newspapers give no idea of the state of affairs in this country; the LINDI forces had 2,000 casualties within a week this month.

I opened all your son's letters enough to see where and from whom they came, and the date, and then burnt them, thinking you would like to know what had become of them. A 'Committee of Adjustment' of 3 officers is usually appointed, but I don't like the idea of a whole committee dealing with a dead man's private letters. He had only a few personal belongings with him on the 16th, which were lost. Everything else is further back and will be dealt with by a committee. They generally sell all clothes, camp kit etc, and send home only small things as have sentimental value or are likely to be of interest to the family.[131]

The conditions the men endured naturally had an impact on morale and at Christmas in 1916, men in the British South Africa Police mutinied. Murray coerced them back into line, but they continued to suffer from the hardships of their circumstances.[132] This mutiny came as something of a surprise given the care and consideration for the personal wellbeing of the troops in the south. This seems to have been the last mutiny in the British forces and coincided with the end of Smuts' command. There had been a mutiny in February 1915 in the north when the Somali Scouts under Berkeley Cole caused trouble. It is not known why this happened but the unit was reconfigured as Cole's Scouts under Lord Cranworth.[133] On 15 April 1916, 29 NCOs and men of the East Africa Maxim Gun Company refused to saddle up en route to Kondoa Irangi due to the conditions and orders they were given. They were placed under arrest.[134]

The campaign in East Africa was a test of endurance for all. This section has focused predominantly on the white forces however, those in the Gold Coast, Nigerian and West Indian Regiments as well as the Cape Corps and mainland Indian troops suffered the same. By far, the biggest group, the carriers and porters, suffered more, dragged into a struggle they did not ask to be part of, yet had no way to avoid. Many died, but many also survived, with some seeing the campaign through to its conclusion.

CHAPTER 8

LAST DAYS, 1918

As with previous years, the war in Europe during 1918 was to mirror that in East Africa, albeit for different reasons. The year started with an optimism which did not reflect reality. In Germany, although peace negotiations were underway with the Russians and an offensive was renewed on the eastern front, Germany was struggling. Production to support the military effort was unable to keep up and it was anticipated that America would have its first troops in Europe by May or June. This left a very small window of opportunity to defeat Britain and France on the Western Front. In March 1918, General Ludendorff launched his final attack across the Somme, moving into Flanders and finally into the area of the Marne, threatening Paris in June. Unable to break through, Ludendorff brought his attack to an end in July. Having successfully defended against the German advance, the allies brought their offensive, planned for 1919, forward and attacked at Amiens. Morale and available manpower were to play their part too – German morale was waning and already the influenza epidemic was starting to make an impact. Pressure was maintained through small offensives as part of the Arras offensive and by October, the German Hindenburg line of defence was broken. Germany was becoming isolated, its Turkish allies agreed peace on 30 October 1918 whilst Austria did so on 3 November. Finally on 11 November 1918 the armistice agreed by Germany and its enemies came into effect and for the third time since war was declared, a decision in Germany directly affected the events in East Africa.[1]

After three years and four months traversing across East Africa, the year 1917 ended on a false high. Van Deventer had offered Lettow-Vorbeck surrender terms which the latter did not receive until the new year. All the forces were exhausted and suffering from poor morale although the surrender notice went some way to reinvigorating the Germans. Lettow-Vorbeck felt sufficiently confident in his followers' morale that he declined the offer. Despite the agreements and plans for co-operation between the British and Portuguese, the latter were too weak and poorly equipped to offer much resistance. Morale, too, was low which enabled the Germans to replenish their stores – equipment and food – at very little cost to themselves although Lettow-Vorbeck noted the effectiveness of British propaganda in the numerous desertions he had to deal with.[2]

After the rains and when Lettow-Vorbeck's forces re-united, on 11 April 1918, the first set battle in Portuguese East Africa was fought at Churimba Hill (Medo; Chirimba). The allied forces faced the Germans without the Portuguese who were dealing with a native uprising. As with previous set battles, both sides suffered losses they could ill-afford.[3] A few other set battles would be fought in Portuguese territory, all with the same effect, over the next two months with a total of ninety-five engagements being recorded between April and June.[4] Thereafter, Lettow-Vorbeck would ensure he stayed out of reach to preserve his small force, living off Portuguese settlements with van Deventer following him. A German Boer described this phase of the war as 'a funny war. We chase the Portuguese, and the English chase us.'[5]

In June 1918, the Portuguese were extremely concerned about the British (and South Africans) being in their colony which led van Deventer formally to reassure the colony that the British and their allies would leave as soon as the Germans were defeated. Diplomacy was clearly called for as Rosa was increasingly sensitive in believing that Smuts' policy of excluding the Portuguese from any action was being continued. He was not far wrong in this assumption, but the reality at the time was not to 'get one over the Portuguese' but rather to ensure the Germans were defeated to release shipping, men and equipment for Europe. Recognising that the Portuguese were not strong enough to tackle the Germans, others took on the task.[6] Portuguese sensitivities had been exacerbated by the publication of the British Labour Party war aims in November 1917 and a scandal in the South African press about a 'women market' organised by Portuguese officials. These tensions led MacDonell to 'insist on returning to his post [as Consul General] in Lorenço Marques', which meant van Deventer had no liaison officer in the Portuguese military camp until Major 'SOS' Cohen, Intelligence Officer, took over.[7]

Rosa, pressured by Lisbon, pushed for joint action but took two weeks to act on van Deventer's instructions regarding the protection of Quelimane and then on 4 July 1918, called a council of war in the town. The British represented by Cohen were insistent that the port be defended, but the Portuguese vacillated.[8] The uncertainty around their involvement meant the Portuguese were unprepared and failed to hold the Germans at Nhamacurra despite the coaxing and coordination by Major Gore-Browne of 2/3 King's African Rifles.[9] Gore-Browne and over one hundred askaris were drowned or shot trying to escape the Germans once the flanking Portuguese troops had broken and fled leading to the decimation of three Portuguese battalions and two British companies. This defeat in early July 1918 was the last straw for Anglo-Portuguese co-operation and van Deventer refused to work with Rosa. Rosa, in turn, was fired by Governor General Mosson de Amorim and recalled on 9 July. He left in August and on his arrival in Lisbon in October was arrested and imprisoned for a couple of months. The British, however, later awarded him the Order of the Bath while the War Office cautioned van Deventer not to take any action that could be construed as an insult to the Portuguese nation.[10] The Gold Coast Regiment also left East Africa in August 1918, on the 13th, the decision to withdraw them demonstrating to the Portuguese that the British had no intention of staying in their territory.

In Africa, in the absence of the Portuguese military commander, van Deventer met with the Portuguese Governor General on 22 July. They agreed separate spheres of operation with the Portuguese being allocated sectors which would have minimum impact on the direction of the fighting.[11] Portugal's official involvement in the East African campaign had come to an end although there were some Portuguese troops mixed with English troops subsequently captured by the Germans.[12]

For Lettow-Vorbeck the attack on Nhamacurra enabled him to restock as well as replace the remaining 1871 weapons. He restructured his forces and had them march in parallel columns as opposed to the single column which marched a few days apart. Although this created new difficulties, he felt they were outweighed by the advantage of having all his troops close to hand which enabled him to attempt encircling his adversaries whilst they were encircling him.[13] This approach was evident at the Battle of Lioma on 30 and 31 August where the King's African Rifles and Kartucol fought their last battle of the campaign. Two months later, the war ended.[14] The last battles to take place in Portuguese East Africa were between Shortcol, on 8 September 1918, and German troops led by Captain Spangenberg and against Captain Koehl near Mahua.[15]

Despite having rejected van Deventer's offer of peace in January, Lettow-Vorbeck was having a relatively difficult time. To protect his forces, he resorted to threatening any natives who were suspected of supporting the British or allies with hanging when they returned to German East Africa. The British, knowing of the threat, exploited this by promising good treatment with the result that ten percent of Lettow-Vorbeck's carriers deserted including his personal servant.[16] Lettow-Vorbeck had also been pushing his men who were suffering from cerebral spinal meningitis and a bronchial virus. Small pox then broke out and at one point the senior doctor succumbed to malaria. Morale was declining which was made worse by the news filtering through from Europe. The situation was so bad that on 20 September 1918, Schnee complained and requested that the most seriously ill and injured troops be abandoned to save the others. Lettow-Vorbeck refused to listen. When he re-entered the German colony on 29 September 1918, desertions increased despite his orders for deserters to be shot. It was clear that the tide was turning – the porters in particular believing the British were now the stronger force.[17]

On 17 October 1918, at Ubena near Mbeya and Iringa, Lettow-Vorbeck left behind his trusted commander Wahle and other injured as he moved towards Rhodesia. Waiting until he was back on German soil to leave men behind was a deliberate move on Lettow-Vorbeck's part so that they were not left to Portuguese but rather to British care.

Their proximity to a major British base would ensure access to medical facilities.[18]

Lettow-Vorbeck had been contemplating moving north, but changed his mind to invade Northern Rhodesia realising that:

> the inner part of Rhodesia had not been affected by the war and hence had enough provisions. [...] What is more, the English would not have reckoned with the Germans heading to Rhodesia and hence would not have been prepared for it. Later from Rhodesia there were many options that opened up for the Germans ... a whole range of possibilities whose effects were not to be underestimated.[19]

One of which was to cut across to Angola and then German South West Africa. The idea of the Germans in South West Africa and East Africa being able to meet up through Angola has met with mixed reactions. Some authors believe it would have been possible[20] whereas other sources suggest it was not. Du Toit in his history of *The Boers in East Africa* notes that those who migrated north after the Boer War did so via the sea as 'no trek had made it overland.'[21] Van Deventer, too, could not have believed the move possible as he was taken by surprise and had no defences in place.[22]

From captured newspapers the Germans discovered that Cambrai had fallen and that the Bulgarians had surrendered but this did not affect Lettow-Vorbeck much as positions could be given up for so many different reasons, and he continued on his way.[23] On 1 November 1918, Lettow-Vorbeck attacked Fife in Northern Rhodesia, experiencing his closest escape from death. He then moved onto Kasama, from where he would make his way into Angola. The seizure of Mwenzo Mission west of Fife, again, allowed the Germans to restock fully, including medical supplies.[24] Schnee summed up the feelings of the Germans in the last days: 'It seems to me that for the main part everyone hopes for peace in the near future, with the deliverance that it will bring us from our situation, which grows ever more unbearable and which consciously or unconsciously will leave its mark permanently on us.'[25] On 9 November, Spangenberg moving slightly ahead of the remaining Germans found the town of Kasama deserted. District Commissioner Croad had evacuated the town sending the women to Mpika and the ammunition to a place thirty miles south of Kasama, Chiwuhuwulu, and then onto Chambezi factory which was fifty-four miles south of Kasama.[26]

Major Hawkins recalled the story of the last days in *The Times*:[27]

On the morning of November 11th (Armistice Day) the column was still forty-one miles from the road junction at Malima River, where we hoped to cut off at least the German rear-guard. Twenty-one miles were covered on the 11th, and touch with the enemy obtained one mile from the cross roads after marching eighteen miles on the 12th.

The position of the force on this day was a peculiar one. The column, consisting of 750 rifles, was probably considerably inferior to the total number of the enemy should he stand at bay. Further, our column had far outstripped all communications, and it would be impossible to pursue beyond Kasama without waiting for food. It was therefore determined to deal as heavy a blow as possible at the enemy before he got out of reach.

There turned out to be six enemy companies on the Malima, who, being attacked unexpectedly in the rear, hastily retired with loss to the north side of the open valley of the Malima, across which a hot fight raged till dark ... 9.30pm ... when fighting ceased.

Nearby, on 13 November, a German advance party arrived south of Kasama and fired at British defenders occupying a rubber factory.[28] A British farmer also joined the defence firing an elephant gun from inside the roof of the factory, leading the Germans to believe that they faced an artillery piece.[29]

News of the armistice was received in Livingstone on the 11th, but owing to a fault in the telegraph did not reach the Chambeshi (Chambezi) till two days later. Croad heard of the armistice at 'about 1 o'clock' when a Mr F Rumsey brought him a wire from the administrator in Livingstone 'saying that we were to carry on till General van Deventer wired me instructions.'[30]

At 11.30am on November 13th one of our KAR native patrol posted on the main road reported that two motor cyclists carrying white flags and with white bands at their helmets passed from the direction of Abercorn going towards the enemy at Kasama. The native patrol shouted to them and tried to stop them, but they took no notice and passed on towards Kasama and the enemy.

This news caused great excitement in the column as no home news had been received for over a week. It was decided to advance slowly and await events.

At 2.45pm, when four miles from Kasama, the advance point reported two German askaris coming in under a large white flag, with a letter for the column commander. This proved to be a telegram received by von Lettow from our motor cyclists announcing the Armistice.

The Germans found it hard to believe and Lettow-Vorbeck cycled off to let Spangenberg, who was ahead of the main German force, know.[31] Whilst he was with Spangenberg, on 14 November, Lettow-Vorbeck met District Commissioner Croad, who explained that hostilities had ceased in Europe following the German government's capitulation. Lettow-Vorbeck returned to his main body where he had to convince some of his senior officers that the war was over. He also arranged for the release of the prisoners including Colonel Dickinson who had spent more than three months with the Germans.[32]

On the morning of 16th November von Lettow arrived at Kasama and handed in to us his written unconditional surrender, provided the terms should turn out as represented to him. [...] At midday the whole German force marched back through our camp *en route* for Abercorn, 100 miles away, where the official surrender was to take place.

His formal submission was received by Brigadier-General W FS Edwards of the King's African Rifles at Abercorn on 18 November, and a formal surrender took place on 25 November 1918.[33] The surrender document was signed by Edwards for the British, whilst Lettow-Vorbeck, Captain Anderson and Captain Walter Spangenberg signed for the Germans. By refusing to allow Schnee, the supreme commander of German East Africa, to sign the document, Lettow-Vorbeck gave the message that his surrender 'did not signify a surrender of Germany's control of its East African colony.'[34]

Lettow-Vorbeck had completed the task set. He had kept the German colony in German hands for as long as he could and attracted numerous troops and their auxiliary services away from the battlefields in Europe including much needed shipping to transport American troops and supplies across the Atlantic. It would now be down to the politicians, including his adversary Smuts to determine the final outcome of German East Africa.

Whilst the discussions were progressing in Europe as to the future of the African territories, back in Africa in the weeks after the armistice, twelve Germans died from flu as did 279 German askari and porters. British deaths were four times greater in October.[35] Surviving soldiers and auxillaries were demobilised, some more slowly than they had hoped or expected, prisoners of war were returned home and societies started to rebuild their communities and buildings. Many of the German residents in East Africa returned to Germany whilst thirty Afrikaners were deported to the same having supported Lettow-Vorbeck during the war. The issue was later raised in the South African parliament during 1920 as part of the Nationalist attack on Smuts.[36] In South West Africa, half of the resident German population, around six of the twelve thousand, were repatriated to Germany including the Schanderl brothers.[37] This was to maintain some level of white continuity in the country whilst giving the message to the natives that the Germans had been defeated.

Some difficulties ensued over the interpretation of the armistice agreement and had to be referred back to Europe. The victors determined the interpretation of Article XVII of the armistice which stated that the East African German forces 'should be "evacuated."' The War

Office insisted this could only happen after 'unconditional surrender and disarmament'.[38] The implication was that Lettow-Vorbeck and his men were in effect prisoners of war. Lettow-Vorbeck though, insisted they be 'granted the honours of war' and be treated as ordinary citizens, and although van Deventer agreed with him, the latter felt his hands were tied.[39]

The issue of whether Lettow-Vorbeck and his men were prisoners of war or not continued to niggle. Van Deventer was in a difficult position. He had already defied the British War Office and allowed Lettow-Vorbeck's officers to retain their weapons, but he could not push too much. He, therefore, wrote to Lettow-Vorbeck on 2 December 1918:

> I beg to acknowledge receipt of your telegram setting forth your formal protest against your troops being treated as prisoners of war [...] I have had no choice but to act in accordance with the orders of the War Office, and fear treat your force as prisoners of war.[40]

The same day the Germans left for Kigoma aboard the *St George* (which Spicer-Simson had commandeered from Banana) where they were entertained by the Belgians and on 8 December 1918 arrived at Dar-es-Salaam. Lettow-Vorbeck left East African soil on 19 January 1919, five years to the date of his arrival. He left on the SS *Transvaal*, previously the *Feldmarschall*, which had been captured in Dar-es-Salaam. Back in Germany, Lettow-Vorbeck and his undefeated Germans rode through the Brandenburg Gate on 2 March 1919 to meet the leaders of the Weimar Republic.[41] They were too late to influence the decision regarding German East Africa which had been made a week after they left East Africa. Having spent the remainder of the year awaiting the outcome of the final peace discussions and Lettow-Vorbeck getting married, the victorious German Commander and Governor Schnee who had stuck with him all through the years of turmoil, embarked on a new struggle from May 1920, to reclaim Germany's colonies.

CHAPTER 9

BEHIND THE SCENES, 1915–1918

The outbreak of war in 1914 had taken everyone by surprise, despite countries having been anticipating war for some time. However, when it did erupt, governments discovered just how unprepared they were for modern war or rather war on such a large scale. The practicalities caused the difficulties. It was one thing to say Britain was an ally of France or Portugal but how would this work in reality? When France made overtures to get involved in East Africa during 1914, Britain was quick to prevent this ensuring French influence was contained in West Africa and the Middle East. Italy, in the 1915 Treaty of London, was eventually promised British and French territory in compensation for any German colonies annexed in an attempt to keep that country out of the war in Africa. It was more difficult, however, to distract Portugal and Belgium with promises of post-war settlements, not least because their colonies were directly involved in the theatre. This chapter focuses on Britain's relations with its allies concerning the war in East and southern Africa. It specifically looks at the coordination of activity between the main players and how Britain had to mediate against South Africa's expansionist and nationalist desires.

Coordination

All through the East Africa campaign there was more than one British authority controlling aspects of it. In at least one instance – 1917 – it is stated that two British columns working in close co-operation in the field were organised, paid and supplied by different authorities. 'Wasteful in supplies, clerical staffs, and in all the rearward services' good intelligence was particularly missing in 1914 and 1918.[1] These are some of the highlights of a report on lessons from the campaign written in 1933 for the official history. Five British departments were involved in 1914 and although the India Office had handed over command of the northern East Africa theatre after the defeat at Tanga in November 1914, it remained involved to varying degrees as India continued to supply manpower and material. In addition, there was each of the allies which needed to be accommodated. This dispersal of function and command would work in Lettow-Vorbeck's favour as agreement took time to achieve. During the campaign, various groups recommended tighter coordination, but not always with success – the individual proving the pivotal link.

Dealing with Portugal in the early stages was relatively straightforward. Portugal needed material support from Britain to be able to participate actively in the war and as Britain was unable to supply enough equipment for its own troops, the solution was for Portugal to remain neutral. This suited Germany and the other belligerents too. Belgium, however, proved a little more tricky. It soon became clear to the Foreign Office which needed to present a coherent position to its Belgian counterpart that the two lead departments, the Colonial and War Offices had different ideas about Belgian involvement. Both were keen on expansion, albeit the Colonial Office without Belgian support. In contrast, the Foreign Office saw the need for compromise providing it did not undermine Britain's position. So, in August 1914, the Foreign Office was prepared to support the decision in Northern Rhodesia to ask the Belgians for assistance against a German attack on Abercorn. This was despite the War and Colonial Offices being against the decision, a situation the Colonial Office described as 'eminently undesirable'.[2] Again, in October 1914, when the Belgians asked for British support in launching an offensive against the German province of Ruanda, the Colonial Office objected. In exasperation, Sperling in the Foreign Office noted that:

> the whole difficulty arises from the extraordinary jealousy of the
> Colonial Office of any action by the Congo troops beyond the

Congo frontier. The result of this policy can only be the pro-
longation of the operations against German East Africa and the
unnecessary loss of a good many lives.[3]

The Belgians were in an difficult position. Their country had been
overrun by the Germans in Europe and they were reliant on the
British for support. Yet, in Africa, they had at the start of the war,
more trained troops than any other country. These troops were sitting idle as transport links were poor and their ally, Britain, could not
decide whether or not it wanted Belgian help. Overall, however, the
general officer commanding in the Congo, Tombeur, appeared to be
in line with the motherland policy and saw his role to keep the Congo
sufficiently active, obtaining what German territory it could for use
by the Belgian government to restore itself after the war. Germany
seemed aware of this situation when, in December 1914, 'William II
made a tentative offer to buy the entire Congo Free State as the price of
German withdrawal from Belgium.'[4] Whether Kaiser Wilhelm made
the offer on behalf of Germany or in the hope that he would be able
to control the territory independently as his cousin Leopold II had
remains unknown. Belgium rejected the offer, believing it would be
in a better bargaining position retaining the Congo and occupying
German territory outside of Europe.

In Central Africa in 1914, for common sense and defence reasons
Governor Sir George Smith kept the Resident Commissioner Salisbury,
Buxton the High Commissioner of South Africa, and Belfield Governor
of East Africa informed of actions in Nyasaland.[5] However, communications did not seem to go any further than the sharing of information and a request for material when required. Following pleas by the
Colonial Office and Buxton in South Africa, the War Office eventually
agreed to 'exchange military information directly with the Governor
of Nyasaland and provide him with advice if required.'[6] However,
when the Governor of Nyasaland approached Portuguese East Africa
for assistance with the Chilembwe uprising, the War Office objected
due to its fear that Portugal's acceptance would lead to it becoming a
belligerent in Europe. The Foreign Office, too, raised concerns about
Smith's ability which the Colonial Office interpreted as sacrificing

Nyasaland to ensure Portuguese neutrality. Eventually a compromise was reached 'whereby the Governor in an extreme emergency could ask for Portuguese assistance whilst simultaneously informing London.'[7]

As the war progressed and South Africans became increasingly involved, Buxton was concerned. In October 1915, the South Africans fighting in the various colonies surrounding the German protectorate were all under different commanders and with different conditions of service and pay. In Central Africa, two hundred South African troops, the 2nd South African Rifles paid for by the British government as imperial service units, were sent to Nyasaland to supplement the meagre forces there as it was feared that the country would barely be able to raise enough troops for its own internal protection, let alone to support other theatres. The situation was exacerbated by troops having left neighbouring territories to fight in German South West Africa and Europe, Nyasaland being land-locked and the Chilembwe uprising in late January/February 1915. In addition, during 1915, six hundred South Africans went to protect the border between German East Africa, Nyasaland and Northern Rhodesia while two hundred were sent to reinforce the 2nd Rhodesian Regiment in East Africa, the latter reinforcements arriving on 4 November 1915.[8]

Buxton, too, was responsible for the troops in Northern and Southern Rhodesia and the protection of the High Commission Territories. Unifying the command of all these groups of troops would make his command easier. He was anxious that the troops in Nyasaland, under the command of Smith, fall under the same control as his troops to ensure the safety of the British territories south of German East Africa. At the time, because no specific military policy existed for East Africa, it was decided to maintain the status quo until a decision was made. This lack of coordination caused Buxton to refrain from approaching the Belgians for assistance despite the threats of attack and his desire that closer co-operation be entered into with them.[9] A month later, on 12 November 1915, at the request of the Colonial Office and Buxton, General Northey was appointed joint commander of the Rhodesian-Nyasaland frontier, which enabled him to plan and prepare for an offensive.[10] Despite the fact that Northey was seconded from the War Office and responsible to the Colonial Office, Buxton had a better hold on what was happening. He now had to communicate with one military commander in the south instead of three and forces could be moved more easily by having at least one layer of communication removed.

In his roles as Governor General and High Commissioner Buxton was involved in the decisions determining where troops were sent. Given the complex relations in southern Africa, he was able to mediate from a wider perspective and provide a link to the home government. This was particularly noticeable concerning the British South Africa Company territories of Northern and Southern Rhodesia. Initially, the company had offered to raise a contingent for service outside of Africa, as it was not directly concerned with the Union's expansionist ideas. However, after the outbreak of the rebellion and the threat of an anti-British government on its border, the company agreed to send men to support the South African government in quelling the rebellion and also to send a contingent, the 1st Rhodesian Regiment, to German South West Africa.[11] It was also around this time that Buxton noticed a subtle change in British South Africa Company director LS Jameson's speeches about future incorporation with the Union.[12]

A problem arose, however, when the company announced that it had a second contingent ready for service. This had been recruited on 21 November 1914 following the 1st Rhodesian Regiment's departure for German South West Africa. South Africa did not need any additional troops for the South West Africa campaign as it had imposed conscription to deal with the internal situation. However, it was felt that the 2nd Rhodesian Regiment could not be sent to Europe before the 1st Rhodesian Regiment in order to avoid upsetting the latter. One option was to send them to Nyasaland, but as the situation there was calm, it was decided that the regiment of four hundred men be sent to East Africa under the command of Major AE Capell. The General Officer Commanding East Africa, General Wapshare, was informed of this decision on 7 February 1915, a week before the Chilembwe uprising erupted.

The question of where to send Rhodesian troops was again raised as the German South West Africa campaign drew to a close in July 1915. The options were East Africa, Nyasaland or Europe. The Union government suggested Nyasaland, possibly to replace South Africans on the border. Buxton felt Europe would be the better destination in order to maintain morale, particularly in the Rhodesias. The War Office decided it was better to send the Rhodesians to Europe rather than break the regiment by deploying it to Nyasaland. However, as the decision took so long to make, the regiment was disbanded with many volunteers joining the South African volunteers to Europe, or making their own way there.[13] Others remained to reinforce northeast Rhodesia which had been weakened by the withdrawal of the Belgian troops.[14]

Belgium

During 1915, the Belgians suggested there be more unity amongst the Imperial troops in East Africa and following a number of threats, removed their forces from Abercorn in Northern Rhodesia. The Belgians had hoped to work with the British forces to realise their aim of occupying German territory. The issue was that until Lake Tanganyika was brought under allied control, the Belgians were contained in the Congo. In reality, although Belgian opportunities increased with access across the lake, they were still relatively constrained in what they could do whilst the British were on the defensive.

Belgium was prepared to work with Britain, but it was concerned about the influence of the South Africans, whom they did not trust.[15] With South Africans involved in defending the Northern Rhodesian border, the desire of the British South Africa Company and the mining company De Beers to expand and its possible inclusion in the Union, the Belgians were wary. Their wariness was exacerbated by there being no guarantee that Britain would support Belgium's ownership of the Katanga region as it had against Rhodes before 1900.[16]

Keen for action towards the end of 1915, the Belgians had started planning an offensive. However, they were short of porters as the natives in the Congo were not keen to volunteer and the Belgian administrators were not in favour of letting Belgian natives out of the Congo boundaries. Discussions had been entered into with Frederick Jackson, Governor of Uganda, to supply porters from there but due to the demand for porters in British East Africa, Uganda would only be able to provide Tombeur with the necessary men in March 1916. They put their plans on hold. On hearing of the potential arrival of the South Africans in 1916, the Belgians reinitiated their plan and when Smuts arrived co-operation or joint action was suggested. Smuts, however, was reluctant. He first wanted to secure the Uganda railway and have control of the Kilimanjaro region which would provide access into the German colony from British East Africa. This he achieved towards the end of March. In April, he was prepared to open negotiations with the Belgians to undertake a two-pronged attack on Tabora and other major towns in the area.[17] Despite their hesitation about working with Smuts, the Belgians welcomed the opportunity to invade German territory.

Relations between the Belgians and British were, therefore, rather strained during the early years of the war. Firstly due to the confusion of what was happening, secondly due to Spicer-Simson on Lake Tanganyika who treated colleagues with disdain and thirdly, Smuts. This was fed back to the respective home governments which had to mediate these tensions within the wider political sphere. To help manage the relations between the two commands, Ewart Grogan, who had travelled through the Congo on a number of occasions, volunteered to act as a liaison. Having gone across in 1914, Grogan helped set up telegraph connections to enable easier communication but during 1915 was back in British East Africa dealing with local issues. Smuts' contribution to strained relations increased when he blamed the Belgians for Wahle's escape from Tabora rather than acknowledge Crewe's role in failing to contain the Germans.[18] It was not until van Deventer asked Grogan to return to the Congo as liaison officer in 1917, that the relationship improved,[19] aided by some German surrenders and subsequently less pressure on the allied forces.

Back in 1915, with the need for troops growing and the ability to replace them reducing, the British were forced to ask the Belgians for assistance. Although there was a new Colonial Secretary, Walter Long, he was also anti-Belgian but the damage caused during Smuts' tenure in East Africa would prove the stumbling block to relations between the two countries. In addition, the Belgians had started to demobilise their troops. In March 1916 they agreed to take over Bismarckburg and send troops to various places along Lake Tanganyika as well as allow the British use of the lake.[20] A meeting in April between the two governments in Europe agreed future co-operation, leaving details to be sorted out on the ground. With the German Wintgens stretching Northey's lines towards Lake Tanganyika, it made military sense for the Belgians to work with the British. If the Belgians did not help, they could lose their bargaining chips – Ruanda and Urundi. Various meetings were held with Colonel Huyghé, initially with Smuts and then with Hoskins. At these meetings it was agreed that the Belgians would remain a distinct unit but follow orders from the British Commander-in-Chief. They, the Belgians would also be dependent on the British for supplies and equipment. However, relations soon started to deteriorate due to the shortage of troops on both sides and the increasing pressure on Iringa.

With van Deventer in command of the British forces, between 20 and 23 July 1917 a conference was held in Dar-es-Salaam to resolve the issues, especially as Belgians were still serving under British commanders and the Belgians did not have their own defined sphere of operations. Further meetings followed on 6 and 9 September. Finally, a meeting on 27 October between Huyghé and van Deventer took place where it was agreed that the Belgians would withdraw before the rains. Matters came to a head in October and London had to step in and ask for greater flexibility.[21] The issue with the Belgians did not seem to be with the commander but rather with the home government which was pushing Huyghé to keep a separate sphere of action.

Belgium's desire to keep its own sphere of action in East Africa was to cause Britain frustration.

> Since Belgium's main ambition in the war was theoretically not the expansion of her African territory but the liberation of her homeland, if Belgium were able to occupy a sufficiently large portion of the East African hinterland, the Belgian government might use this advantage as a pawn to gain European concessions from Germany at the conference table. If Belgium were to exchange her advantages in German East Africa for additional

territory in Europe, Britain might find that the Belgian-occupied portion of German East Africa had been bargained away to post-war Germany to the detriment of British interests in the area without Britain's having any say in the matter.[22]

For this reason, Tombeur, the Vice-Governor of Katanga Province, was appointed overall commander of the East African Belgian forces. His task was to claim as much territory as possible by capturing regional administrative centres and other major strategic points.[23] This was in line with Colonial Secretary Paul Hymans' view, expressed on 4 January 1916, that:

> [t]he duty of the government . . . is to speak loudly and firmly and to study all these questions [concerning the territories Belgium wanted]. A decisive hour is at hand for the monarchy and for the country. We must seize it and take advantage of it before it is too late. The country [will] never pardon is leaders for a peace without advantages and aggrandisements.[24]

Hyman's statement was to encourage King Albert to endorse action in East Africa even if joint Anglo-Belgian operations were delayed. With pressure from America that Belgium sell the colony to obtain finance to fund the war, they found themselves on the defensive. Britain was of the belief that if it had not been for issues of prestige, Belgium would have surrendered the Congo. In reality, Belgium had no thoughts of ridding itself of the Congo but rather to obtain Portuguese territory in West Africa to further develop access to the sea.[25] To obtain the territory, they would exchange captured East African land. What they did not need, could be sold to restore the motherland.

Portugal

Relations with the Portuguese were more trying for Britain than those with the Belgians. Despite being Britain's oldest ally, recent events had strained relations between the two countries and both were uncertain where exactly the other stood. Britain desired Portuguese territory but whether it was for the motherland or its South African dominion was unclear. Portugal was too weak to protect itself without British assistance and until Britain felt it would benefit from Portugal's involvement in the war, it was easier for that country to remain neutral.

Reluctantly Portugal agreed. However, this did not prevent its politicians from working to further Portuguese colonial aims within the constraints of neutrality especially given Germany's progress in Europe. Under most circumstances, these acts would have been regarded as a declaration of war, but as the situation suited Germany, nothing was done to escalate Portugal's involvement until March 1916. Whilst Portugal was neutral, it allowed German ships to use its harbours and also knowingly permitted German passengers to enter its territory using false passports. In this way, Captain Sorrenson and others were able to return to Germany and goods and news to be smuggled into the German colony.[26] This annoyed Smuts who looked for ways to legitimately assume control over the Portuguese colony. He was only prevented from doing so by Britain's moral obligation to protect the integrity of its ally's possessions. It is, therefore, not surprising that the Portuguese were petrified about South African intentions regarding their colony. They explained that it was not 'unreasonable to fear that the Union might cherish ambitions and schemes which would be anything but acceptable to Portugal.' The Union was after the port and district of Lorenço Marques in Delagoa Bay.[27]

To ease relations, when Smuts proposed sending his political officer Major Hayes Sadler across in October 1916, Gil refused as Lisbon had not approved the appointment.[28] Eventually to help ease pressure, van Deventer decided to send the French liaison officer attached to his headquarters, Colonel Viala, to the Portuguese. Sheppard noted, 'The Portuguese are probably less suspicious of the French than ourselves, and I think VIALA's visit will have excellent results, for he is a first class fellow, and very keen on helping the campaign in any way possible.'[29] The success of the visit was seen in Rosa's idea that he could launch a three-pronged attack on German East Africa. Van Deventer had to appeal to London for help as well as Viala, particularly as the Portuguese liaison officer did not like Rosa and so purposefully made things difficult.[30]

During 1916, the Portuguese had agreed to Britain controlling captured German territory, however, during November 1917, when it appeared that the Germans would surrender, the Portuguese changed their mind, insisting that Portugal keep any territory it occupied.[31] At the same time, the Portuguese announced that they were happy to have a liaison officer attached to their headquarters providing they could send one to the British.[32] Errol MacDonell filled the role from March 1917 until January 1918 when he resumed his position as Consul to the Portuguese colony. He was used to dealing with the sensitive Portuguese but his appointment as liaison was made more difficult when he was given an interpreter who was Royalist whilst the officers, such as Rosa, were Republican.[33] MacDonell was well placed to influence actions in Portuguese East Africa. As Consul, he had managed to obtain control over Portuguese activities through his relationship with the Governor General. This had frustrated Lothar Bolen, a German agent directed by Schnee to obtain goods from Portuguese East Africa. Bolen complained that despite the Portuguese being friendly, their 'hands {were} tied one every side'.[34] When MacDonell returned to his position as Consul, Major Cohen took over MacDonell's role as liaison.[35]

The German agent had a good case. Apart from the control that MacDonell exercised, van Deventer asked on 1 January 1918 for the Portuguese forces to report directly to him. This would enable van Deventer to overcome resistance and misinterpretation of orders. Although the Portuguese government was supportive, the German-owned local Niassa Company officials were not. Eventually, the British Ambassador to Lisbon, Sir Lancelot Carnegie, was instructed to obtain:

> Entire control of everything connected with movements of troops and stores at Porto Amelia, including hiring and management of dhows. Control, by arrangements with local Portuguese Authorities of the Base and lines of communication inland. ... It is important that Portuguese Government should agree the actual engagement and payment of carriers &c. should be done by British Authorities, experience having shown danger and inefficiency of Portuguese methods.[36]

The Colonial Office had continued to express its dismay at Portugal wanting the Kionga Triangle. As a result, the Foreign Office ordered an enquiry into the significance of the territory to inform later negotiations. The outcome was that the territory was of benefit to German East Africa as it enabled easier smuggling but nothing more.[37] The Foreign and War Offices were, therefore, prepared to concede Portugal getting Kionga. However, the Colonial Office felt, despite the findings of the Foreign Office, that if the Germans had been insistent on retaining this piece of land, it had to be valuable and so encouraged Smuts to capture it in 1917 from the Germans who had forced the Portuguese out.[38] There were some British Colonial Office officials who viewed Portugal's greater involvement more positively. They felt that when it came to the bargaining table they would be able to push for administrative and human rights reform in Portuguese colonial territory.[39]

Apart from the wider political issues Portugal had to deal with and its relations with neighbouring allies, it also had to contend with native uprisings. Portugal's relations with its native population were strained, and only two commanders saw any value in employing natives in the war effort. Amorim, Commander of the first Portuguese Expeditionary Force to East Africa recruited natives into his forces. When he was recalled, Major Moura Mendes, his successor, stopped the practice. However, when, in 1916, Mendes tried to organise a native garrison of Kionga to allow him to advance further into German territory, Governor General Alvaro de Castro overrode him.[40] This put extra pressure on the already stretched Portuguese troops and led to a further reduction in their morale.

Unlike the situation before the war, where neighbours would send assistance to help subdue native uprisings during the war, Portugal's neighbours now refused due to the mistreatment of its colonial inhabitants and the pressures of war.[41] The Barue rebellion was just such a case. It erupted in Portuguese East Africa against the recruitment of 5,000 carriers and lasted from March to November 1917. In June the Makonde revolted.[42] The Portuguese were, therefore, forced to deal with the internal situation before looking to extend into German territory, whilst its British neighbours had to manage the large number of

Portuguese East Africa refugees entering their territory. With pressure from Lisbon, Gil tried to manage both the internal unrest and support of the allied aims. He failed and was recalled.

At Carnegie's request, the Sidonio Pais' government agreed to the Portuguese Expeditionary Force reporting to van Deventer. His government was made up of men who had been in the frontline as opposed to politicians.[43] Rosa was promoted to General and Massano de Amorim, Commander of the 1st Portuguese Expeditionary Force, took over as Governor General in place of de Castro.[44] On 29 January 1918, van Deventer met the acting Governor General at Lourenço Marques to discuss arrangements. Two weeks later, on 12 February, van Deventer and Rosa met to finalise details. As before, Rosa was not happy to subordinate to van Deventer, but, had little choice given the state of his troops' health. Dealing with the Portuguese was not easy as 'they expressed much confidence in themselves and their troops affected eagerness to take the field and appeared to resent being kept in the background. ... In short there was a good deal of high-flown talk, but very little practical keenness', which meant British troops having to pick up the action.[45] The result was the defeat at Nhamacurra.

Rosa was caught between the politicians and the military and this was not helped by the fact that 'the Portuguese hate and suspect all foreigners, and [...] they hate the British most of all because they fear them.'[46] The distrust between the government and army was such that the government was 'attempting to run the campaign by cable, from Lisbon'.[47] Whilst MacDonell was in Lorenço Marques, the diplomatic relationship could be managed despite the military relationship fluctuating. However, the border area remained troublesome as the Niassa Company which controlled the territory was pro-German. The Germans made the most of this situation and invaded into Portuguese East Africa.[48]

As it appeared that the campaign would move into Portuguese East African territory, the Belgians considered taking their campaign into Portuguese territory in support of Britain. Before committing themselves, though, they reconnoitred the area and decided against seeking permission for their troops to enter Portuguese territory.[49] This was probably just as well. Belgian involvement may have impacted on what amicability there was between the Portuguese and British.

France

On 3 January 1916, the French Deputy and ex-Minister of Finance, Dumont, let Lord Bertie the British Ambassador in France know that providing France obtained Alsace and Lorraine in Europe, it was prepared to leave decisions regarding the German colonies to Britain.[50] However, on 24 February 1916, Paul Cambon, French Ambassador to Britain, posed a question over the administration of the Cameroons, which had capitulated a week earlier on 15 February 1916. Cambon felt France should be given administrative responsibility providing the country with a port in Central West Africa. If granted, France would relinquish all interest in East Africa.[51]

France believed it was entitled to a claim over East Africa as a result of Kitchener's request for troops from Madagascar to assist in that theatre, despite the request being withdrawn and the troops used elsewhere.[52] Further, when the British re-launched the offensive in East Africa without informing France, the latter felt it was purposefully being excluded from the eastern half of the African continent. This France was prepared to accept on condition that it was given control over the Cameroons. Britain acquiesced on the understanding that it was accepted that all territory captured during the war would be administered on a temporary basis pending the final allocation at the peace table.[53]

Soon after, in June 1916, the French requested that one of their officers be attached to Smuts' command; the reason for this request remains unclear. Despite this, the British agreed and the officer joined Smuts' command for a few months.[54] In response, Smuts requested that he have officials attached to the Belgian and Portuguese headquarters. These officials, he believed, would administer any territory the allies captured. Not surprisingly, the allies objected but did agree to exchange liaison officers.[55]

South Africa

South Africa's leaders had determined at the outset of war that once German South West Africa was captured they were not prepared to hand it back to Germany. The territory had been desired from before

the turn of the century and it was well known in British circles that
South Africa had aspirations of incorporating the territory into the
Union.

As early as 3 August 1914, before war was officially declared, CP
Crewe was predicting that Britain would be entering the fray and
'That means of course an expedition to German South West Africa'.[56]
On 9 August, Sir Duncan McKenzie wrote that he expected South
Africa:

> will do all in its power to assist the Imperial Government, and
> the simplest and most efficient way of doing so, is to send forces
> to capture and annex East and West Africa. This chance of unit-
> ing South Africa should not be missed . . .[57]

Advice even came from England courtesy of David Graaff who dined
with Colonial Secretary Harcourt on 20 August 1914:

> [Harcourt] hinted that if South Africa is able to send anything
> over he will see to it that very full publicity is given to the
> gift. [...] True we are doing a good deal by agreeing to take
> German South West Africa, but we should not lose sight of the
> fact that we are taking the country for ourselves and not for
> anyone else.[58]

In the aftermath of the German South West Africa campaign, Smuts
advanced publicly:

> There is now the prospect of the Union becoming almost dou-
> ble its present area. If we continue on the road to union, our
> northern boundaries will not be where they now are, and we
> shall leave to our children a huge country in which to develop.
> [...] a people who will be a true civilizing agency in the dark
> continent.[59]

Expanding the country's borders was definitely on the South African's
agenda.

The Imperial government responded in a formal communication to the Union that it would not be able to claim the territory until the end of the war and that it was for the Empire to decide. At the same time, Harcourt secretly wrote to Governor General Buxton:

> Of course, everyone knows it would be almost impossible for the British government to deprive any Dominion of territory which they had actually taken during the war, if they wished to retain it. We have certainly not begun to think here about terms of peace or distribution of the spoils but has it ever occurred to you that if, at the end of the war, German SWA is in the hands of the Union, it might be a good thing to try to exchange with Portugal, offering them a part or the whole of GSW for a part or the whole of their possessions on the East coast of Africa [...] probably Portugal would not look at it.[60]

Playing the political game was a sensitive one in South Africa. The need to reconcile the nationalists whilst maintaining positive relations with Britain proved tricky as seen by the different messages given to the variety of participants about the same issue. For example, the South African cabinet sanctioned South African involvement in conquering South West Africa provided that two conditions, using volunteers only and that parliament grant its approval, be met. Yet, the correspondence which went to London agreeing South Africa's participation made no mention of these conditions.[61] The conquest of German South West Africa, South Africa's 'Cinderella colony', although requested by Britain, suited South Africa's leaders at the time as it would ease the Union's attempts to incorporate the German colony, Bechuanaland, Rhodesia and eventually Nyasaland.[62] 'It is doubtful that a fully conscious imperial policy existed at this date, and the territory was probably desired more as an expansion into what was perceived as rightfully the Union's backyard.' Silvester continues that the year '1915 represented another and very symbolic "Act of Union"' – the incorporation of German South West Africa – a point South Africa re-iterated on 10 December 1918 when the country assumed Britain would obtain the rights to German South West Africa and then give it to South Africa.[63]

South Africa, although subordinate to Britain, was a major player in southern Africa. Smuts and Botha were quite open about supporting the British Empire providing it was of benefit to South Africa as well. For this reason, the two leading South African politicians saw their way to continue supporting Britain's war effort on the African continent.

South Africa had desires for German East Africa, but not necessarily for South Africa. Seemingly somewhat out of character, South Africans such as JX Merriman believed that at best German East Africa could become a 'second Natal', or 'a colony with a planter aristocracy resting on black labour'. If this did not happen, an alternative was for it to become 'a dumping ground for the overspill of British India'.[64] By September 1916, Merriman was suggesting that 'the best that could happen to [South Africa] from our own selfish point of view' would be to exchange German territory with the Portuguese for Delagoa Bay. This could possibly lead to South Africa becoming a 'nursery from which would be drawn the administrators of the tropical regions of Africa'.[65] Writing to Lord Bryce, an influential Liberal in December 1916, Merriman noted that the 'ideal plan' would be to govern East Africa in the same way that India was, by a 'selected, well paid, and pure civil service, under whose regime it might become the dumping ground for those restless Indians who give so much trouble in the European self-governing colonies.' This would potentially help South Africa resolve its Indian problem if Indians moved north from South Africa.[66] This would not have gone down well with the South Africans in East Africa as:

> the English-speaking South Africans, mostly from Natal, "arrived before the Boers and obtained the land nearest to Nairobi and the railway. ... They were determined to create a white man's country like South Africa: like the Cape without its liberalism, and Natal without its Indians."[67]

In addition, C Percy Smuts, a South African in Uasin Gishu wrote to the press on 26 August 1916 that it 'would make much more sense ... to join the Union of South Africa as it could handle the color questions.'[68]

The demands for Portuguese East African territory were further complicated for the British government in 1917 when the British South Africa Company, under Dr LS Jameson's directorship, indicated that it was interested in the Moçambique province for itself. Including this territory into the Rhodesias as well as that of Nyasaland, would enable the chartered company to have easy access to the ocean. Jameson argued that South Africa did not deserve the Moçambique territory given its 'anti-native' stance and that the territory was contiguous with the German territory.[69] Walter Long, Colonial Secretary, did not seem to pass Jameson's letter on. He had a habit of not passing private correspondence on to the public office but may also have been concerned that the criticism the chartered company was making against South Africa was applicable to the company too. In addition, the Colonial Office was known to be resistant to anyone but itself controlling territory and this may well have been an influencing factor.[70] With Jameson dying on 26 November 1917, the idea was not pursued.

South Africa's desire for East Africa was restricted to those in government or 'high politics' as noted by Merriman.[71] As this was Smuts' area of expertise, it was left to him to do the negotiating. However, he was prompted by colleagues such as T Watt, Minister for Public Works, who wrote to him about Portuguese East Africa, 'Can you find a way to convince the British Government to enter negotiations with Lisbon's ambassador?'[72] Despite Smuts being in London and in the inner circle determining the future peace discussions, Merriman in early 1918, was concerned:

What has Lloyd George been doing by talking about the future of the German Colonies? Does he not know that the retrocession of German S.W. Africa would certainly lead to the loss of South Africa, while the abandonment of East Africa would lead to the establishment of a hostile Power bent on the destruction of our Eastern Empire? [...] However, I do not suppose the gentleman whom you call the 'clever little Welshman' either knows or cares much about imperial politics. I wonder whether you in the military intelligence know anything of the anti-British pro-German propaganda in South Africa. ... We are all very glad that the East African campaign has come to an end, at least we hope so. Von Lettow has made a great reputation; he must be a gallant soul; take some comfort from the fact that he had a Scotch mother and put in some time at Oxford.[73]

India

Another country interested in the East African territory was India. On 29 September 1916 the Indian government let the Secretary of State, Lord Montagu, know that East Africa would be 'an admirable field for Indian expansion'. If this could not be arranged, then they asked that Indian emigration be permitted on the same conditions as that for whites.[74] Others who supported the idea included Harcourt, who had already suggested in March 1915 that East Africa would be ideal for Indian emigration,[75] and the Johannesburg *Herald* which thought in March 1918 that India would expand into German East Africa. This, it felt, would not be a problem for South Africa provided the territory remained administered as it was.[76]

In India, too, 'there were hopes amongst instructed Indians at least of the foundation on the other side of the Indian Ocean of a daughter country. But these were disturbed by the conflict of interest which led the white colonists to impose restrictions and disabilities upon the Indian communities.'[77] GK Gokhale, of the Indian National Congress, had recommended that British East Africa and German East Africa be given for Indian commerce in his last political testament, which was made public in summer 1917, despite recognising that the Union would have first claim to the territory as it had sent a larger army.[78]

As with the South African population, the Indian population seemed to be unconcerned about the future of East Africa. It was of most concern to those Indians resident in East Africa and a small group of politicians. There were four reasons given for India being awarded German East Africa: India had contributed large numbers of men to the war in that theatre, the country had a two-hundred year relationship with the territory, Indians needed an area to emigrate where they would not conflict with the dominions' views on who should be able to enter their territory and that it would benefit the 'indigenous population' by educating them in small scale farming.[79] This put India's leaders in a difficult position as men like Viceroy Chelmsford could see both sides of the story but were unable to suggest a workable solution. The colonists in East Africa were keen on Indian labour but under indentured conditions where after a specified time, the Indians returned to India. This naturally did not suit the Indian leaders who were starting to demand the same rights as the white dominions especially as they had contributed so much to the war effort.[80] Charles Lucas of the Colonial Office felt it 'at least conceivable that [German East Africa] might be a sphere for India and South Africa.'[81]

With Britain being the dominant power over its dominions and allies, decisions made in London were crucial to the conduct and outcome of the war. During the preparations for the peace discussions, India's case was put forward by the Secretary of State for India, Lord Montagu. His argument was based on the contents of Council of India member Sir Theodore Morrison's memorandum which had been tabled at the War Cabinet in June 1918, and set out above.

CHAPTER 10

THE WAR IN LONDON, 1915–1917

Whilst the war was being fought in Africa and elsewhere, another struggle was taking place on the diplomatic front, both within each country concerned and between the various allies. What happened on the diplomatic front would invariably impact on the military struggle as it was 'behind the scenes' that decisions were made about what supplies and reinforcements were to be sent to a specific theatre of war. Invariably these behind the scenes wranglings also determined where fighting would take place, or at least where war would be waged and to what extent. As Britain was the most involved power in East Africa, the decisions made in London had a major impact on the direction of the campaign in Africa. This chapter explores the discussions and tensions prevalent in Britain concerning the East Africa campaign and how they related to the overall conduct of the war. In exploring the tensions and decisions, the role of the individual comes to light demonstrating that war is directed, not by a group, but by individuals either working alone or collaboratively to achieve a common goal.

As will be recalled, 1914 was a year of indecision and disaster for the British in East Africa as different views dominated discussions at various times. The defeat at Tanga in November 1914 went some way to reducing confusion but not completely. With Kitchener so focused on the Western Front and any theatre which directly impacted on it such as Egypt, little was done to coordinate the various interested parties in East Africa. All decisions had to pass through the relevant office, Colonial, India or War, and then through the Foreign Office to the Portuguese or Belgian ally for a response. This resulted in delay and much frustration.

Although clear that they wanted to defeat German East Africa, the Colonial and War Offices were not in agreement over the detail of the campaign. The Colonial Office continued to object to the War Office taking command of the colonial forces in the area and to placing all British troops under one single command, if it was the War Office. This meant that actions in the north and south remained uncoordinated and appeals to Prime Minister Asquith 'to force a decision', did not help. At least the battle of Tanga removed the India Office from the equation. Charles Callwell, of the War Office, summed up the position:

> As far as I can make out, HM Government have no definite military policy in that part of the world [Africa]. However, [...] the Colonial Office appears throughout to have been to discourage Belgian efforts for fear of their setting up claims at the end of the war ... We have tried to deal with German East Africa by ourselves and we have failed. We have no additional troops to spare to send in reinforcement. The wisest course would seem to be to get the French and Belgians to help us.[1]

The Foreign and War Office position was in effect: win the war and then deal with the detail. In mid-December 1914, Colonial Secretary Harcourt gave his approval for limited formal military co-operation which the Belgians accepted willingly.[2] When faced with the options, the Colonial Office felt it was better to contain the war in East Africa to countries already directly involved than bring in outsiders. Making use of French or Italian troops would only complicate matters later on.[3]

Troops

The main issue affecting the war in Africa was the availability of troops; the supply of which was determined by the War Office, whose main concern was the Western Front. The availability of troops had been a factor in deciding whether to launch a campaign in East Africa over and above putting the German wireless stations out of action. In 1915, it was the lack of reinforcements which caused the Imperial troops to remain on the defensive. As manpower was desperately needed on the Western Front, any troops identified as possibly useful in East Africa were declined and sent to Europe. This meant that for any action to take place in East Africa, the Colonial Office had to source its own recruits from the local or other colonial territories. The stumbling block, in the early years of the war, was the reluctance of the Colonial Office and the colonists to recruit blacks ('natives') *en masse* as this could undermine the idea of white superiority and provide blacks with the ability to use firearms against their white subjugators. The blacks in the King's African Rifles had been specifically selected from certain tribes for their military ability and loyalty, it being recognised that loyalty was to the local commander or regime and not necessarily to Britain and the Empire.[4]

In the south of the theatre, the Colonial Office was responsible for the colonies and the campaign. Despite this, the Colonial Office was restricted by the availability of local troops as the War Office still had first call on the Imperial troops for the Western Front. Invariably though, when the War Office did offer troops for the campaign, the Colonial Office often objected, not least because their use would incur a cost which the Colonial Office or the colony would have to pick up after the war.[5] The Colonial Office was also faced in 1915 with the fact that the India Office refused to remove the troops which had failed at Tanga and that the volunteer sources in British East Africa, Northern Rhodesia and Nyasaland had already been recruited to the maximum.[6]

The biggest hindrance to an increase in action in East Africa, however, was Lord Kitchener, Secretary of State for War. He could not see why territory which had been given to Germany in 1885 and which could be annexed at the peace table if Britain felt strongly about it, now had to be fought over. For him, the priority was the Western Front and the Dardanelles, which had been sanctioned by the cabinet. Further, he had to counteract proposals by David Lloyd George to open the Eastern Front as an alternative means to defeat Germany. As far as Kitchener was concerned, any costs incurred in fighting the war could be dealt with at the end providing Britain won and if Britain did not, the cost would be immaterial.[7] The Colonial Office, however, was extremely protective of its territories and attempted to ensure that as many issues were resolved as soon as possible to ensure there were few problems and costs to be met after the war ended. An example was seen in 1915/1916 when some difficulty arose over who would pick up the costs incurred in the charter company territory of Southern and Northern Rhodesia. The Imperial government had already picked up the costs incurred by the British South Africa Company to defend Nyasaland in November 1914 and as the British South Africa Company had covered the costs of the initial defence of their territories, the Colonial Office eventually convinced the Imperial government to pay for the new troops, the discussions taking five months to resolve. Finally, a thousand Malawians joined the Rhodesian Native Regiment. Until then, the Colonial Office was prepared to forego the troops needed to bring the campaign to an end or protect the territory.[8]

Major-General Wapshare who, in November 1914, had replaced Aitken as General Officer Commanding the forces in East Africa, believed that troops could still be raised in East Africa. He acknowledged that many of the colonials had not joined the armed forces due to their farming commitments, but that they were prepared to defend their country if needed.[9] This contradicts the reports from 1914 when at least 85 per cent of settlers enlisted to protect their country and from letters available it appears that the numbers on the roll were not reflective of reality as many men were away from the front on authorised absence.[10] In addition, the recruitment number was increased by one thousand to give the Germans the impression that there were greater numbers than there really were.[11] The result was that before Wapshare reported on the volunteer situation and asked for troops from India, the War Office refused stating that if he adopted a 'defensive attitude along the Anglo-German border', he would have sufficient troops to launch a campaign in conjunction with the Belgians in northern Congo or from Uganda.[12]

Ostensibly to ascertain what was happening in East Africa about recruitment and whether additional troops could be raised, Lord

Kitchener sent out 'a limited number of officers and selected civilians with East African experience' in the form of his brother Colonel Henry Kitchener and Lord Cranworth. Wapshare and others in Africa, including Meinertzhagen, felt Henry Kitchener had been sent to Africa to either keep him out of the Secretary of State's way or to feedback on what was happening in East Africa.[13] Cranworth writes that Colonel Kitchener was resented by the headquarters staff and that he 'was very far from appreciating their attitude towards himself'.[14]

Having arrived on 13 February 1915, Colonel Kitchener reported on 18 March that more European troops could not be raised in British East Africa and that although a thousand men could be found in Uganda, the length of time it would take to train them would pose a problem. Colonel Kitchener did not confirm Wapshare's idea of expanding the King's African Rifles, and was later accused of coming under the influence of Governor Belfield who was against the arming of blacks and the need to keep the colony out of the war. It was therefore suggested by General Callwell, Director of Military Operations, that troops be raised in Madagascar for an attack on Dar-es-Salaam. Following complaints from headquarter staff, Colonel Kitchener was refused permission to travel there to agree this with the French authorities and within five months, Lord Kitchener had been persuaded by his staff and French procrastination that Madagascan troops for East Africa would not be a good idea.[15] Finally, Ewart Grogan and Lord Delamere, leading settlers in the colony, organised a meeting of their compatriots, the outcome of which was a unanimous vote for conscription.[16]

The Colonial Office was soon to be provided with a different scenario by Lord Delamere when he returned to the United Kingdom for medical treatment in August 1915. He believed that Wapshare, who was not 'man enough for the job', had written numerous letters to the press complaining that the settlers were not enlisting. However, by the time Delamere spoke to the Colonial Office, Wapshare was in Basra having been replaced by Brigadier-General MJ Tighe on 3 April 1915. Although Kitchener wrote to Wapshare that the transfer had nothing to do with his running of the forces in East Africa, the timing seems to suggest otherwise. Counteracting Wapshare was Governor Belfield who was seen to be obstructive.[17] He did this by encouraging the settlers to remain on their farms rather than enlist, with the newspaper, the *East African Leader* taking the lead in supporting the Governor. The result was that despite being promised two months' training and two months' service, volunteers remained scarce.[18] The situation in the colony was one of confusion. Individual experiences, too, support this state. JJ Dough, an intelligence scout, who had enlisted before war was declared, wrote to the War Office following his discharge in 1919 to have his enlistment date corrected.[19]

The shortage of recruits, their loyalty and reliability, including of the local inhabitants was to tax the Colonial Office and those departments it dealt with. The biggest concerns were over the Indians, natives and Boers. Regarding the Indians, Wapshare believed the 130th Baluchis to be mutinous and given their religious beliefs felt they would disrupt other Arab and Muslim troops. He felt the same about the 46th Sikhs and did not want them sent to East Africa.[20] The India Office, however, held the opposite view, claiming that the troops in East Africa were 'excellent fighting material and should give ... very good service indeed.' If the troops were not used soon, it would be 'harmful politically'.[21] It is interesting to note that these troops were sent from India at the time given the growing concerns over the safety of Mesopotamia and India's security. Sir Hartmann Just of the Colonial Office interpreted this as a political move stating that 'the policy in India [was unfortunately] to get every native regiment with any suspicion of loyalty attached to it out of the country.' East Africa rather than Europe, he continued, seemed to be the preferred destination with the War Office concurring. Just's feelings may have been exacerbated by his having recently received the report on Tanga in which the Indians were blamed for the defeat.[22] During 1916, another eight companies of the Transfrontier Pathans suspected of 'Turkish sympathies' were sent to East Africa from Mesopotamia, although on that occasion little objection was raised.[23]

In January 1915, Kitchener ordered troops newly arrived in East Africa from India to return. They had 'questionable loyalty'. Despite this, Harcourt of the Colonial Office objected as he felt their removal would result in the 'murder of all the settlers there' and destabilise the area. This would be more detrimental to the empire than ridding Mesopotamia of the Turks. With India Office pressure added, Kitchener reversed his decision and the 130th Baluchis and 46th Pathans were given permission to proceed to East Africa.[24] This added to the concerns of the Governors and others who worried about potential uprisings.[25] Later requests by Bonar Law, Harcourt's successor, for reinforcements from Australia and New Zealand were rejected.[26]

Change in British government

As a result of the interplay between politics and the military in Britain, a change in government occurred from Liberal under Herbert Asquith to a coalition between the Liberals and Conservatives, first under Asquith and then, from December 1916, under David Lloyd George. These political manoeuvrings were to see the undermining of Kitchener's role as Secretary of State for War by the introduction of General William (Wully) Robertson as Chief of the Imperial General Staff on 23 December 1915. Robertson, who replaced AJ Murray after the latter had been in post just three months, was initially seen as favourable but with time, he too became a problem for the politicians and following pressure from Lloyd George, the Department of War Munitions was set up to influence the military through alternative means. The real issue was that Asquith, as Prime Minister, believed his role was 'the preservation of national unity'.[27] He was, therefore, hesitant to make major decisions, believing that if problems were left long enough they would resolve themselves. However, given the pressures he was under, he was soon arranging for Kitchener to be out of the country when important decisions were to be made. One of these occasions concerned the decision to go on the offensive in East Africa.

On 25 May 1915, the Liberal government under Asquith formed a coalition with the Conservative Party in an attempt to allay Conservative concerns about the direction of the war, given the failure of the attack on the Dardanelles, the resignation of Admiral Jackie Fisher as First Sea Lord and the Western Front ammunition crisis. However, little changed regarding the direction of the Western Front, although attempts were made to open the Russian Front and to bring Italy into the war as an ally. The formation of the coalition led to a change in Colonial Secretary with Andrew Bonar Law replacing Lewis Harcourt and Arthur Balfour assuming the mantle of First Lord of the Admiralty. Edward Grey, a Liberal, remained Foreign Secretary. As Grey had been in office for some time, the new Secretaries of State tended to defer to him based on his experience and relationships with the various governments. Once Grey left office in 1916, this deference no longer occurred and the War and Colonial Offices determined their policies without input from the Foreign Office which they ignored until they had agreed between them on a line of action.[28]

The role of individuals in determining the future of the East Africa campaign was significant. As mentioned previously, Lord Kitchener was the voice against action in East Africa, whilst others such as Sir George Fiddes, Assistant Undersecretary of State for the Colonies had a greater influence than the Secretary of State, especially once Harcourt left office.[29] At the Foreign Office, Sir Edward Grey and Sir Eyre Crowe, his Assistant Undersecretary of State, played an instrumental role as did Lord Hardinge once he arrived back from India. When Balfour took over the Foreign Office, Maurice Hankey, Secretary of Imperial Defence, noted that 'so long as Balfour and [Robert] Cecil are at the Foreign Office, peace is virtually impossible, owing to their ultra caution and laziness and lack of drive.'[30] Once Kitchener was side-lined, the Director of Military Operations and Intelligence, General CE Callwell, became influential regarding military policy. In this, he was supported by General AJ Murray even after his time as Chief of the Imperial General Staff from 27 September to 22 December 1915.

Lord Kitchener

Kitchener had reluctantly become Secretary of State for War on 6 August 1914. He had no interest in the position, having announced on a number of occasions that he would prefer to be a street-sweeper than go to the War Office.[31] He had no faith in the War Office believing it to be incompetent and that if a rival office was to be set up, it would take the War Office at least three months to realise.[32] The only reason he assumed the post was because the king had asked. He was not the right person for the role and knew it. He was not a politician but a

soldier and even there, the wars he was used to fighting were different
to the one he was now faced with. Kitchener was used to fighting in
Africa against untrained troops such as the Madhi and the Boers. As
a Boer War soldier, commenting on a mounted infantry charge at the
battle of Paardeburg noted, 'We all thought Kitchener a bad tactician
but a good organiser.'[33] An analysis of his successful expeditions shows
they were carefully planned before any action was undertaken. During
the Great War, he did not have the luxury of time to meticulously
plan operations.

Kitchener was used to running his own show with a small group
of trusted and devoted followers and in the same way that the General
Staff would complain about Smuts not working with them, so the War
Office staff complained that Kitchener kept information to himself,
put very little in writing and refused to delegate. As Callwell, tasked
with finding troops, noted on 22 November 1914 when the War Office
had assumed control of the East Africa campaign, 'It is not easy to get
"K" to do what one wants but I have managed to get him to press
for assistance from Madagascar.'[34] Not long after, Callwell reflected
'[Kitchener] has Egypt on the brain. He told me I must get troops for
East Africa from somewhere, and I succeeded in extracting the Malay
States Guides out of the Colonial Office and went to him with great
pride to announce my triumph. "Send them to Egypt," he said and my
prayers were to no avail.'[35] When Callwell suggested that he had found
'a Boer Contingent to go [to East Africa] from South Africa' he noted
that 'K does not seem to favour the idea.'[36]

Kitchener could not see any point involving East Africa in the larger
struggle than the extent to which it already was. He felt it important
to retain a strong Germany in Europe as a counterbalance to other
potential enemies and that leaving Germany's colonies in its control
would help rebuild British-German relations after the war.[37] He was
supported in his attempt to keep East Africa out of the war by Balfour
who felt that an attack on Austria would do more to further Britain's
war aims than increasing action in East Africa.[38] Kitchener had
ordered the troops onto the defensive following the defeat at Tanga in
November 1914 and his view was reinforced in 1915 when the attack
on Jasin Basin was repelled.

We will not know what really motivated Kitchener to take the stance he did regarding East Africa, but Lord Kitchener had invested in a large coffee farm, Songhor Estates, near Muhoroni on the Uganda railway about 120km from the German East African border in 1908. He negotiated the detail whilst a guest of Percy Girouard, Governor, in Nairobi.[39] On 7 January 1915, Khan Bahadur wrote to the Governor enclosing coffee seeds saying 'I suppose the cultivators of Lord Kitchener's estate know how to do it. I gave a sample of the seeds to Colonel Hawker to show you.[40] Kitchener's estate did seem to 'know how to do it' as on 15 August 1914 the *East Africa Standard* noted: 'The growth of the coffee trees (on Lord Kitchener's estate) strike [the correspondent] as being little short of marvellous ... Settlers will rejoice to hear that a further sum of £400 is to be spent during the current year to improve the bridges between the station and Lord Kitchener's estate.'[41] Two days before he drowned on 6 June 1916, Kitchener signed a document authorising the formation of a limited company to control the farm.[42] His intention was to retire to the farm as he felt more at home in Africa than in England. As it was, his brother Henry remained in East Africa and died on the farm in March 1937.[43]

On occasion, Kitchener was known to put personal interests before state and military. The High Commissioner to Cyprus' secretary Charles King-Harman wrote during the 1890s, that 'if conscience came into conflict with self interest, self interest would win where Kitchener was concerned.[44] Although he may have been motivated by personal interest to keep East Africa out of the war, his personal experience of the territory supported his case. He had visited East Africa as a representative of the Zanzibar Boundary Commission which divided the British and German territories in 1885. This commission had been instrumental in giving Germany control of Mount Kilimanjaro and the island of Heligoland in exchange for Witu and the islands of Zanzibar and Pemba.[45] In addition, he was friends with the former Governor, had friends resident in the colony and had visited the territory in 1885, 1908 and 1911 for work and on leave. He could see no reason to now fight for control of the territory.

Kitchener's African experience of warfare alerted him to the need for large numbers of troops and other support mechanisms, such as carriers and shipping, to ensure the army could manoeuvre. This was vital manpower which, in his opinion, could best be used serving Europe. If sufficient troops could be found in Africa without detracting from the European manpower needs then he was amenable to offensive action in East Africa. This was evident in his approach to the French for troops from Madagascar when he heard they might be available. Ultimately, on this occasion, it was the Foreign Office which vetoed their use to prevent future French claims for a portion of conquered German East Africa.

Kitchener's biggest difficulty was in dealing with the politicians. He dealt with his cabinet colleagues in the same way he did his General Staff. With Britain at war and his task to direct the military activity, he saw no reason for having to debate issues in the same way the other heads of departments did. Withholding information from his cabinet colleagues led to frustration and to Asquith exploring ways to bypass Kitchener so that appropriate political decisions could be made.[46] The dilemma Asquith had was that he could not remove Kitchener from office due to the public outcry there would be, but this had to be balanced with the threats of resignation he was faced with from cabinet colleagues. So, Asquith organised for Kitchener to see the Dardanelles. This enabled him, as Prime Minister, to assume control of the War Office for a while and, together with cabinet, agree to the War Council recommendation that an offensive be launched in East Africa.

The decision to launch the East Africa campaign

The factor which enabled this decision to be made without diverting manpower from Europe, despite Kitchener's objections, was South Africa. The South Africans had defeated German South West Africa in July 1915 and Prime Minister Louis Botha and his deputy, Jan Smuts, were looking for a place to employ redundant soldiers of mainly Afrikaans or Dutch origin favourable to Britain. For South African political reasons, these men would not fight in Europe as that would be directly supporting Britain which would result in their being ostracised at home. East Africa seemed ideal as it was on the African continent and could be explained as protecting South Africa. If the Germans were not contained, they could override the forces in Southern and Northern Rhodesia, Nyasaland and Portuguese East Africa, thereby threatening the Union. This argument suited commanders in Europe who felt the Boers were unmanageable and ill-disciplined based on their experiences during the 1899–1901 war.[47] Having them fight in Europe could be more troublesome than helpful.

Having first written to the Colonial Office in April 1915 that South Africans, mainly Boers, could well be sent to East Africa after the German South West Africa campaign was over, Governor General Buxton in August 1915 reiterated the point to the Colonial Office pending the outcome of the South African election in October. The timing of Buxton's communication tied in with a new attempt to find troops for East Africa following Delamere's visit and a suggestion by Arthur Steel-Maitland, Parliamentary Undersecretary of State for the Colonial Office, that for every South African sent to Europe, someone from the New Armies being trained in Britain be sent instead to East Africa. Callwell, at the War Office, suggested that Bonar Law approach Kitchener on the matter as he personally felt Kitchener 'would have a fit' when he heard about it.[48] The Army Council considered the plan at its meeting feeling 'it would be advantageous if the forces in East Africa could be strengthened.' It also suggested that South Africa be approached following Buxton's report that 'Ministers trust, […] that it will be possible before long for His Majesty's Government to utilise the military resources of the Union in other directions in the African continent.'[49] By the end of August, Smuts was writing to Merriman that the British government 'now practically intimate that in future German East Africa will be our destination.' This would enable the country to 'consolidate our territories south of the Zambezi and Kunene.'[50]

The receipt of Buxton's report and the unanimous decision on 6 September 1915 by a group of 'prominent' settlers in British East Africa, under the guidance of Lord Delamere and Ewart Grogan for conscription was well timed to support decision-making in London. The war in Europe had not progressed in the allies' favour, the British Expeditionary Force had been pushed back to the coast in September 1914 and by October 1915 a stalemate had set in. Turkey had joined the German alliance in November 1914 and Belgium had been over-run. More positively, Togoland was under joint British and French control by the end of August 1914 and the campaign against the Germans in Cameroons was progressing successfully in favour of the British and French. In December 1914, the German Pacific Islands had been occupied by the Australians and in July 1915 the Germans in South West Africa had been defeated.[51]

On 13 August 1915, the Army Council wrote to the Colonial Office accepting the idea of South African troops for East Africa 'at an early date'. Bonar Law, despite being Colonial Secretary, did not seem keen on colonial issues, and delayed actions as a result. It was only after Delamere's visit that he seemed to take an interest in East Africa. Having received Army Council acceptance, Bonar Law asked Buxton whether South Africa would be prepared to send the troops on offer to East Africa rather than Europe. He felt that 'East Africa and the surrounding districts is of a nature to cause a good deal of anxiety' and that the South Africans could affect a victory 'well worth securing' at minimum cost. Once he had received Buxton's response, Bonar Law would raise the issue formally.[52] In his response, Buxton reminded the Colonial Secretary that the suggestion had already been made that South Africans be sent to East Africa but that Britain preferred a contingent for Europe. This was the condition under which the latest troops, the South African Infantry Brigade, had been raised. Changing the destination of this contingent would cause 'serious difficulties' according to Smuts, as many of these troops were English speakers and had enlisted specifically as the contingent was destined for Europe.[53] It included many of the 1st Rhodesian Regiment who had been sent to German South West Africa rather than Europe in 1914 and they would be resistant to any other theatre. The change in destination would also raise financial issues which Smuts and Botha were keen to avoid as they had recently settled the rate of pay for troops in Europe. Further, any change just before the election would play into the Nationalists' hands, especially as Botha and Smuts did not think that South Africans would enlist for East Africa unless at the Union rate of pay which was three times the Imperial rate.[54]

Each group of South Africans serving in the war was on a different rate of pay dependent on who had employed them.[55] To overcome the issue of pay for the contingent raised specifically for service in East Africa, Bonar Law, believing the situation in East Africa to be a 'serious concern', forced a compromise with the British Treasury given that South Africa could not afford to pay the difference between the Imperial rate of pay of 1s a day and that of the Union rate of 3s per day. That Bonar Law's claim was contrary to the reports from East Africa that the locals were feeling the most secure they had since the war's outbreak was not taken into account. Further, he claimed that if a solution was not found, Botha's government would collapse.[56] The British government accepted this argument and gave permission for a South African brigade to be raised for service wherever required. This gave Botha an open hand to recruit troops after the election was held.[57] The Nationalists remained quiet. Given that Britain was paying for the South Africans to be deployed outside of South Africa, and that South Africa was not incurring debt on behalf of the Empire, the Nationalists had no real complaint. They had fought the same issue over the price of wool, with less success, when it was discovered that Britain had been promised the whole wool export at reduced market prices. The Nationalist stance was in total contrast to the Unionist Party which felt that South Africa should incur whatever debt was necessary to support Britain in its time of need. When Botha did have to ask for money and additional troops as he did in April 1916, he had a fight on his hands.[58] Internally, however, the National Party was more concerned about the impact on natives if they were told they could determine their own future in the captured colonies.[59] Britain had to deal sensitively with its newest dominion to ensure it remained within the Empire fold.

Kitchener was on his way to the Dardanelles when, on 8 November 1915, an interdepartmental conference was called for by the Foreign Office. It was to consider a Belgian proposal for action on the German East African coast to draw attention away from the Congo border. The outcome was that there should be sufficient reinforcements for any future actions and that the War Council should consider control of the operations in the East Africa theatre given that the Admiralty felt the proposal was not feasible.[60] It was suggested by Callwell, who had not attended the meeting, that the Committee of Imperial Defence address the issue. This was approved by General AJ Murray, Chief of the Imperial General Staff until 22 December 1915, who instructed Maurice Hankey, Secretary of the Committee of Imperial Defence, to make the arrangements. Hankey met with Arthur Steel-Maitland and George Fiddes, both of the Colonial Office, on 10 November to discuss the issue of East Africa and on 11 November set up a sub-committee of the Committee of Imperial Defence to thrash out the issue.[61] The sub-committee met on 12 November with Callwell as chair. It was agreed that steps 'be taken to ensure the conquer of this German colony with as little delay as possible', and that this could only happen with the 'assumption of a resolute offensive with an adequate force'. At this meeting Steel-Maitland's suggestion that a South African brigade be substituted with a New Army brigade was discussed. In addition, Belgium would be asked to assist.[62] Preparations were started, including the appointment of General Sir Horace Smith-Dorrien by the Army Council as commander of the forces in East Africa on 23 November. Others who had been considered included Smuts and Winston Churchill, both of whom suggested themselves.[63] Kitchener arrived back in England on 30 November.

The War Council, renamed from the War Committee on 11 December 1915, dealt with the question of East Africa on 15 and 16 December 1915, when it considered two papers. One, an appreciation by the General Staff, dated 10 December, and another by Kitchener, dated 14 December. The main difference between the two papers concerned the position of the war in Europe and the role of East Africa at the peace table. The Colonial Office was in support of the paper submitted by the General Staff as it was more straightforward whereas Kitchener's 'left too much to chance.'[64] The General Staff paper in addressing issues such as morale and prestige avoided the issue of territorial aggrandisement which met the August 1914 requirements for new actions. This was also achieved by not addressing the question of why go to war in that theatre but rather how the campaign should be won and the forces needed to do so. The delay of a few months imposed by the rainy season moved the decision in the General Staff's

THE WAR IN LONDON, 1915–1917

favour.[65] Kitchener's paper counteracted the General Staff, claiming that action in the theatre would present a 'very dangerous project' and would result in a similar situation to the one India found itself in Mesopotamia, namely demanding more troops than were available. He reiterated the arguments he had raised previously about obtaining the German colony at the peace table, the pointlessness of fighting over territory Britain had previously given away and the wasteful loss of life conquering the territory would entail.[66] Kitchener's pleas were in vain as Smith-Dorrien had already been appointed and the South African government notified of the situation.

The discussion on 16 December, therefore, only confirmed the November decisions made during Kitchener's absence. During the December meeting, Bonar Law felt it necessary to apologise to Kitchener for having acted without the latter's views being known and explained that it would be difficult to reverse the decision given the trouble such an announcement would cause in South Africa. When the meeting turned nasty, Lloyd George as Minister of Munitions suggested a compromise, despite himself being against the campaign; that the conquest of German East Africa be delayed until the Germans had been evicted from British East Africa (all the Germans actually held was the small border town Taveta). The War Committee gave its approval on 18 December 1915, including the decision that a British brigade would be sent to East Africa to replace the South African one sent to Europe.[67] The military plans were agreed on 23 December and confirmed on 28 December 1915. By this time the undermining of Kitchener's position had been completed with the appointment of General Robertson as Chief of the Imperial General Staff.[68] The importance of British East Africa was summed up by Bonar Law who 'in agreeing to the East Africa proposal said sadly, "We have bigger things than EA to quarrel about."'[69]

Towards the end of 1915, Smith-Dorrien, the new Commander-in-Chief planned the East African campaign as he had experienced the war in Europe, around trenches. Chief of Imperial General Staff, General Robertson approved the plans on 23 December 1915 failing to correct Smith-Dorrien's assumption. Given Britain's experience of colonial wars in the area and the recent 1899–1901 war in Southern Africa as well as the failure of the set battles in East Africa during the current war, this seems strange. Perhaps it was the thought that the enemy they were facing in Europe would use the same tactics in Africa that influenced the planning. Or perhaps it was felt that a few decisive battles would be all that was needed to decide the outcome. More likely it was due to pressure on General Robertson who gave his approval on his first day on the job. As he had missed much of the preceding discussion and given the pressing need for action to start, Robertson had little choice. Whilst on board ship to East Africa, Smith-Dorrien fell ill.

Smith-Dorrien was in an unenviable position. He had agreed to command a campaign he did not fully agree with, believing all efforts should be concentrated on Europe. But, as the decision had been made to fight in East Africa and he was without a job, he would do it. What he did not realise at the time was how little support he would get from the War Office, that is Kitchener. He had been told there were no additional resources and the requests he put in were in fact met by the Admiralty.[70] But this did not ease the fact that Kitchener was totally hostile. When Smith-Dorrien wrote to him regarding final arrangements and his salary, Kitchener 'told me that I must refer the matter to you [Asquith], as he had no idea what was in your mind at the time you made the appointment, but that, if you would let him know what your wishes on the subject were, he would carry them out.'[71] Having to balance the demands of the politicians and War Cabinet with no support from his superior, it is little wonder he fell ill.

Although too ill to travel to Pretoria, Smith-Dorrien continued to plan his offensive and liaise with the South Africans, via his secretary Baikie, over logistics. Meanwhile, Josiah Wedgwood, British Member of Parliament and on the staff heading out to British East Africa, wrote an illuminating account to the Prime Minister on 25 January 1916:

> We land at Mombasa today. So far as I can make out the Indian troops in British East Africa are a failure, and the South African troops coming out are excellent and almost over confident. They want to get it all over, on the rounding up principles employed in SW Africa, before the rains in April. So do Smuts and Botha who want a quick success cheap...

I gather that the relations between the Indian troops Officers and the Colonial troops officers are not particularly good; but of this I shall know more when I land.

You might think of sending Winston as Governor and CiC if Smuts still resolutely refuses to come. I saw Smuts privately. He would like to come as General but their position seemed to me bad and the danger of "ratting" among their followers in Parliament is evident. Smuts is the one the nationalists hate most, but Botha could hardly stand without him.

Anyway don't send any Indian Generals but somebody who will get on with the colonials.[72]

Within ten days, it was felt that to delay action any further pending Smith-Dorrien's health would have a negative impact in South Africa. The result was that when Smuts was offered as commander of the allied forces in East Africa, this was accepted, including by Kitchener on 3 February 1916.

Britain's interest in East Africa

The decision having been made in Britain to reactivate the campaign in East Africa, attention turned to fighting the war until Smuts suggested that Britain assume complete control over the East African territory. His suggestion was prompted by discussions with France over the Cameroons in February 1916 and justified by his belief that neither Belgium nor Portugal would be able to achieve any victory without British, and South African, support.[73] Before agreeing to Smuts' proposal, Britain approached Belgium and Portugal in April 1916 to determine their views on war-time control of the territory.[74]

The Colonial Office used the opportunity opened by the discussions to make its desires known. It did not want the Belgians involved in the administration of East Africa as the territory was wanted for Britain to complete the Cape Town to Cairo railway.[75] Given that the territory was the most fertile in the area, adding it to British territory

would be a bonus. In case there were any further doubts over the territory, the Colonial Office noted that Germany had intended to use the
same territory to build a railway across the breadth of Africa, and this
supported the strategic importance of the area.[76] This was an important claim as the cabinet had been quite clear at the start of the war
that no campaign or action was to be undertaken purely for territorial
gain. The Colonial Office was concerned that if the Belgians were
allowed to control the territory during the war, it would be almost
impossible to remove them afterwards.[77] That there were other strategic considerations meant that the Colonial Office's proposal could
be taken seriously. The War Office, therefore, supported the Colonial
Office in wanting to keep the Belgians out and proposed that Britain
control all captured territory for the duration of the war, except for the
area where the Belgian communication lines ran.[78]

The procrastination and indecision of the British hardened the
Belgians' attitude who then demanded payment in return for assistance
offered. To bring the campaign to an end, the War Office was prepared
to pay the price, whilst the Colonial Office, again, objected. When
Bonar Law asked Smuts' opinion, the latter naturally agreed with the
Colonial Office and rejected further Belgian assistance.[79] Further problems ensued as the Foreign Office did not want to upset the Belgians and
so they delayed formally notifying them of the changed position. The
Belgians, frustrated at British indecision, ceased military operations and
consolidated what they held.[80] To protect Britain's long-term interests in
the area and keep its southern African dominion happy, the British government was prepared to limit its co-operation with Belgium. However,
soon after Smuts left East Africa negotiations were resumed regarding
the use of Congolese troops in subjugating the German forces.[81] Smuts
had been wont to demand services from the Belgians rather than ask for
help or acknowledge their contribution in capturing Tabora. This did
not make for good working relations. With Smuts gone, Hoskins and
Colonel Huyghé met in April 1917 to discuss future operations with
Huyghé suggesting Hoskins take overall command. When Hoskins
left, these discussions continued with van Deventer.[82]

In August 1916, the new Permanent Undersecretary of the Foreign
Office, Lord Hardinge, convinced Prime Minister Asquith to determine

the territorial gains Britain wanted from the war. The request for the commission to determine Britain's interests had been pre-empted by Smuts' request to offer the Germans peace terms at the end of July 1916 and a note by Sir Edward Grey on 12 July 1916 stating that 'The war has to be regarded as a whole and the fact that we hold all German SW Africa and are in process of getting German E. Africa and have German colonies in the Pacific south of Equator *puts us in a weak position for bargaining about Cameroons and Togoland.*'[83] Despite there being a recognition that something needed to be done about Britain's war aims, Hardinge's predecessor, Arthur Nicholson, was a poor administrator who did not get along with his Secretary of State, Grey.[84] Hardinge, now in post was able to get things moving.

The surrender terms Smuts proposed, namely that civilians and reservists be released on parole while the rank and file were interred, were rejected by Colonial Parliamentary Undersecretary Arthur Steel-Maitland.[85] A War Committee meeting on 1 August 1916 showed just how divided the British departments were over East Africa. Steel-Maitland believed that the terms Smuts was proposing would cause difficulties in the future and would be seen as a sign of weakness. Robertson, though, was prepared to accept the surrender as it would bring the campaign to an end, reduce costs and enable greater concentration on the war in Europe. Bonar Law at the Admiralty wanted unconditional surrender to ensure the natives were not confused whilst Colonial Secretary Balfour thought Bonar Law's concerns would be dealt with if Britain occupied the major cities such as Dar-es-Salaam and Tanga. For Curzon, Minister without Portfolio, the decision was dependent on what Britain ultimately hoped to see happen with the captured colony. He also noted that the longer South Africa remained in the colony, the less eager they would be to leave and the greater their claim to the territory (the same concern Smuts had about Belgian and Portuguese involvement). In response to Curzon's appreciation, Bonar Law suggested that native troops be used to complete the campaign, especially as he had heard that the 'South Africans all thought they would get land'.[86] As the Germans were already using armed askaris, as were the British, the arguments presented on the outbreak of war against arming blacks no longer held. The committee had also been aware of the minute by George Fiddes of the Colonial Office which suggested that Smuts' offer of surrender was possibly an indication of his boredom with the campaign and that he wanted to return home. This matter had already been mentioned at the 11 July War Committee meeting when Smuts had announced that he thought the campaign would be over by December and that General Hoskins could replace him as Commander-in-Chief.[87] Smuts proceeded to offer Lettow-Vorbeck terms on 30 September 1916 which were, as predicted, rejected.[88]

As a result of these discussions, Asquith asked Sir Louis Mallet to chair a Committee on Territorial Changes to determine Britain's territorial needs from the war. The committee issued three reports by April 1917 and concluded that Germany's colonies should not be returned.

> The political objections to the restoration of German East Africa [were] hardly less strong, irrespective of considerations of a geographical and strategic character which [made] its retention a matter of great importance to the cohesion of the British territories in Africa and to the security of our shipping in the whole Indian Ocean.[89]

The findings from the Mallet committee were not discussed by the cabinet in the confusion brought about by the change in prime minister from Asquith to Lloyd George, but were later used by the committee set up by Lloyd George under Lord Curzon in March 1917 to consider the future of the German colonies.

Early in 1917, Lloyd George invited the prime ministers of the dominions and an Indian representative to London to participate in discussions about the war given that they were contributing large quantities of resources and manpower to the war effort. These meetings were to be held under the title of the Imperial War Cabinet. The bringing together of these representatives started a process which led to the defining of the Empire's war aims. The Colonial Office took the opportunity of having the heads of state in London to convene a series of meetings which became known as the Imperial Conference.

The two series of meetings would be alternated to enable visitors to attend both. With the political situation in South Africa still volatile, Botha not comfortable in formal settings and Smuts itching to get away from German East Africa, the Imperial War Cabinet meetings provided a good reason to recall Smuts. He left German East Africa in January 1917 and after a short stopover in South Africa, to meet his wife and Botha, left for Europe arriving in February 1917.[90]

When it became apparent that the number of delegates attending the meetings was going to make them unwieldy, Lloyd George set up subsidiary groups to occupy his guests. He asked Lord Curzon to chair the Territorial Desiderata Committee and Lord Milner, leading imperialist and administrator, to chair the Non-Territorial Desiderata Committee. They were both sub-committees of the War Cabinet, set up to deal with detail which would enable the Imperial War Conference and Cabinet attendees to focus on the main issues affecting the war. Curzon's committee met five times before submitting its final report on 28 April 1917.[91]

The German East Africa colony was determined to be too important to be given back to Germany for strategic, economic and political reasons. Handing German East Africa back to Germany after it had been defeated would cause political unrest in South Africa and upset in India, British East Africa and have a negative impact on natives throughout the area. The action would be seen as a betrayal of those who had given their lives for the Empire struggle. The committee also felt that neither Belgium nor Portugal should gain any territory apart from Portugal getting the Kionga Triangle. This was despite the belief that Portugal had only entered the war to retain its colonial empire and not for territorial aggrandisement.[92]

During these discussions, Smuts attempted to obtain the Portuguese territory for South Africa. He

considered [it] very important to secure the elimination of Portugal from the southern part of her present East African territory. This was because '[t]hat territory of seaboard of 2000 miles, [...] interfered directly with the natural development of the Union of South Africa and of Rhodesia. It had occurred to the South African Government that an exchange might be arranged by which, in return for the southern part of German East Africa, Portugal might be willing to cede her territory up to the Zambezi including Delagoa Bay and Beira ... [along the] lines of the secret agreement made with Germany in 1898.

He admitted it would probably need to be 'supplemented by a money consideration' too.[93] Following discussion, with input by Walter Long of the Colonial Office and G Clerk of the Foreign Office, the final report stated:

> The possibility of the acquisition or lease of Delagoa Bay and of Portuguese East Africa up to the Zambezi, or the securing of special concessions in this region whether in exchange for the southern portion of German East Africa, or in return for financial assistance is a matter deserving the consideration of His Majesty's Government more particularly in view of the advantages that would accrue to the Union of South Africa. Great Britain already enjoys the right of pre-emption in the case both of Delagoa Bay and of all the Portuguese colonies in southern Africa in the event of Portugal deciding to sell.[94]

These formal discussions enabled the Colonial Office to put forward its case which it had been discussing from at least the outbreak of war and gives insight to the 'general' views circulating in imperial circles at the time.

> Harcourt and his once pro-German staff at the Colonial Office demonstrated surprising speed in deciding that Germany's colonies in Africa must be forfeited, if possible to the British Empire. Just three days after Britain's entry into the war, following discussions with Reginald Butler, his official Private Secretary, Sir John Anderson, the Permanent Undersecretary, and William Lambert, the Chief Clerk and head of the South African Department at the Colonial Office, Harcourt decided that Germany could no longer be permitted to hold colonies in Africa.[95]

Harcourt 'observed that "Belgian compensation must (and will) come in Europe (and in cash) not in German East Africa."'[96] The Colonial Office had an 'extraordinary jealousy' of other nations' intentions in East Africa as Harcourt wrote to Buxton on 22 September 1914: 'From a political point of view it is eminently undesirable to have Belgians taking part in operations against German colonies in Africa, either by themselves or in cooperation with British forces.'[97] He, Harcourt, was also surprised at himself standing 'in front of the map of Africa and carving it up.'[98]

Correspondence between Long and Robertson in November 1917 was further enlightening about the British government's view of East Africa. Long questioned on 24 November:

> when will British politicians understand how to conduct a war?! We are sacrificing life in East Africa because we won't give the Natives any hope for the future. We are short of men in France and we are at the same time recalling good soldiers to make bad ploughmen and grow weeds!![99]

Robertson responded two days later.

> But you know what the Cabinet decided, and why they so decided, namely because Col House [American emissary] objected to our taking the proper line. This is the kind of thing that turns up almost every day in the week in connexion with one or other of our allies. We never do the right thing because we are afraid of offending the feelings of either one Ally or another. In trying to please and help our friends we shall ruin ourselves if we are not careful. I am always saying this and the answer I get is that I am narrow minded and do not pay suf-ficient attention to the political side of this question. That may be so but I remain convinced all the same that we shall never win this war until we beat the Germans, and we cannot do that unless we have adequate men, and we are not likely to have them if we allow them to die in East Africa and other places where they are doing no good.[100]

Pressure was maintained on Hoskins and van Deventer to bring Lettow-Vorbeck to order as soon as possible to ease the drain on shipping and material from the Western Front. Following the Imperial War Cabinet and Conference meetings and the success of Smuts in clearing the Germans out of German territory in East Africa, the discussions moved into determining what would come out of the peace discussions.

CHAPTER 11

ALL FOR WHAT?

Very few histories of World War One chisel below the surface to ascertain what the individual players, and hence countries, really hoped to get out of the war. The current chapter looks at how these aims, formulated over the years of war as discussed in previous chapters, were articulated and dealt with at the Paris peace talks in 1919. As important as the stated aims, were the sacrifices the negotiating teams were to make and why. Here again, the influence of certain individuals can be identified in directing government policy.

On 6 April 1917, the United States of America, led by President Woodrow Wilson, entered the war, following, but not a result of, Russia's withdrawal in February of the same year. The balance of power materially changed and Britain had to take America's views into consideration or risk losing its most financially stable ally.[1] British Foreign Secretary Arthur Balfour believed American views had to be taken into account if post-war peace was to be maintained.[2] Given the divergent views of the two countries and the fact that French and others' views, not least those of the dominions and India, would need to be taken into account, finding a satisfactory middle path would not be easy.

On 8 January 1918, Wilson made public his Fourteen Points which were to become the basis of the peace settlement. The fifth clause concerned the colonies: 'A free, open-minded and impartial adjustment of all colonial claims, based on the principle that the interests of the population concerned have equal weight with the equitable claims of the government whose title is to be determined.'[3] The ensuing difference in interpretation by Wilson and the dominions was to cause difficulties, particularly as the British government had announced on 4 January 1918 that it was not prepared to see Germany's colonies returned. Britain was, however, prepared to see the ex-German colonies allocated according to native or local inhabitant wishes.[4]

The cabinet was divided over how to pacify Wilson and thought in terms of land. Prompted by Balfour to find a means of pacifying the United States, Prime Minister David Lloyd George and his colleagues determined that if America accepted territory as a spoil of war, the dominions and Britain would be justified in doing so. The dilemma though, was which territory could be safely given to America? Jan Smuts felt it should be given Palestine, whilst Lloyd George and Winston Churchill thought East Africa was best. The latter two were supported by Colonial Secretary Walter Long. In addition, all except Churchill toyed with the idea of America obtaining Armenia. This latter idea appealed to Wilson, although he felt he would have to obtain Congress' permission before agreeing to the United States accepting colonies.[5]

Smuts was obviously against the idea of German East Africa being given to America as it would get in the way of his imperialist designs. In this he was supported by JX Merriman, as mentioned previously.[6] Leo Amery, Assistant Secretary to the War Cabinet, too was so disgusted with the idea that he prepared a paper entitled the 'United States and British war aims'. Rather than German East Africa, he suggested the United States be offered the Belgian Congo as the restoration of Belgium could not 'be considered apart from the restoration and development of the immense tropical territory (the Congo).' This would be well suited to 'American enterprise and organising ability'. He then proposed that Britain should retain German East Africa as it would ease administration of the area which he believed was of 'the very greatest importance' to Empire security.[7] Amery submitted his paper and discussed it with sympathetic colleagues, Smuts and Lord Milner, as he, Amery, was not able to participate in cabinet discussions due to his role as secretary.

The idea of giving the Congo to the United States had been prompted by Smuts, before Amery's paper, who suggested that the United States head up a 'Development Board' overseeing all of tropical Africa.[8] To Amery's horror, Lloyd George ignored the arguments and wishes of members of his cabinet and 'offered East Africa to Colonel House' in October 1918. He did this 'because he is now convinced that the Americans would be a nuisance in Palestine and upset all our Moslems. After dinner [Amery] had a great go at him over East Africa and Lord Milner and Hankey backed [him] up.'[9] Amery foresaw America expanding into Portuguese East Africa within a few years of the country assuming control of the German colony and clashing with South Africa over the Portuguese territory.[10] Lloyd George as Prime Minister would ultimately have the final say on British and dominion wishes in any discussions with other countries where he was their representative. Lloyd George's offer to give East Africa to the United States, despite the issue not having been resolved at cabinet level, demonstrated this and later in the peace discussions led to systems being put in place in an attempt to restrict Lloyd George acting on a whim.

E Morel summed up the dilemma the politicians faced: 'In the ultimate resort, Africa is a bigger question than the Balkans, bigger even than the question of the fate reserved for the Turkish possession in Asia Minor.'[11] '[D]espite the continent's remoteness, the activities of the European colonizing powers in Africa were the key to international peace.'[12] America was a relatively new player to the international scene and how its involvement in other continents would pan out was yet to be seen. Britain, the experienced international player, was determined to work out where America would least impact on its own desires. In trying to reconcile the differences between Britain, South Africa and America, Smuts proposed the mandate.

Mandates

Smuts developed the idea of an international board or mandate system from an idea put forward in July 1916 by his American philosopher friend WE Wolstenholme. The latter suggested the captured territories be put under 'international co-operation in which all nations [would] be on an equality, as regards the work and its rewards as well as its responsibilities.'[13] Two years later, in August 1918, Smuts tentatively suggested the idea of an international board to the British cabinet as a means to reconcile Wilson's proposals for peace (Fourteen Points) and the Empire desire for German territory. He followed up his suggestion with a paper in November. Before circulating the paper, Smuts wrote to Curzon to clarify his thoughts. He proposed that no colonies be returned to Germany, some were to go to 'our Dominions' and the rest retained by the administering country. If this was not acceptable, then he proposed the mandate be adopted as this would still allow Britain to control the territory. Smuts was ensuring that sub-imperialist ideals could be met within the wider imperial desires. This had been his intention all along as noted by the politically astute who had fought with him in East Africa:

> Smuts and [van Deventer had] never really tried to catch [Lettow-Vorbeck], but have deliberately herded him down south into [Portuguese East Africa], because the Dutch want to get a footing in Delagoa Bay. This [was] apparently the common talk out there.[14]

The peace discussions provided Smuts with the opportunity to realise South Africa's desires. Whilst he had been in London, he had tended to subordinate South Africa's desires within the wider empire context, however, with the peace looming, he started to manipulate the situation to further South Africa's aims. Lord Bertie of Thame, the British ambassador to France astutely recognised in 1916 that: South Africa 'had not spent life and treasure in German East Africa for no object [and] would insist on it being retained for the British Empire.' He was proved correct in 1918 when Smuts was the only person to vote against the United States of America being offered control of the German colony. Others who were against the idea, Amery and Milner, were not in a position to vote.[15]

In any event the United States, in keeping with Wilson's Fourteen Points, was not interested in colonies.[16]

Smuts' paper was delayed getting to the cabinet as Long, who had also been sent a draft, objected to the idea that Britain should 'suggest [the] setting up in some form ... [of] international control [for] Central Africa.'[17] Long's objection was over Britain suggesting the idea of 'international control'. For Long, Britain was far too superior to do such a thing and would undermine its position as a world player. Rather than blame Smuts for this idea, though, he blamed Sir Erle Richards, a senior Foreign Office official, who had been assigned to help Smuts. Discussions soon started between Smuts and Wilson with the result that Long's concern was subsumed by bigger issues – namely whether or not the system applied to the African colonies or only to what was previously the Austro-Hungarian Empire. Smuts' initial thoughts about the mandate system, written in November 1918, had excluded the German colonies. It was Wilson who insisted on including the German colonies and resisted all pressures to the contrary. With the amalgamation of the two ideas, the mandate system became seen as an 'Anglo-American agreement', which Britain felt it could not renege on. Management of the mandates would be the responsibility of the proposed international body, the League of Nations.[18]

Paris

From January 1919, the delegates from the various countries and their staff began to converge on Paris to prepare and agree the peace terms to be presented to Germany. This included the dominions which were not to be represented individually at the peace talks but as part of the British Empire. Lloyd George would have to accommodate the dominions' views and these were bound to be far-reaching, as expressed by Botha to Smuts:

> I have only one desire and that is to be there [in Europe] when peace is discussed, for then I shall support you in person in getting many things and seeing difficulties solved for which we shall perhaps never have another chance – especially the question of Mozambique. Jannie, there is no doubt about it, this is a matter which we must bring up and settle in our favour. The region

must be bought out and we must pay for it. Then there is German West – we must keep this, for we and the Germans will not again live together on a friendly footing if they keep German West.[19]

To accommodate the dominions, Lloyd George continued the imperial meetings in Paris, the group becoming the British Delegation. The delegation met almost daily and, invariably, a representative of the dominions accompanied Lloyd George to the council meetings. As a result, the Empire heard of Council of Four and Ten decisions almost immediately and was able to thrash out differences prior to council meetings so that a united Empire view could be presented. In this regard, Hankey, secretary to the delegation, had his work cut out for him as the Canadian Prime Minister Borden did not want any territory from the war, whereas Hughes of Australia, Botha and Smuts did.[20] The British Empire, therefore, presented a strongly considered case having had to reconcile its differing views before discussing them publicly and in effect had covered many of the arguments put forward by other countries. In addition, Britain's position was strengthened by having a representative from the dominions form part of Britain's negotiating team as it could claim it was not just speaking for itself. By including its dominions, it technically had smaller nations' interests at heart.

The general sentiment expressed by Botha was the same for virtually every other country attending the peace talks. The talks were, therefore, bound to be lively, and possibly heated, especially as the German, Russian and Turkish empires which existed in 1914 were no more in 1918.

The first meeting of the Paris peace talks took place on 18 January 1919. As a number of the main players, Britain, France, Japan and Italy were interested in German colonies, this was one of the first issues addressed. It was also a relatively straightforward decision to make and by the time the Second Plenary Session took place on 25 January 1919, Britain and France had forced the decision of what to do with the captured German colonies: they would not be returned to Germany. However, Wilson managed to delay the allocation of the colonies.

Perhaps not surprisingly, given the number of countries involved in its conquest, German East Africa featured rather substantially in the discussions of how to allocate the ex-German colonies. As Britain desired the territory and France had agreed in 1916 to keep out of East Africa in return for Togoland and the Cameroons, this left South Africa, Belgium, Portugal and India as the other main claimants for the German territory.

Before the Council of Ten met on 30 January 1919, the British Delegation had fully debated the mandate issue and as the outcome suited Britain, Lloyd George was prepared to support their case despite the ultimate desire of South Africa, New Zealand and Australia being to control territory in their own right. The result was that Lloyd George presented the Council of Ten with a compromise settlement, agreed by the Empire Delegation team purely so that a decision could be reached. He pointed out that the decision to accept all territories to be allocated as mandates did not represent the Empire's true feelings. If the mandate was 'merely a general trusteeship upon defined conditions' and that the League would have the 'right to interfere' only when these conditions were 'scandalously abused', the British Empire would accept the mandate system.[21] The position had been reached following Botha's main contribution to the peace talks. In a moving speech he explained that one had to 'give way in the little things to achieve the highest ideals'.[22] South Africa was once again, as in 1902, prepared to sacrifice its dreams to ensure a lasting peace – it would forego annexing German South West Africa, seen as integral to the Union, in favour of a mandate so that the peace discussions would not falter. The implication was that William Hughes of Australia and William Massey of New Zealand had to sacrifice their annexation-desires for New Guinea and Samoa too. The same day, on 30 January 1919, Belgium submitted a request to retain the German territory it was administering.[23]

Belgium and Portugal had noticeably been excluded from the discussions on mandates. Neither Belgium nor Portugal sat on the Council of Ten, despite Belgium's complete involvement in the war. The two countries were, therefore, reliant on the goodwill of the two major colonial powers, but soon discovered that they would have to fight for recognition of their contribution.[24]

On 7 May 1919, Germany was presented with the news that the colonies would not be returned but would be distributed under the supervision of the 'Allied and Associating powers'. The same day, Lloyd George presented Wilson with a note allocating the colonies. It was as expected, although, the French initially objected to the wording over the Cameroons and Italy complained that it did not receive territory as promised in the 1915 Treaty of London. By pointing out that the Treaty did not refer to mandates but to French and British territory, Balfour was able to deflect further discussion.[25] The one notable award was the whole of German East Africa to Great Britain, despite the Belgian request to Lord Milner in March for territory.[26]

Belgium discovered that the colonies had been allocated as mandates in the published reports of the proceedings a day later and lodged the 'most emphatic protest'. Lloyd George called Milner from London to resolve the issue and find a way to prevent the United States supporting a settlement in Belgium's favour.[27] In other words, Milner had to find a solution outside of the formal discussions. On 15 May 1919, Milner and Baron Pierre Orts of the Belgian Colonial Office met to work out how all the claims for German East African territory could be met. This was to be at the expense of Portugal, which did not submit objections to the 7 May colonial allocation until 29 May.[28]

The Portuguese objection to the allocation of the colonies was submitted three days after Milner had presented Baron Orts of Belgium with his idea of a four-way territorial swap. Milner was prepared to concede that if Portugal rejected the idea, Britain would accept Belgium's proposal to divide German East Africa between the two countries, Belgium and Britain.[29] If Portugal accepted the proposal Belgium would get part of Cabinda including the Portuguese Angolan southern bank of the Congo River in West Africa. As compensation, Portugal would obtain German East African territory along the borders of Northern Rhodesia and the Congo. The territory Portugal received would also 'pay' for South Africa obtaining Delagoa Bay. Once the exchanges had taken place, Belgium would cede to Britain the German East African territory that it would receive as mandates, namely Ruanda and Urundi.[30]

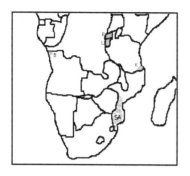

The proposed four-way territorial swap

B = Belgium's claim
R = Ruanda initially granted to Belgium as mandate and then given to Britain in payment
U = Urundi initially granted to Belgium as mandate and then given to Britain in payment
K = Kionga Triangle awarded to Portugal
SA = South Africa's claim to Delagoa Bay & Moçambique Province

The decision to divide German East Africa between Britain and Belgium was made on 24 August 1919 and there the territorial realignment ended. When presented with the Milner-Orts proposal, Portugal refused to part with its territory on the West African coast despite receiving the Kionga Triangle and Rovuma River enclave as proprietor. The new Portuguese government under the new and unstable presidency of João do Canto e Castro (16 Dec 1918–5 Oct 1919) could not give up any territory without political repercussions despite needing to obtain finance to develop its existing East African colonial territory.[31] The result was the map of southern and eastern Africa remained unchanged except that German South West Africa was allocated to South Africa and German East Africa was divided between Britain, Belgium and Portugal. All, except the Portuguese award, were mandated.

The mandate system allowed each country to nominally control the territory it had conquered, the extent to which was determined by the category allocated to the mandate – A, B or C. Category A was the least controlled whilst Category C allowed for the occupied territory to be governed almost as an integral part of the governing country. Category A mandates, reserved for the Middle East were the only ones which had a limited occupancy, the others would be determined by the League of Nations, on whose behalf the territories were being governed.[32] Allocating the level of control for each territory took time. The dominions having won their case in the imperial discussions saw their move to autonomous nationhood squashed by Wilson's idealism. For those countries interested in acquiring African territory, they were deprived of obtaining the territory they desired by Portugal's inferiority fear.

Belgium had upset Britain's plans on 8 May 1919 when it complained about the East African allocation. However, it was Portugal's distrust of the colonial powers which resulted in the best post-war solution for Africa failing. As it turned out, Britain, which received German East Africa as a B-type mandate, obtained less territory than it had hoped for when it surrendered Ruanda and Urundi to Belgium. Belgium had to settle for more, Ruanda and Urundi, without achieving its desired territorial adjustments on the West African coast and despite needing finance to rebuild the home country did not seem to consider selling or exchanging any of its African territory. South Africa and India were both left empty-handed, although South Africa received South West Africa as a C-type mandate on 17 December 1920 acting on Britain's behalf.[33] In contrast to the concerns about the Union not getting territory, the backlash predicted by Smuts did not materialise as the national situation was more volatile, particularly after Botha had died in August 1919.[34] India saw some settlement of Indians in the East African territories but not the freedom of movement hoped for. Despite India's large contribution to the campaign in terms of men and supplies, it paid the largest price in terms of not seeing its desires in Africa fulfilled.

The Paris peace talks had provided an opportunity to remove as many potential causes of future conflict as possible. This was the ideal, but the reality proved otherwise. Lloyd George despite wanting 'a just peace' was soon caught up in a war of words with Clemenceau, demanding the Kaiser's head and reparations. Had they been left to conclude the peace, Germany may well have been removed from the map of Europe. However, as they had to take others into account, the best they could hope for was to remove Germany from the map of Africa and other non-European areas – and in this they succeeded.

Ultimately the allocation of the mandates depended on the League of Nations coming into being which still had to be agreed by the peace delegates. When it was, Germany's African colonies were officially siphoned off to Britain, France, South Africa and Belgium with Portugal obtaining a slither of territory, the German Pacific Islands went to New Zealand, Australia and Japan, which also received the naval base at Shangtung. German East Africa, the territory involving the most number of interested parties and being the most complex of settlements was allocated as three mandates early on. The last mandate was finalised in 1923.[35]

Instrumental in getting the mandates allocated as they were, was a number of individuals – Smuts, Hughes, Massey – who collectively as the British Empire Delegation were able, with the support of significant others such as Lord Milner, Leo Amery and Maurice Hankey, to pressurise Lloyd George to argue their case. Baron Orts ensured Belgium got the recognition he felt the country deserved, whilst Portugal's ruling elite felt too insecure in their position to agree any radical changes to the country's empire. All these decisions, made behind the scenes, were to prevent President Wilson of the United States of America from exercising the power he held, personally through his convictions and institutionally as head of the most financially stable government at the time. The Senate's refusal to join the League of Nations was a serious blow to Wilson's influence, but, by then, he had seen the allocation of Germany's colonies as mandates where the wishes of the local inhabitants would need to be taken into account regarding any future decisions about their status.

CHAPTER 12

CONCLUSIONS

Should the war have been taken to East and southern Africa? The answer is 'yes' if you follow the British war book or listen to Lettow-Vorbeck. Beyond that, the answer is debatable and outside the scope of this book. In tangible costs, the war against German South West Africa cost £23 million whilst that in East Africa cost £72 million, the latter being four times the 1914 British war budget. In human terms, the German South West Africa campaign resulted in the death of 2,266 men (German and South African) and the East Africa campaign over 100,000 in total (South African, British, Portuguese, German, Belgian, askari and carrier). These figures exclude those maimed physically and emotionally. They also exclude the number killed in the South African rebellion, the direct result of South Africa's involvement in South West Africa, the Chilembwe, Makonde, Barue and other localised rebellions. The associated manpower- and intangible costs resulting from the breakdown in relations between various groups such as the English and Afrikaans speakers, as well as the impact on the local inhabitants in each of the dependencies and the economic disruption both during and after the war has not been addressed, despite being alluded to in the earlier discussion.

One of the challenges this book undertook was to explore the role of the individual in determining the outcome of the war. At all levels, individuals of all races – armed, auxiliary forces, carriers, local inhabitants, civil servants and politicians – all influenced the development of the campaign. Some such as Aitken were responsible for the needless loss of life due to their failure to take opposing forces and terrain seriously. Caufeild of the navy insisted on sweeping for mines and notifying the Germans that a treaty had not been ratified allowing the enemy time to prepare its defences. Others, such as Smuts, failed to listen to their subordinates about supply lines in the rush to get the job done, again leading to a needless loss of life; although in this instance, not due to military action which he judged would ruin his reputation more. Those, such as Lettow-Vorbeck recognised the importance of keeping their men healthy whilst others such as Kitchener foresaw the long-term implications of increasing military action in the theatre. King-Hall risked using aeroplanes in conditions not previously considered, while men like Wienholt, Arnoldi, Delamere, Grogan, King, MacDonell, WG Hughes, P Erskine and Noel all contributed to the success of the allied forces in East Africa. Similarly, the actions of Wahle, Kurt, Looff and Rosenthal ensured Lettow-Vorbeck was able to achieve his goal of attracting as many men and supplies away from the Western Front. The interplay of all these individuals and others resulted in the war developing the way it did.

During the first seventeen months of war, our protagonists Smuts and Lettow-Vorbeck were operating in different parts of the continent. Yet, both showed what they were made of. Both were seen as arrogant or confident in their beliefs. They were intolerant of sensitivities and human emotion and whether they realised it or not, were reliant on trusted colleagues to mediate. Smuts had Botha, and Lettow-Vorbeck, after 24 November 1914, had Schnee. The two men, Smuts and Lettow-Vorbeck had been instrumental in setting up the military systems their countries would use: Lettow-Vorbeck only since January 1914 and Smuts since 1912. Given the issues both had to overcome in their countries to set up effective military structures, by the time they got to 'meet' in 1916, the opposing forces were technically evenly balanced. How they were managed proved the difference.

The two men, as with others involved, were products of their time, constrained by the contexts within which they functioned. Smuts, as deputy Prime Minister, was unable to do much in the public eye without the opposition commenting on it back in South Africa, whilst Lettow-Vorbeck was instructed by his superiors to defer to Governor Schnee. Military and political protocols dictated how people interacted. Had it not been for the Admiralty and Colonial office who were concerned about the impact of the war in East and southern Africa and the confusion within the territories themselves, it is unlikely decisions would have been made in London to rush into action as they did. For the War Office, Kitchener in particular, the war in Europe remained the priority and a strong case had to be presented before subsidiary actions were sanctioned.

The end of 1915 saw preparations being made for Smuts' move to East Africa and for his first encounter with Lettow-Vorbeck. During the year, neither had been idle. Smuts had worked with Louis Botha to wrap up the 1914 South African rebellion and launch the campaign against German South West Africa. In April, he felt the situation in the Union was sufficiently calm for him to join Botha in the campaign. Having spent five months on commando coordinating the southern attack he returned to South Africa to fight the election and recruit troops to fulfil promises made to Britain. Lettow-Vorbeck spent the year coordinating skirmishes and putting structures in place. These would be useful in future months when, and if, the campaign moved into German territory. He ended the year with the German colony in the ascendancy except in the far south where, although, undefeated, British tenacity ensured local support. Lettow-Vorbeck's incursions into British East Africa and Northern Rhodesia were the 'only instance[s] during the war when German colonial forces actually took the offensive against adjoining British territory'.[1]

The year 1915 was the year of the politician. Buxton had settled into his role as Governor General and High Commissioner of South Africa. He pushed for coordinated action in Central Africa which saw the appointment of Northey as commander and was able to influence South Africa sending troops to East Africa. In South Africa, Botha and Smuts won the election, albeit with a smaller majority than before, which ensured the Union remained in the war supporting Britain. In Britain, Asquith in response to pressure by others outmanoeuvred Kitchener to activate the campaign in East Africa. In Germany, too, the politicians dominated the military, while for a short time longer, the Admiralty still held sway.

By February 1916, all the German colonies except German East Africa had been conquered. This soon gave rise to questions over control of the territory especially in West Africa where France had been as involved as Britain in subjugating the German territories. It took the remainder of the year to determine the territorial aims of each of the allied countries involved in Africa and until the peace discussions to finalise how they would be met.

Politics clashed with military requirements. Smuts was too scared to engage Lettow-Vorbeck for fear of 'butchering' the South African forces and the impact this would have on him politically. He, therefore, resorted to encircling movements in an attempt to capture the German troops. His other motivation was to incorporate Portuguese East Africa territory into the Union. With Portugal an ally, he had to tread carefully. Forcing the campaign into the southern territories would aide his, and South Africa's, expansionist agenda. The fact that Botha had won the 1915 election with a smaller majority than anticipated reduced South Africa's potential claims in East Africa even before its involvement in the campaign when both Botha and Smuts felt they could not argue for complete control of the theatre, but had to work in conjunction with the War and Colonial Offices to defeat Lettow-Vorbeck. It was also the year that liaison officers, MacDonell, Grogan and Viali, were appointed to allied forces in an attempt to align the wishes of the home governments with the need for co-operation on the ground.

In Europe, the allied governments, prompted by their foreign envoys and ministers, realised the need to compromise politically in order to ensure the military victory, after which they could resolve their political differences. During this time, Lettow-Vorbeck continued with his policy of trying to attract as many forces to Africa as he could. Although large numbers of men were sent to East Africa, Lettow-Vorbeck failed to realise that many of these troops were seen, by the British, as unsuitable to fight in Europe. The need to import equipment and material to support these forces, however, achieved his aim of drawing shipping supplies away from Europe.

In some ways 1917 was no different to other years, but following on from 1916 when Smuts drove his forces across Africa in pursuit of Lettow-Vorbeck, the significance of the changes have easily been lost. These years while proving the tenacity of the soldier to do his best for his country, demonstrated the impact of politics on the direction of the campaign, especially where the military leaders were not politically astute. In effect, the East Africa campaign saw the fall of Smith-Dorrien, Hoskins and Kitchener for purely political motives. Smuts left East Africa to fight another, different, war – to obtain the recognition of South Africa as a force to be reckoned with on the African continent.

During most of 1918, military action in East Africa centred on the Portuguese colony as all German troops which had not surrendered crossed into that country. The home military governments, particularly Britain, pushed for an early end to the campaign to release vital material for Europe whilst the Germans recognised the benefit to their cause having attempted to send additional supplies to Lettow-Vorbeck. Relations between the allied forces on the ground had been strained for most of the war, but during 1918 hit breaking point. The home governments, although distrustful of each other, were able to put aside their concerns to work things out. Much of this was down to ambassadors who understood the host government and were able to push the right buttons. For example, Belgium's decision not to send troops to assist with the campaign in Portuguese territory, helped to reduce further potential conflict especially given Portugal's sensitivities.

Political events in Europe, following the military capitulation of the German forces under Ludendorff, brought the campaign to an end in November. Different interpretations of the surrender terms caused some resentment amongst Lettow-Vorbeck and his men, although the mutual respect the military men had for each other helped ensure a conducive relationship until the Germans were officially able to return home.

Finally, the peace discussions around East Africa shed light on the values of each of the main countries. Britain and France believed they were the strongest powers and that having sacrificed the most, deserved the greatest say. However, they were both economically subordinate to the United States of America which had its own agenda for the developing world. Belgium was concerned with not being recognised or valued despite its involvement and participation throughout the war years, and as a result subordinated its real desires for Africa. Portugal was realising that it was no longer a super power and that its empire was crumbling which is why it refused to surrender territory it could ill-afford to maintain. South Africa pushed to be recognised as a country in its own right, to realise dreams it had nursed for decades and to potentially solve the white race problem it had. The other allied countries were subordinate to Britain, and as they lacked dominion status were unable to get their way unless it suited Britain. As in the scramble for Africa, the boundaries were determined by men sitting in Europe with very little concern for the local inhabitants. Their decisions were based on economic desires and even where advisors, such as Grogan and Meinertzhagen were used to determine boundary markings these had little to do with the real desires of the local inhabitants despite the announcements that native views would be taken into account.[2]

The campaign and peace discussions around East and southern Africa are significant, not for what they contributed to the overall war effort, but for the lessons that can be learnt from its conduct, and the wider implications. This account has attempted to demonstrate the impact of politics on military action. It is striking that those who were for action in East Africa were the politicians whilst the military men, particularly at the senior levels, were against taking the war to East Africa once radio and wireless security had been ensured. Given the involvement of politicians on such an insignificant theatre of war raises a question over their involvement and impact on the developments of the Western Front. Would a study of the relationships between the politicians in London, Haig, French and other senior military leaders show that the British forces were in fact not 'led by donkeys?'[3]

For reasons of time and space, this history is incomplete. Allusion has been made to the impact of the campaign on black inhabitants of East and southern Africa as well as white civilians resident in the various territories. It is regretted that more attention could not be given to them within the scope of this study, or to the economic impact of the campaigns given the mine-employment contracts between South

Africa, Moçambique (Portuguese East Africa) and Malawi (Nyasaland), for example. What has been significant whilst researching this book, is the consideration senior individuals paid to the indigenous peoples. They may not have made their views public at the time and their views may not be wholly acceptable today, but there was a significant group who were grappling with the impact of the war on those who were governed. JX Merriman wrote to Bryce, an influential liberal, 'Poor wretches! Is it not strange to see rival bands of black men shooting each other in order to decide which set of Europeans shall have the right to despoil them of their land and simple possessions?'[4]

And Wills succinctly sums it up:

> [It is] ironical that violent conflict should have been brought to the African continent by those European Governments that thirty years before had imposed their administrations in the name of peace and order. The official record referred in extravagant terms to the Africans' "wholehearted loyalty and affection for the white leaders whom he has come to know and trust, and to his even deeper and more devoted loyalty to the sovereign empire he serves." A glimpse of the other side of the picture appeared in the *Nyasaland Times* after the Karonga fighting. "The poor Africans," wrote John Chilembwe, "who have nothing to own in this present world, who in death leave only a long line of widows and orphans in bitter want and dire distress, are invited to die for a cause which is not theirs."

Farwell is blunter:

> [Lettow-Vorbeck] succeeded in what he set out to do, yet what he did was in the end worse than useless, for he could not prevent the victory of his country's enemies; he cost the lives of thousands and the health of tens of thousands more. He tore the social fabric of hundreds of communities and wrecked the economy of three countries. His splendid military virtues were devoted to an unworthy cause and his loyalty given to a bad monarch.[5]

Returning to Wills:

It is likely that the campaign made at least as great an impact
on the African consciousness as on that of Europeans, for whom
it was part of a greater whole; certainly it appeared in a different
light. The white man's government, as opposed to individuals,
was no longer seen as infallible, having descended to warfare of
a kind that its first consuls had condemned among the tribes.
Africans, sometimes with considerable reluctance, had been persuaded to fire on a European enemy; what was for many a taboo,
had been broken.[6]

The campaigns enabled the politicisation of subordinate groups within
the different countries involved. In South Africa, the South African
Native National Congress offered to raise 5,000 infantry in the Cape
to support Louis Botha and the war effort, and the African People's
Organisation representing coloureds had raised a corps of 10,000 men
by September 1914.[7] They hoped that by demonstrating their loyalty they would be regarded as citizens of equal standing to whites.
That they were not gave birth to ideas of nationalism, most notably
in India, which were to be further developed during World War Two.
In 1933, the British War Office produced a report on the operations in
East Africa during World War One recognising the value of the native
troops.[8] Although, a close reading of the report indicates that the War
Office still did not fully appreciate the involvement of blacks as soldiers. Lettow-Vorbeck is regarded as having the first fully integrated
modern force where he started appointing askari to NCO positions
based on merit and was quite upset when his black askaris were not
treated with the same respect as his white officers.

Women, too, as with those in Britain and other more developed
countries, came into their own. The English women in the colonies,
as with those in Britain, put their struggle for suffrage on hold for
the duration of the war and performed war-related work. The war
saw women in South Africa move into office and shop employment
whilst young Afrikaans girls moved from the farms into factories.[9] In
East Africa, the women, as explained by Elspeth Huxley and Karen

Blixen, took over the running of the farms whilst the men were away and in German East Africa, the women supported the men by taking over various auxiliary roles to allow the men to focus on engaging the enemy.[10] Camp followers, too, were important for maintaining the morale and loyalty of the men as recognised by Lettow-Vorbeck.

The long term impact of the war has been more difficult to determine. The peace discussions provided an opportunity to re-align the African continent's boundaries and potentially remove areas of contention. That this did not happen, as witnessed by the civil wars in Ruanda and Burundi amongst other conflicts, confirms that the powers of the day were less interested in their dependencies than in their own gains. Having orchestrated possession of a strip of land to build the Cape Town to Cairo railway, Britain handed the strip back to Belgium in 1923. It was no longer needed to build the railway as the Cape Town to Cairo air route had opened in September 1919. The first successful flight from London to Tanganyika (previously German East Africa and later Tanzania) took place in 1920 and from Cairo to Cape Town in February of that year by the South African Sir Pierre van Ryneveld.[11]

The men who participated in the East Africa campaign, except for the Germans and 2nd Rhodesian Regiment,[12] returned home to little fanfare or welcome. Given that their experiences of the war were so different to comrades who had fought in Europe, and that their achievements did not suit the political powers in the respective countries, not much was done to acknowledge their involvement. There are a few monuments in Kenya (British East Africa), Tanzania and Zimbabwe (Southern Rhodesia) to the campaign, but as Stapleton notes there is a 'general amnesia about the First World War in Zimbabwean society', and most monuments have been pulled down.[13] The amnesia has not just been in Zimbabwe. It is only within the past decade or so that the campaign has come to light and to be studied as a campaign rather than side-show. There were a number of autobiographies written in the years after the war and a few novels were written based on incidents from the campaign and these today provide a valuable insight.

The South West Africa campaign still requires the same military investigation that the East Africa campaign is now receiving. To date, too much has been taken for granted from the myths, official histories and popular accounts which have been produced. Significantly, the men who fought in South West Africa were welcomed home when they landed, despite nothing further having been done publicly to acknowledge their contribution to the war effort.[14]

It is difficult to say which of the two campaigns, the East African or South West African, had the biggest impact. Although little has been done to remember South West Africa, it in effect became part of South Africa until 1990 when the country became the independent Republic of Namibia. The mandate seems to have been sufficient reward for the Union given that anything more could potentially have resulted in another civil outburst. East Africa, however, has regularly featured in remembrances. In 1929, Lettow-Vorbeck was invited to a dinner in London, and to stay as the guest of Richard Meinertzhagen. Lettow-Vorbeck noted 'I arrived on time to the minute at the Holborn Restaurant in London, where 1,100 former soldiers had assembled, and where for the first time I met face-to-face my long-time opponent General Smuts.'[15] This meeting marked the start of a life-long friendship between the two men and although it is not clear whether they met again, they certainly remained in touch with Smuts sending Lettow-Vorbeck food parcels during the Second World War and writing to him two weeks before his own death. In 1950, Smuts died and three years later, Lettow-Vorbeck made his final visit to Africa. During the same year, on 14 November 1953 the Chambeshi monument was unveiled on the spot where Croad and Lettow-Vorbeck met to discuss the surrender. A decade later, in 1963, it was moved to its present position and a year on, Lettow-Vorbeck died, the same year, the German government agreed to pay the surviving askari for their services during the war.[16] Half a century later, the impact these two men had on the African continent remains, although, their names may no longer be associated with much of what they set in place. The same could be said for the man who tried to keep East Africa out of the war, Lord Kitchener.

NOTES

Introduction

1. PJ Pretorius, *Jungle man* (1947) p.27
2. Lecture at British Staff College, 1901 in E Durschmied, *The hinge factor: How chance and stupidity have changed history* (2003) p.212
3. PJ Pretorius, *Jungle man* (1947) p.28
4. JJ Collyer, *Official History: Campaign in German South West Africa, 1914–1915* (1937)
5. For example a section of ES Thompson's diary does not exist as he ran out of paper whilst on the march in East Africa, ES Thompson, 'A machine gunner's odyssey through German East Africa: The diary of ES Thompson part 3, 18 September 1916–26 February 1917' in *South African Military History Journal* 7:6 (1988)
6. E Trzebinski, *The Kenya pioneers* (1985) p.182
7. Belgian Government, *The Belgian campaigns in the Cameroons and German East Africa* (1917)
8. TNA: CAB 45/65; Richard Wapshare's papers are at the Imperial War Museum
9. R Anderson, *The forgotten front: The East African campaign 1914–1918* (2004); H Strachan, *The First World War in Africa* (2007); E Paice, *Tip and Run: The untold tragedy of the Great War in Africa* (2007); G Foden, *Mimi and Toutou go forth: The bizarre battle of Lake Tanganyika* (2005)
10. CJ Charlewood, 'Naval action on the Tanganyika coast, 1914–1917 Part 1' in *Tanganyika Notes and Records* 54 (1960) p.133
11. CJ Thornhill, *Taking Tanganyika: Experiences of an Intelligence Officer 1914–1918* (2004) p.11

Notes and bibliography content

Text

NOTES

12. R Anderson, *Forgotten front* (2004); H Strachan, *War in Africa* (2007);
E Paice, *Tip and Run* (2007); G Foden, *Mimi and Toutou* (2005); C Hordern,
Military operations East Africa, August 1914–September 1916 vol 1 (1941/1990);
H Fecitt, *The soldier's burden: Harry's Africa* [online: kaiserscross]
13. Clemenceau in FR de Meneses, 'Too serious a matter to be left to the
Generals? Parliament and the army in wartime Portugal 1914–1918' in
Journal of Contemporary History 33:1 (1998) p.84
14. H Strachan, *War in Africa* (2007) p.vii
15. R Anderson, *Forgotten front* (2004) p.11
16. P von Lettow-Vorbeck, *My reminiscences of East Africa: The campaign for
German East Africa in World War 1* (nd) p.16; H Strachan, *War in Africa*
(2007) p.103 notes Lettow-Vorbeck had visited the Boer Republics but does
not go into detail about timing or in what capacity or for what purpose.
17. RV Dolbey, *Sketches of the East Africa campaign* (1918) p.30
18. R Anderson, *Forgotten front* (2004) p.25 using Lettow-Vorbeck's *Mein Leben*;
U Schulte-Varnedorff, *Kolonialheld für Kaiser und Führer: General Lettow-
Vorbeck – Mythos und Wirklichkeit* (2006) p.14
19. P von Lettow-Vorbeck, *My reminiscences* (nd) Preface
20. J Listowell, *The making of Tanganyika* (1965) p.63; WK Hancock, *Smuts: The
fields of force 1919–1950 vol 2* (1968) pp.525–529
21. WK Hancock, *Smuts: Fields of force* (1968) p.525
22. G Corrigan, *Mud, blood and poppycock* (2003); H Fecitt (personal correspondence); C Hordern, *Military operations* (1941) pp.219–221
23. R Anderson, *Forgotten front* (2004) pp.26–27

Chapter 1   Position on the eve of war

1. *Parliamentary Debates* (1921) in B Porter, *The lion's share: A short history of
British imperialism 1850–1995* (3rd ed) (1997) p.242
2. H Harmer, *Makers of the modern world: The peace conferences of 1919–1923 and
their aftermath: Friedrich Ebert* (2008) p.106
3. T Packenham, *The scramble for Africa 1897–1912* (1992) pp.349–361,356;
R Connaughton, 'The First World War in Africa (1914–1918)' in *Small wars &
insurgencies* 12:1 (2001) p.111
4. U Schulte-Varnedorff, *Kolonialheld* (2006) pp.14,43
5. T Packenham, *Scramble for Africa* (1992) pp.342–344
6. BM Du Toit, *The Boers in East Africa: Ethnicity and identity* (1998) p.15
7. R Anderson, *Forgotten front* (2004) p.23
8. C Hordern, *Military operations* (1941) pp.525–528
9. A Samson, *Britain, South Africa and the East Africa campaign 1914–1918: The
Union comes of age* (2006) p.18

10. A Seegers, *The military in the making of modern South Africa* (1996) p.8
11. T Packenham, *Scramble for Africa* (1992) pp.138,340
12. KJ Harvey, *The Battle of Tanga, German East Africa, 1914* (2003) p.35
13. TNA: CAB 103/86, 24 Jan 1911 memorandum
14. CAB 38/8/6, 10 Aug 1901 Altham paper in A Samson, *Britain, South Africa and East Africa* (2006) p.20
15. C Hordern, *Military operations* (1941) p.30; K Ingham, *A history of East Africa* (3rd ed) (1965) p.245; *The East African Leader*, 1 & 8 Aug 1914; H Strachan, *War in Africa* (2007) p.2
16. KJ Harvey, *Battle of Tanga* (2003) pp.25–26
17. TNA: CAB 38/4/9, memoranda 7 & 23 Feb 1904
18. T Packenham, *Scramble for Africa* (1992) p.606
19. CAB 38/4/9 in A Samson, *Britain, South Africa and East Africa* (2006) p.21
20. See JD Vincent-Smith, 'The Anglo-German negotiations over the Portuguese colonies in Africa, 1911–1914' in *Historical Journal* 17:3 (1974) pp.620–629; RTB Langhorne, 'Anglo-German negotiations concerning the future of the Portuguese colonies, 1911–1914' in *Historical Journal* 16:2 (1973) pp.361–387
21. Viscount Grey of Fallodon, Foreign Secretary sent the provisional agreement to Conservative leader Arthur Balfour who sat on the CID; ME Townsend, *The rise and fall of Germany's colonial empire, 1884–1918* (1930) p.191
22. FR de Meneses, *Makers of the modern world: The peace conferences of 1919–1923 and their aftermath: Afonso Costa* (2010) chapter 1
23. D Wheeler, 'The Portuguese army in Angola' in *The Journal of Modern African Studies* 7:3 (1969) p.427; FR de Meneses, 'Too serious a matter' (1998) pp.85–96
24. JP Cann, 'Moçambique, German East Africa and the Great War' in *Small wars & insurgencies* 12:1 (2001) pp.114–143; R Anderson, *Forgotten front* (2004) p.49; E Paice, *Tip and run* (2007) pp.139–142
25. JP Cann, 'Angola and the Great War' in *Small wars & insurgencies* 12:1 (2001) p.145
26. JP Cann, 'Angola and the Great War' (2001) pp.144–165
27. TNA: FO 371/2599/72511, 17 Apr 1916 FO minute
28. WA Hance & IS van Dongen, 'Lorenço Marques in Delagoa Bay' in *Economic Geography* 33:3 (1957) p.245
29. Grey Papers FO 800/61 in RTB Langhorne, 'Anglo-German negotiations' p.369
30. T Packenham, *Scramble for Africa* (1992) pp.656–663
31. R Anderson, *Forgotten front* (2004) p.23
32. K Smith & FJ Nöthling, *North of the Limpopo: Africa since 1800* (1993) pp.238–241

33. H Fecitt, *The Uganda Volunteer Reserve 1914–1916* [online: kaiserscross]
34. B Porter, *The lion's share* (1997) pp.232–233
35. BM Du Toit, *The Boers* (1998)
36. H Moyse-Bartlett, *The King's African Rifles: A study in the military history of East and Central Africa, 1890–1945* (1956) p.137
37. H Strachan, *War in Africa* (2007) p.104; K Ingham, *East Africa* (1965) p.245
38. IWM: 06/88/1 LES Ward, *Summary note*
39. PA: MSS Dav 9, 30 Jul 1914, telegram Governor EAP rec 7.6pm
40. IWM: 06/88/1 LES Ward, *Summary note*
41. BM Du Toit, *The Boers* (1998) p.18
42. KJ Harvey, *Battle of Tanga* (2003) p.26
43. KJ Harvey, *Battle of Tanga* (2003) p.26
44. P von Lettow-Vorbeck, *My reminiscences* (nd) p.10
45. P von Lettow-Vorbeck, *My reminiscences* (nd) p.15
46. M Page, *KAR: A history of the King's African Rifles* (1998) p.27; W Lloyd-Jones, *KAR: Being an unofficial account of the origin and activities of The King's African Rifles* (1926) p.169; R Anderson, *Forgotten front* (2004) pp.26–28; ME Page, *The Chiwaya war: Malawians and the First World War* (2000) p.70
47. R Anderson, *Forgotten front* (2004) pp.23,49; JP Cann, 'Moçambique, German East Africa and the Great War' (2001) p.116; JP Cann records 1,527 men in PEA.
48. AJ Wills, *An introduction to the history of Central Africa: Zambia, Malawi and Zimbabwe* (4th ed) (1985) for an overview of the history of the area
49. DD Phiri, *Let us die for Africa: An African perspective on the life and death of John Chilembwe of Nyasaland/Malawi* (1999); O Ransford, *Livingstone's Lake* (1966) pp.228–229; G Shepperson & T Price, *Independent African: John Chilembwe and the Nyasaland rising of 1915* (2000)
50. TNA: CO 525/57/76 note on cover re GG Nyasaland letter 14 Aug 1914
51. DD Phiri, *Let us die for Africa* (1999); O Ransford, *Livingstone's Lake* (1966) pp.228–229; ME Page, *The Chiwaya war* (2000) p.70
52. TNA: CO 525/44/434, 12 Nov 1912; CO 525/55/14671, 14 Mar 1914; CO 525/55/14662, / Nov 1913; ME Page, *The Chiwaya war* (2000) chapter 2
53. KJ Harvey, *Battle of Tanga* (2003) p.35; R Davenport & C Saunders, *South Africa: A modern history* (5th ed) (2000) p.42
54. JJ Collyer, *South West Africa* (1937) p.1
55. A Seegers, *The military in the making* (1996) p.17
56. H Spender, *General Botha* (1919) pp.259–260; FV Engelenburg, *General Louis Botha* (1929) p.258

57. A Samson, *Britain, South Africa and East Africa* (2006) pp.69–72; P Lewsen (ed), *Selections from the correspondence of JX Merriman 1905–1924* (1969); AP Cartwright, *The first South African: The life and times of Sir Percy Fitzpatrick* (1971)

58. A Samson, *Britain, South Africa and East Africa* (2006) p.76; H Spender, *Botha* (1919) p.331

59. Round Table, *Commonwealth Quarterly* 17 (1914) pp.491–496

60. A Seegers, *The military in the making* (1996) p.18

61. A Seegers, *The military in the making* (1996) Chapter 1

62. I van der Waag, 'Rural struggles and the politics of a colonial command: The South African Mounted Rifles of the Transvaal Volunteers, 1905–1912' in Miller, Stephen M (ed), *Soldiers and settlers in Africa, 1850–1918* (2009) pp.281–282; B Nasson, *Springboks on the Somme: South Africans in the Great War* (2010) p.38

63. WK Hancock and J van der Poel, *Selections from the Smuts papers June 1910–November 1918 vol 3* (1966) p.303; JJ Collyer, *South West Africa* (1937) pp.18–19

64. A Seegers, *The military in the making* (1996) p.22

65. R Hyam, *The failure of South African expansion 1908–1948* (1972) p.26

66. A Seegers, *The military in the making* (1996) p.20

67. A Samson, *Britain, South Africa and East Africa* (2006) p.81; BJ Liebenberg & SB Spies (eds), *South Africa in the 20th Century* (1993) p.95; B Cloete, *Die lewe van Senator FS Malan (President van die Senaat)* (1946) p.318; KW Grundy, *Soldiers without politics: Blacks in the South African armed forces* (1983) p.53

68. J Silvester, M Wallace & P Hayes 'Trees never meet: mobility and containment: an overview 1915–1946' in P Hayes et al (eds) *Namibia under South African rule: Mobility and containment 1915–1946* (1998) pp.3fn,4fn; Germany had its own towns in the territory before World War One and to all intents and purposes seemed to manage the Caprivi Strip. J Butler, 'The German factor in Anglo-Transvaal relations' in P Gifford & WMR Louis, *Britain and Germany in Africa: Imperial rivalry and colonial rule* (1967) p.195; Britain ceded control of the territory to Germany in 1890 as Britain did not believe giving Germany access would prove a threat to Britain.

69. H Strachan, *War in Africa* (2007) pp.76–77

70. R Cornwell, 'The war for independence' in J Cilliers & C Dietrich (eds) *Angola's war economy: The role of oil and diamonds* (2000) [online: www.issafrica.org] pp.43–48; JP Cann, 'Angola and the Great War' (2001) pp.149,161

71. JP Cann, 'Angola and the Great War' (Spring 2001) pp.147,149; P Southern, 'German border incursions into Portuguese Angola prior to the First World War' in *Portuguese Journal of Social Science* 6:1 (2007) pp.5–6; N Stassen,

Afrikaners in Angola (2009) p.84; R Pélisier, 'Campagnes militaries au Sud-Angola (1885–1915)' in *Cahiers d'etudes Africaines* 33:9 (1969) pp.54–123

72. C Lucas, *Empire at war* (1921)
73. Bod: MSS Harcourt 473, 24 Dec 1914
74. A Roberts, *A history of Zambia* (1976) pp.157–158
75. Northern Rhodesia, officially formed in 1911, refused amalgamation with the South. A Roberts, *A history of Zambia* (1976) p.182
76. H Wilson Fox, 'The development of Rhodesia from a geographical standpoint' in *The Geographical Journal* 48:4 (1916) pp.302–303
77. BM Du Toit, *The Boers* (1998) p.24; K Ingham, *East Africa* (1965)
78. BM Du Toit, *The Boers* (1998) p.24
79. G Hodges, *Kariakor: The Carrier Corps* (1999) explains the attitude of blacks to male labour in East Africa
80. For overview of Gandhi's time in South Africa, see PF Power, 'Gandhi in South Africa' in *Journal of Modern African Studies* 7:3 (1969) pp.441–455

Chapter 2   To war, 1914

1. H Strachan (ed), *The Oxford illustrated history of the First World War* (1998); M Gilbert, *First World War* (1994)
2. E Paice, *Tip and run* (2007) p.14 quoting David and Robinson, *Chronicles of Kenya* (1928)
3. IWM: PP/MCR/150, Norman King diary, 12 Aug 1914; K Forster, 'The quest for East African neutrality in 1915' in *Africa Studies Review* 22:1 (1979) p.76
4. E Trzebinski, *Kenya pioneers* (1985) p.177
5. IWM: PP/MCR/62, GB Buxton, 26 Sep 1914; H Fecitt, *Cole's scouts 1914–1915* [online: kaiserscross]; R Anderson, *Forgotten front* (2004) p.43
6. WE Wynn, *Ambush* (1937) p.38
7. H Fecitt, *The Magadi Defence Force 1914* [online: kaiserscross]
8. BM Du Toit, *The Boers* (1998) p.100; E Trzebinski, *Kenya pioneers* (1985) p.179
9. A Davies & HJ Robertson, *Chronicles of Kenya* (1928) p.101
10. CJ Thornhill, *Taking Tanganyika* (2004) p.64
11. Lord Cranworth, *Kenya Chronicles* (1939) p.93
12. RH: MSS Meinertzhagen, 31 Oct 1914
13. BM Du Toit, *The Boers* (1998) pp.99–102
14. Pieterse (1942) in BM Du Toit, *The Boers* (1998) pp.95–96
15. CJ Thornhill, *Taking Tanganyika* (2004) p.138; PJ Pretorius, *Jungle man* (1947) pp.150–160

16. BM Du Toit, *The Boers* (1998) pp.93–98; P von Lettow-Vorbeck, *My reminiscences* (nd) p.174 refers to Booyen, not Rooyen

17. PA: MSS Dav 9, 30 Jul 1914, telegram Governor EAP rec 7.6pm; KJ Harvey, *Battle of Tanga* (2003) pp.15,36; The Western Front extended 400 miles

18. W Lloyd-Jones, *KAR* (1926) p.172; C Hordern, *Military operations* (1941) p.15

19. H Fecitt, *The Uganda Railway Volunteer Reserve 1914* [online: kaiserscross]

20. H Strachan, *War in Africa* (2007) pp.114–115

21. H Fecitt, *The Uganda Volunteer Reserve 1914–1918* [online: kaiserscross]

22. K Ingham, *East Africa* (1965)

23. TNA: WO 106/573, 4 Aug 1914 telegram CO to India; C Hordern, *Military operations* (1941) pp.29–30; H Moyse-Bartlett, *King's African Rifles* (1956) p.264

24. TNA: CAB 38/28/51, 1 Nov 1914 Report

25. TNA: WO 106/573, 5 Aug 1914 Recommendations

26. A Samson, *Britain, South Africa and East Africa* (2006) pp.17–25

27. TNA: CAB 38/13/16, 4 Apr 1907 CID Paper 47C

28. TNA: WO 106/573, 8 Aug 1914 telegram IO to Viceroy; C Hordern, *Military operations* (1941) p.30fn

29. G Corrigan, *Mud, blood and poppycock* (2003) pp.108–122; G Corrigan, *Sepoys in the trenches* (1999) pp.8,14,18,27 – A large number of Indian Army officers were on leave in the UK when war broke out as it was the Indian holiday season due to the prevailing monsoons; WE Wynn, *Ambush* (1937) pp.30–31; CUL: Crewe Box I/18 file 4, pp.1–3; file 3, 6 Aug 1914 Hankey to Crewe; file 4, Tanga, p.3; CUL: Hardinge 101, 8 Aug 1914 telegram 375 SoS India to Viceroy (Army Dept) f.19; IOR: Barrow MSS EUR E 420/36, 5–8 Aug 1914 diary entries; TNA: CAB 38/28/41, 18 Sep 1914 Barrow memorandum

30. SR Mehrotra, *India and the Commonwealth, 1885–1929* (1965) p.65

31. C Hardinge, *My Indian years 1910–1916: The reminiscences of Lord Hardinge of Penshurst* (1948)

32. EP Hoyt, *The Germans who never lost* (1970); P von Lettow-Vorbeck, *My reminiscences* (nd) p.18

33. E Paice, *Tip and run* (2007) p.15

34. TNA: CAB 42/2/5, 10 Mar 1915 CID Minutes, p.6; ADM 123/138 pp.29–30; JS Corbett, *Official history of the war: Naval operations vol 1* (1920) p.154; S Roskill, *Hankey: Man of secrets 1877–1918 vol 1* (1978) pp.107–108; H Strachan, *War in Africa* (2007) p.vii; The first bullet fired by a British subject in the war was on 12 August 1914 in Togoland.

35. EP Hoyt, *The Germans who never lost* (1970) p.52 claims it was Lettow-Vorbeck who ordered the destruction of the *Möwe*.

36. P von Lettow-Vorbeck, *My reminiscences* (nd) p.28
37. GW Hatchell, 'Maritime relics of the 1914–1918 war' in *Tanganyika Notes and Records* 36 (1954) p.7; EC Holtom, *Two years' captivity in German East Africa, being the personal experiences of surgeon ECH, Royal Navy* (nd) p.23 noted that the patient had a recovering wound under his clothing and that the Germans had put him to bed to make it look more authentic.
38. EP Hoyt, *The Germans who never lost* (1970) pp.19,38,51; KJ Harvey, *Battle of Tanga* (2003) pp.15,29; E Paice, *Tip and run* (2007) pp.14–16; WO Henderson, *The German Colonial Empire 1884–1919* (1993)
39. H Strachan, *War in Africa* (2007) p.101; The historical novel *The ghosts of Africa* by William Stevenson (1980) provides a vivid account of the conflict between the two men.
40. M Page, *KAR* (1998) chapter 2; P von Lettow-Vorbeck, *My reminiscences* (nd) p.249; E Michels, *Der held von Deutch-Ostafrika: Paul von Lettow-Vorbeck, ein preußischer Kolonialoffizier* (2008) pp.98–99
41. R Anderson, *Forgotten front* (2004) p.37
42. R Anderson, *Forgotten front* (2004) pp.37,41; JP Cann, 'Moçambique, German East Africa and the Great War' (2001) p.120; PJ Pretorius, *Jungle man* (1947) p.159
43. FR de Meneses, *Afonso Costa* (2010) pp.41–48
44. P von Lettow-Vorbeck, *My reminiscences* (nd) pp.18–28
45. R Anderson, *Forgotten front* (2004) p.43
46. H Strachan, *War in Africa* (2007) p.102; R Anderson, *Forgotten front* (2004) pp.44–47; C Hordern, *Military operations* (1941) p.58fn; C Lucas, *The empire at war vol 5* (1921) p.319
47. R Anderson, *Forgotten front* (2004) pp.44–45; Royal Naval Society, 'A backwater: Lake Victoria Nyanza during the campaign against German East Africa' in *Royal Naval Review* 9:2 (1921) pp.287–337
48. JP Cann, 'Moçambique, German East Africa & the Great War' (2001) p.116
49. H Strachan, *War in Africa* (2007) p.100; K Forster, 'East African neutrality' (1979) p.78; JE Helmreich, *Belgium and Europe: a study in small power diplomacy* (1976) pp.176–190
50. R Anderson, *Forgotten front* (2004) p.41; G Foden, *Mimi & Toutou* (2005) p.9; C Hordern, *Military operations* (1941) pp.55–56
51. TNA: WO 106/573, 3 Oct 1914; WO 158/483, 4 Oct 1914; FO 371/1882/56308, 3 Oct 1914; R Anderson, *Forgotten front* (2004) p.45
52. JE Helmreich, *Belgium and Europe* (1976) p.183; R Anderson, *Forgotten front* (2004) p.39
53. C Harding, *Frontier patrols: A history of the British South African Police and other Rhodesian forces* (1938) pp.215–216

54. R Anderson, *Forgotten front* (2004) pp.45,47; C Harding, *Frontier patrols* (1938); L Wallace, 'Northern Rhodesia and the last phase of the Great War' in C Lucas, *The empire at war* (1926)

55. R Anderson, *Forgotten front* (2004) p.46; WV Brelsford (ed), *The story of the Northern Rhodesia Regiment* (1990) pp.30–31; C Harding, *Frontier patrols* (1938) p.228; ME Page, *The Chiwaya war* (2000) p.1

56. WV Brelsford (ed), *Northern Rhodesia Regiment* (1990) pp.30–31

57. WV Brelsford (ed), *Northern Rhodesia Regiment* (1990) pp.29,49–50; TNA: CO 417/543 Rhodesian Contingent

58. PA: MSS Dav 11, 22 Sep 1911 telegram SoS Colonies to HCSA sent 6pm; TNA: CO 417/543 Rhodesian Contingent

59. C Harding, *Frontier patrols* (1938) p.216; TNA: CO 417/543 Rhodesian Contingent

60. C Harding, *Frontier patrols* (1938) pp.216–225,235; AE Capell, *The 2nd Rhodesian Regiment in East Africa* (1922) p.1

61. TNA: CO 616/15/32010, 22 Aug 1914, *Defence of North Rhodesia*; C Hordern, *Military operations* (1941) p.168 has three double companies, a battery of four muzzle body guns.

62. See chapter 'Personal, personnel and material'

63. TNA: CO 525/57/38176, 14 Aug 1914 GG Nyasaland to CO

64. O Ransford, *Livingstone's Lake* (1966) p.241; AJ Wills, *Central Africa* (1985)

65. E Paice, *Tip and run* (2007) p.20; O Ransford, *Livingstone's Lake* (1966) p.24; GM Sanderson, 'Gunfire on Nyasa' in *The Nyasaland Journal* 10:2 (1957) pp.25–39. According to GW Hatchell, 'Maritime relics' (1954) p.134, the captain of *Guendolen* was Collins whilst according to TNA: CO 525/57/38176, 14 Aug 1914, GG Nyasaland to CO, f.87 Collins was Captain (RFA) KAR, the other captain on board was Caldecott (RGA) ADC.

66. R Anderson, *Forgotten front* (2004) p.47

67. C Harding, *Frontier patrols* (1938) p.233

68. GM Sanderson, 'Gunfire on Nyasa' (1957) p.31; O Ransford, *Livingstone's Lake* (1966) pp.244–248

69. C Harding, *Frontier patrols* (1938) p.232; O Ransford, *Livingstone's Lake* (1966) p.251

70. R Anderson, *Forgotten front* (2004) p.38

71. H Strachan, *War in Africa* (2007) p.79; R Pélissier, 'Sud-Angola' (1969) p.97

72. R Anderson, *Forgotten front* (2004) pp.48,57; JP Cann, 'Moçambique, German East Africa and the Great War' (2001) p.119

73. R Anderson, *Forgotten front* (2004) pp.49,57; JP Cann, 'Moçambique, German East Africa and the Great War' (2001) p.119

74. JP Cann, 'Moçambique, German East Africa and the Great War' (2001) p.120

75. KJ Harvey, *Battle of Tanga* (2003) pp.1,3,46; R Anderson, *Forgotten front* (2004) pp.22,49; WE Wynn, *Ambush* (1937) chapters 1–10

76. H Strachan, *War in Africa* (2007) p.108; WE Wynn, *Ambush* (1937) p.44

77. KJ Harvey, *Battle of Tanga* (2003) p.48

78. WE Wynn, *Ambush* (1937) pp.23–24

79. KJ Harvey, *Battle of Tanga* (2003) p.48

80. G Corrigan, *Sepoys* (1999) chapter 1

81. R Anderson, *Forgotten front* (2004) pp.41,56; H Strachan, *War in Africa* (2007) p.107; JS Corbett, *Official history: Naval operations vol 2* (1923) p.234

82. R Anderson, *Forgotten front* (2004) p.41; KJ Harvey, B*attle of Tanga* (2003) pp.29–30,49

83. H Strachan, *War in Africa* (2007) p.109

84. H Strachan, *War in Africa* (2007) p.110

85. R Anderson, *Forgotten front* (2004) pp.51–55; H Strachan, *War in Africa* (2007) pp.101–111; EP Hoyt, *The Germans who never lost* (1970) pp.87–97

86. P von Lettow-Vorbeck, *My reminiscences* (nd) p.44

87. CJ Charlewood, 'Naval action Part 1' (1960) p.130

88. For a short description of the attack on Tanga, see H Strachan, *War in Africa* (2007) pp.108–111; KJ Harvey, *Battle of Tanga* (2003)

89. WE Wynn, *Ambush* (1937) p.79

90. H Strachan, *War in Africa* (2007) pp.105–106

91. C Hordern, *Military operations* (1941) pp.97–99

92. R Anderson, *Forgotten front* (2004) pp.52,62

93. R Anderson, *Forgotten front* (2004) p.59

94. RH: MSS Meinertzhagen, 19 Jan 1915; C Hordern, *Military operations* (1941) p.121; R Anderson, *Forgotten front* (2004) p.60

95. EP Hoyt, *The Germans who never lost* (1970) p.65; CJ Charlewood, 'Naval action Part 1' (1960) pp.120–138

96. EP Hoyt, *The Germans who never lost* (1970) pp.87–97

97. RD Layman, *Naval aviation in the First World War: Its impact and influence* (1994) pp.132–133; KJ Harvey, *Battle of Tanga* (2003) p.29; EP Hoyt, *The Germans who never lost* (1970) pp.98–103; B Farwell, *The Great War in Africa 1914–1918* (1987) p.135; HA Jones, *Official history: The war in the air vol 3* (1931) pp.3–5

98. RD Layman, *Naval aviation* (1994) p.132ff

99. AMD Howes, 'Some details of the first twenty-five years of flying in Tanganyika, 1914–1939' in *Tanganyika Notes and Records* 50 (1958) p.39

100. EP Hoyt, *The Germans who never lost* (1970) pp.98–103 B Farwell, *Great War* (1987) p.135; HA Jones, *War in the air* (1931) pp.3–5
101. IWM: MSS Misc 164 (2541) Diary of an unidentified Petty Officer Stoker in HMS Weymouth 1914–1916, 1 Jan 1915; EP Hoyt, *The Germans who never lost* (1970) p.107; CJ Charlewood 'Naval action Part 1' (1960) p.138; B Farwell, *Great War* (1987) p.137
102. WV Brelsford (ed), *Northern Rhodesia Regiment* (1990) pp.49–51; AJ Wills, *Central Africa* (1985) p.234; C Harding, *Frontier patrols* (1938) p.220
103. WV Brelsford (ed), *Northern Rhodesia Regiment* (1990) p.28; ME Page, *The Chiwaya war* (2000) p.71; According to TNA: CO 417/543 Occupation of Caprivi Strip, Buxton appointed a special commissioner from Bechuanaland to oversee the administration of Schuckmannsburg.

Chapter 3   The outbreak of war: Southern Africa, 1914

1. Earl Buxton, *Botha* (1924) p.336
2. SANA: PM 1/1/12 4/37/14, 7 Aug 1914, minute 9/15 by de Villiers
3. B Cloete, *FS Malan* (1946) pp.318–320
4. Earl Buxton, *Botha* (1924) p.125; FV Engelenberg, *Botha* (1929) p.291
5. BJ Liebenberg & SB Spies (eds), *South Africa* (1993) p.98; B Cloete, *FS Malan* (1946) pp.318–20
6. CFJ Muller, *500 years: A history of South Africa* (1990) p.400
7. EA Walker, *A history of Southern Africa* (3rd ed) (1957) p.559; M Brien, *An uneasy anger: De la Rey and the Foster Gang* (2009) p.154ff
8. HS Webb, *The causes of the rebellion* (1915); SANA: UG 10 (1915) CD 7874, *Report on the outbreak of Rebellion and the policy of the government with regard to its suppression*; UG 46 (1916) *Report of the Judicial Committee relating to the recent Rebellion in South Africa*; PJ Sampson, *The capture of de Wet, 1914* (1915); Earl Buxton, *Botha* (1924)
9. WK Hancock and J van der Poel, *Smuts papers vol 3* (1966) in JG Calitz, *Deneys Reitz (1882–1944) Krygsman, avonturier en politikus* (2008) p.198
10. A Seegers, *The military in the making* (1996) pp.20,29
11. RH: MSS Afr s. 2175 George Farrar Box 12/1, 20 Sep 1914
12. SANA: GG 678/9/95, 11 Sep 1914; SRP 3/1, 9–12 Sep 1914
13. JJ Collyer, *South West Africa* (1937) pp.27–28
14. HS Webb, *The causes of the rebellion* (1915) pp.24,30; JJ Collyer, *South West Africa* (1937) p.22
15. PJ Pretorius, *Jungle man* (1947) p.161
16. RH: MSS Afr s. 2175 George Farrar, Box 12/1, 20 Sep 1914
17. RH: MSS Afr s. 2175 George Farrar, Box 12/1, 20 Sep 1914

18. M Brien, *An uneasy anger* (2009) p.154ff

19. Earl Buxton, *Botha* (1924) pp.41–42; Bod: MSS Harcourt 473, 17 Sep 1914

20. HS Webb, *The causes of the rebellion* (Pretoria, 1915); SANA: UG 10 (1915) CD 7874, *Report on the outbreak of Rebellion and the policy of the government with regard to its suppression*; UG 46 (1916) *Report of the Judicial Committee relating to the recent Rebellion in South Africa*; PJ Sampson, *The capture of de Wet, 1914* (1915); Earl Buxton, *Botha* (1924)

21. *East Africa Standard*, 26 Sep 1914 Manifesto issued by Mr van der Horst, leader of Hertzog's followers

22. A Seegers, *The military in the making* (1996) p.29

23. TNA: WO 32/5026, document 32A

24. A Seegers, *Military in the making* (1996) p.29

25. GJ Calitz, *Deneys Reitz* (2008) p.184 The Reitz's were a prominent Boer family; WO Henderson, *German Colonial Empire* (1993) p.123; Earl Buxton, *Botha* (1924) p.45

26. GJ Calitz, *Deneys Reitz* (2008) p.182

27. A Seegers, *Military in the making* (1996) pp.22–29; C Hordern, *Military operations* (1941) p.30; K Ingham, *East Africa* (1965) p.245; *The East African Leader*, 1 & 8 Aug 1914

28. RH: MSS Afr s. 2175 George Farrar, Box 12/1, 20 Sept 1914; This is an interesting point as many of the English speakers had left the country on the outbreak of war to return to Britain to fight in Europe.

29. A Samson, *Britain, South Africa and East Africa* (2006) p.85; EM Ritchie, *The unfinished war: The drama of Anglo-German conflict in Africa in relation to the future of the British Empire* (1940) p.161

30. RH: MSS Afr s. 2175 George Farrar Box 15/2, f.10, typed record

31. D Reitz, *Trekking on* (1933) p.91

32. C Harding, *Frontier patrols* (1938) p.217; WV Brelsford, *Northern Rhodesia Regiment* (1990) p.28; M Maritz, *My lewe en strewe* (1939)

33. WK Hancock and J van der Poel, *Smuts papers vol 3* (1966) p.275; BJ Liebenberg & SB Spies (eds), *South Africa* (1993) p.103; R Davenport, *South Africa* (1991) p.246; C Hordern, *Military operations* (1941) p.196; C Harding, *Frontier patrols* (1938) p.226

34. H Strachan, *War in Africa* (2007) pp.75 76

35. H Strachan, *War in Africa* (2007) p.75; EP Hoyt, *The Germans who never lost* (1970) p.166

36. RH: MSS Afr s. 2175 George Farrar Box 15/2, f.10, typed record

37. R Keiser, *The South African Governor General 1910–1919* (1975) chapter on rebellion

38. SS Swart, *The rebels of 1914: Masculinity, republicanism & the social forces that shaped the Boer rebellion* (1997) chapter 7

39. GJ Calitz, *Deneys Reitz* (2008) p.194; WO Henderson has the bombing of Swakopmund on 18 September 1914 and Walfisch Bay on Christmas Day 1914, p.123

40. R Keiser, 'The South African Governor General' (1975) chapter GSWA

41. RH: MSS Afr s. 2175 George Farrar Box 12/1, 20 Sep 1914

42. H Strachan, *War in Africa* (2007) p.79; R Pélissier, 'Sud-Angola' (1969) p.97

43. SANA: GG 9/77/3, 18 Aug 1914 Lisbon to FO

44. N Stassen, *Afrikaners in Angola* (2009); R Pélissier, 'Sud-Angola' (1969) p.98

45. R Pélissier, 'Sud-Angola' (1969) p.98; JP Cann, 'Angola and the Great War' (2001) pp.149–160

46. SANA: GG 9/77/3, 26 Oct 1914 Consul General LM to GG Pretoria

47. JP Cann, 'Angola and the Great War' (2001) pp.149–160

48. R Pélissier, 'Sud-Angola' (1969) pp.99–101; JP Cann, 'Angola and the Great War' (2001)

Chapter 4   German South West Africa, Angola and Southern Africa, 1915

1. EM Ritchie, *Unfinished war* (1940) p.160; Bod: MSS Harcourt 471, 2 Jan 1915, 4 Jan 1915

2. T Macdonald, *Ouma Smuts: The first lady of South Africa* (nd); E Truter, *Tibbie: Rachel Isabella Steyn, 1865–1955: Haar lewe was haar boodskap* (1997); FJ Pretorius, *Life on commando* (1999) chapter 10; JC Steyn, *Trowe Afrikaners* (1987); SS Swart, *The rebels of 1914* (1997) chapter 7

3. Bod: MSS Harcourt 474, 13 May 1915 Buxton to Harcourt

4. WK Hancock and J van der Poel, *Smuts papers vol 3* (1966) p.271

5. R Wingate, 'In Memoriam: Sydney Charles, Earl Buxton, GCMG (Sometime Governor General of South Africa and for Twelve Years President of the African Society)' in *Journal of the Royal African Society* 34:134 (1935) pp.1–6

6. JJ Collyer, *South West Africa* (1937) p.152

7. WK Hancock and J van der Poel, *Smuts papers vol 3* (1966) p.275; IWM: MSS 87/47/8 Smith-Dorrien, File B, 16 Nov 1915 Buxton to Bonar Law

8. H Strachan, *War in Africa* (2007) pp.82–83

9. JJ Collyer, *South West Africa* (1937) p.9

10. JJ Collyer, *South West Africa* (1937) pp.155–156

11. The official history and Buxton's notes have four prongs with Smuts in overall command of the Southern forces and Botha in charge of the North. For a summary of the campaign, see H Paterson, 'First allied victory: the

South African campaign in German South West Africa, 1914–1915' in *South African Military History Journal* 13:2 (2004)

12. Bod: MSS Harcourt 473, 11 Sep 1914 Buxton to Harcourt
13. GJ Calitz, *Deneys Reitz* (2008) p.194; JJ Collyer, *South West Africa* (1937) pp.54–56
14. RH: MSS Afr s. 2175 George Farrar Box 15/2; f.18; Farrar is not mentioned in Collyer's history of GSWA.
15. RH: MSS Afr s. 2175 George Farrar, note on file
16. JJ Collyer, *South West Africa* (1937) p.52; H Strachan, *War in Africa* (1997) p.91
17. J Sutton, *Wait for the wagon: The story of the Royal Corps of Transport and its predecessors, 1794–1993* (1998) pp.87–88
18. JJ Collyer, *South West Africa* (1937) pp.137,144
19. RH: MSS Afr s. 2175 George Farrar Box 12/1, 3 Jan 1915 to Lady Farrar; S Monick, 'The third man: Willy Trick and the German Air Force in South West Africa in World War One' in *South African Military History Journal* 5:3 (1988) dates the attack as 17 Dec 1914; V Alhadeff, *South Africa in two World Wars: A newspaper history* (1979) p.20
20. JJ Collyer, *South West Africa* (1937) p.139
21. H Strachan, *War in Africa* (2007) pp.81–82
22. Bod: MSS Harcourt 474 f.181, 25 Apr 1915 Buxton to Harcourt; A Wienholt, *The story of a lion hunt; with some of the hunter's military adventures during the war* (nd) pp.30–31
23. H Strachan, *War in Africa* (2007) pp.88–89; P von Lettow-Vorbeck, *My reminiscences* (nd) Preface; A Wienholt, *Lion hunt* (nd) pp.46–48; W Matten-Klodt (translator: Oakley Williams) *A fugitive in South West Africa, 1908–1920* (1931); C Hordern, *Military operations* (1941) pp.195–196
24. H Strachan, *War in Africa* (2007) p.91
25. P von Lettow-Vorbeck, *my reminiscences* (nd) pp.18–28
26. JJ Collyer, *South West Africa* (1937) pp.146–152
27. JJ Collyer, *South West Africa* (1937) pp.146–154
28. Cd 7873 p.4 in MW Swanson, 'South West Africa in Trust 1915–1919' in P Gifford & WMR Louis, *Britain and Germany* (1967) p.632
29. H Strachan, *War in Africa* (2007) pp.91–92
30. SANA: PM 1/5/714, 21 Jan 1918; H Strachan, *War in Africa* (2007) pp.91–92
31. FR de Meneses, 'Too serious a matter' (1998) p.91; R Pélissier, 'Sud-Angola' (1969) pp.99–101
32. JP Cann, 'Angola and the Great War' (2001) p.162
33. WV Brelsford, *Northern Rhodesia Regiment* (1990) pp.28–29

34. MW Swanson, 'South West Africa' (1967) p.635
35. Bod: MSS Harcourt 471 various papers
36. SAL,CT: MSC 15 Merriman box 39 doc 329
37. TNA: CO 616/23/17379 & Bod: MSS Harcourt 474, 14 Apr 1915 GG SA to SoS Colonies (rec 11.40am); BLM: MSS Buxton 9930 [Provisional listing, box 21, file May–Aug 1915] 26 Apr 1915 Buxton to Lulu [Harcourt]. Bonar Law replaced Harcourt in Jun 1915; PA: MSS Dav 27/21, 11 Aug 1915 Buxton to Bonar Law
38. WSA: MSS Long 947/469, 19 Apr 1915 Crewe to Long (President of the Local Government Board following the formation of Asquith's coalition government. He became Colonial Secretary in Autumn 1916)
39. TNA: CO 616/23/17379, 14 Apr 1915 telegram GG SA to SoS Colonies (rec 11.40am)
40. G Corrigan, *Mud, blood and poppycock* (2004) p.230
41. *De Volkstem* (Pretoria) 27 Apr 1915, 'Hier en daaroor'
42. PA: MSS BL 50/1/24, 29 Dec 1915 John Simon to Bonar Law enclosing letter dated 28 Nov 1915
43. PA: MSS BL 50/1/24, 29 Dec 1915 John Simon to Bonar Law
44. A Samson, *Britain, South Africa and East Africa* (2006) pp.104–105
45. Bod: MSS Harcourt 474 various correspondence Mar–May 1915
46. TNA: CO 616/23/17379, 11 May 1915 Kitchener private & personal draft; PA: MSS Dav 27/5, 8 Jun 1915 Buxton to Bonar Law
47. A Samson, *Britain, South Africa and East Africa* (2006) p.115
48. Various in Bod: MSS Harcourt 471–475
49. Bod: MSS Harcourt 472, 5 May 1915 meeting with Graaff and Burton
50. TNA: CO 616/23/17379, 14 Apr 1915 GG SA to SoS Colonies (rec 11.40am); 9 May 1915 GG SA to SoS Colonies (rec 3.15pm); DDA: DC 744 box 1717, 26 Nov 1915 report; C Hordern, *Military operations* (1941) p.165
51. SANA: DC/2/74/1717, 26 Nov 1915 Report
52. See C Hordern, *Military operations* (1941) p.601 for list of Imperial Service and Indian Regular troops
53. The tension between South Africa and India was over South Africa's attitude towards Indian immigration and marriages. Gandhi had been fighting for Indian rights from the late twentieth century until 1914 when he left for India on the outbreak of war.
54. *De Burger*, 15 Feb 1918 'Eie litsbeskikking vir inboorlinge in duitse kolonies,' p.4; R Hyam, *South African expansion* (1972) pp.1,23
55. TNA: CO 616/27/35472, 31 Jul 1915 telegram GG SA to SoS Colonies (rec 10.30pm); SANA: GG 667 9/93/14, 31 Jul 1915 minute 995 signed by Botha and Smuts; A Grundlingh, *Fighting their own war: South African blacks*

and the First World War (1987) discusses black involvement, his PhD thesis (University of South Africa, 1981) includes the involvement of Indians and coloureds.

56. SANA: GG 667 9/93/14, 12 Aug 1915 telegram SoS Colonies to GG (copied to Ministers 13 Aug); A Grundlingh, *Fighting their own war* (1987) pp.96–114

57. B Nasson, *Springboks* (2007) pp.157–159

58. TNA: CO 616/28/44145, 28 Aug 1915 minute 1136, SANA: GG 667 9/93/14, 29 Aug 1915 secret GG to SoS Colonies

59. A Grundlingh, *Fighting their own war* (1987) p.40

60. A Grundlingh, *Fighting their own war* (1987) pp.40,58; KW Grundy, *Soldiers without politics* (1983) p.55

61. TNA: CAB 45/44, Fendall diary, 1 Jun 1917, f.76; AE Capell, *2nd Rhodesian Regiment* (1922) p.94

62. N Clothier, *Black valour: The South African Native Labour Contingent 1916–1918 and the sinking of the Mendi* (1998) p.1. A total of 625 lives were lost, this figure includes ten whites.

63. The SANNC became the ANC. Grundlingh, *Fighting their own war* (1987) focuses mainly on natives sent to France, although general comments have also been made. Not much information has been kept on the native forces sent to East Africa.

64. SANA: GG 667 9/93/14, 29 Aug 1915 secret telegram GG to SoS Colonies; *De Volkstem*, 5 Oct 1915 'Generaal Botha te Potchefstroom'

65. *De Volkstem*, 5 Oct 1915 'Generaal Botha te Potchefstroom'; As reported in *De Volkstem* on 18 Oct 1915, he reiterated this point in Rustenburg

66. KW Grundy, *Soldiers without politics* (1983) p.53

67. DF Malan, in the years before 1948, was in favour of keeping the coloureds on his side. When he decided that Afrikaner nationalism was more important, he sacrificed his political relationship with coloureds.

68. Earl Buxton, *Botha* (1924) p.223

69. TNA: CO 616/28/44145, 28 Aug 1915 minute 1136

70. SANA: DC/2/74/1717, 26 Nov 1915 Report

71. SANA: GG 667 9/93/14, 25 Aug 1915 APO to Buxton; GG 574 9/41/17, 12 Aug 1914 J Curry, South Africa Coloured Union to Botha; GG 575 9/41/30, 30 Aug 1914 Natal Indian Society to Acting GG; A Grundlingh, *Fighting their own war* (1987) p 14. KW Grundy, *Soldiers without politics* (1993) pp.50–2

72. TNA: CO 616/31/49709, 26 Oct 1915 Bonar Law to Chamberlain

73. Supported by A Grundlingh, *Fighting their own war* (1987) p.14

74. TNA: CO 533/161/35755, 12 Aug 1915 note by Steel-Maitland; CO 533/161/37457, 13 Aug 1915 WO to CO; CO 533/160/7814, 15 Feb 1915 Wapshare to WO (rec 3.55pm); SANA: GG 667 9/93/7, 10 Aug 1915 secret minute 1037; PA: MSS Dav 27/10, 29 Jun 1915 Buxton to Bonar Law; C Harding, *Frontier patrols* (1938) pp.216–225

75. HJ Simons & RE Simons, *Class and colour in South Africa 1850–1950* (1969) pp.176–186

76. PA: MSS Dav 27/5, 8 Jun 1915, Buxton to Bonar Law; *The Bloemfontein Post*, 6 Aug 1915 'Poor recruiting'

77. This is not mentioned in Meinertzhagen's original diaries at RH

78. TNA: CO 533/161/21958, 13 May 1915 CO by Fiddes

79. *De Volkstem* (Pretoria) 21 Sep 1915, 'Generaal Botha beantwoord vragen'; WA Kleynhans, *Election manifestos* (1987); *Bloemfontein Post*, 13 Nov 1915, p.3; *De Volkstem*, 19 Jan 1915, 'Expedisie naar DOA,' A letter by 'Ou Philip' suggests farms to entice recruits

80. PA: MSS Dav 27/21, 11 Aug 1915 Buxton to Bonar Law

81. TNA: WO 106/572, 15 Jul 1915 GG SA to SoS Colonies; WA Kleynhans, *Election manifestos* (1987)

82. TNA: CO 616/27/32634, 15 Jul 1915 HC SA to SoS Colonies (rec 1.45pm)

83. TNA: CO 616/27/32634, 16 Jul 1915 CO minute; *De Volkstem*, 5 Oct 1915 'Generaal Botha te Potchefstroom'

84. SANA: MSS Smuts vol 13, 30 May 1915 Botha to Smuts; WA Kleynhans, *Election manifestos* (1987)

85. TNA: CO 616/27/34016, 23 Jul 1915 GG SA to SoS Colonies (rec 1.10am); WO 106/572, 23 Jul 1915 GG SA to SoS Colonies; CO 616/27/32634, 16 Jul 1915 Sperling minute; WO 106/572, 20 Jul 1915 SoS Colonies to HC SA; Earl Buxton, *Botha* (1924) pp.238–239; FV Engelenburg, *Botha* (1929) p.310

86. Bod: MSS Harcourt 472, 19 May 1915 meeting with Graaff and Burton, f.263

87. PA: MSS Dav 27/59, 1 Dec 1915 letter Buxton to Bonar Law; *Matatiele Mail* Dec 1915 various

88. TNA: CO 533/162/53575, 9 Nov 1915 WO to Smuts (sent 11.40am)

89. IWM: MSS 87/47/8 Smith Dorrien, Extract private and personal Lord Buxton to Bonar Law, 16 Nov 1915; PA: MSS Dav 27/21, 11 Aug 1915 Buxton to Bonar Law; MSS Dav 27/46, 9 Nov 1915 meeting with Smuts

90. TNA: CO 533/162/53957, 12 Nov 1915 personal GG SA to SoS Colonies, 13 Nov 1915 SoS Colonies to GG SA (sent 5.35pm); PA: MSS Dav 27/51, 9 Nov 1915 Buxton meeting with Smuts

91. PA: MSS Dav 27/21, 11 Aug 1915 Buxton to Bonar Law

92. PA: MSS Dav 27/46, 9 Sep 1915 Bonar Law to Buxton; MSS Dav 27/51, 9 Nov 1915 Buxton to Bonar Law; WK Hancock and J van der Poel, *Smuts papers vol 3* (1966) pp.325–326

93. AJ Smithers, *The man who disobeyed: Sir Horace Smith-Dorrien and his enemies* (1970)

94. PA: MSS Dav 27/21, 11 Aug 1915 Buxton to Bonar Law

95. TNA: CAB 45/35 file I, refers to telegram of 28 Jun 1915

96. PA: MSS Dav 27/27, 3 Sep 1915 Buxton to Bonar Law; various biographies on Smuts

Chapter 5   War on the waters and in the air, 1915–1917

1. B Nasson, *Springboks* (2010); K Robbins, *The First World War* (1993); H Strachan (ed), *The Oxford illustrated history of the First World War* (1998); M Gilbert, *First World War* (1994); J Keegan, *The First World War* (1999)

2. GH Cassar, *Kitchener's war: British strategy from 1914–1918* (2004) pp.160–161

3. E Paice, *Tip and run* (2007) pp.104–106; GH Cassar, *Kitchener's war* (2004) pp.160–161; P von Lettow-Vorbeck, *My reminiscences* (nd) pp.88–91; EP Hoyt, *The Germans who never lost* (1970); H Fecitt, *The East African Maxim Gun Company* [online: kaiserscross]; Royal Naval Society, 'A backwater' (1921) pp.287–337

4. EP Hoyt, *The Germans who never lost* (1970) p.109; CJ Charlewood, 'Naval action on the Tanganyika coast, 1914–1917' Part 1 & 2 in *Tanganyika Notes and Records* 54 & 55 (1960); AMD Howes, 'Twenty-five years of flying' (1958); C Weber & D Lint (exec producers) *The jungle navy* (1999)

5. B Farwell, *Great War* (1987) p.142

6. EP Hoyt, *The Germans who never lost* (1970) pp.112–125,160; GW Hatchell, 'Maritime relics' (1954) pp.1–2; CJ Charlewood, 'Naval action on the Tanganyika coast, 1914–1917 Part 2' in *Tanganyika Notes and Records* 55 (1960) pp.162–164; P von Lettow-Vorbeck, *My reminiscences* (nd) p.86

7. PJ Pretorius, *Jungle man* (1947) pp.14,161–162

8. GW Hatchell, 'Maritime relics' (1954) p.10

9. PJ Pretorius, *Jungle man* (1947) pp.15–27

10. R Anderson, *Forgotten front* (2004) pp.56–57; H Strachan, *War in Africa* (2007) pp.116–117; RD Layman, *Naval aviation* (1994) pp.132–136; B Farwell, *Great War* (1987) pp.137,148; HA Jones, *War in the air* (1931) pp.3–14

11. PJ Pretorius, *Jungle man* (1947) pp.15–18,26–27

12. EP Hoyt, *The Germans who never lost* (1970) pp.127–129,191–202; CJ Charlewood, 'Naval action Part 2' (1960) p.165; GW Hatchell, 'Maritime

relics' (1954) pp.13–17; G Foden, *Mimi & Toutou* (2005) p.76 refers to Rosenthal as captain of the *Königsberg*.

13. CJ Charlewood, 'Naval action Part 2' (1960) p.160
14. EP Hoyt, *The Germans who never lost* (1970) pp.150,161,165,197–202; G Foden, *Mimi & Toutou* (2005) p.76
15. GW Hatchell, 'Maritime relics' (1954); CJ Charlewood, 'Naval action Parts 1 and 2' (1960)
16. G Foden, *Mimi and Toutou* (2005) p.22
17. Summary in DO Stratford, 'Naval ships move overland up Africa' in *South African Military History Journal* 1:4 (1969); G Foden, *Mimi and Toutou* (2005); C Weber & D Lint (exec producers) *The jungle navy* (1999)
18. TNA: CO 417/567/23315 Note to HCSA
19. G Foden, *Mimi and Toutou* (2005); P Shankland, *The phantom flotilla* (1968); EP Hoyt, *The Germans who never lost* (1970) pp.182–183; RD Layman, *Naval aviation* (1994) pp.135–136 states four planes
20. E Paice, *Tip and run* (2007) pp.147,149; B Farwell, *Great War* (1987) pp.241–242
21. WV Brelsford, *Northern Rhodesia Regiment* (1990) p.60
22. R Anderson, *Forgotten front* (2004) pp.109,133–134; E Paice, *Tip and run* (2007) pp.151,235; EP Hoyt, *The Germans who never lost* (1970) pp.184–192; GW Hatchell, 'Maritime relics' (1954) pp.11,18; B Farwell, *Great War* (1987) p.242; The *Gotzen* was later raised, refurbished and in 2011 still serving as the ferry *Liemba*. Note: Hoyt's details conflict with the other sources in terms of names.
23. R Anderson, *Forgotten front* (2004) p.107
24. EP Hoyt, *The Germans who never lost* (1970) p.178; supported by R Anderson, *Forgotten front* (2004) p.107; E Paice, *Tip and run* (2007) pp.209,211
25. R Anderson, *Forgotten front* (2004) p.182
26. CJ Charlewood, 'Naval action Part 2' (1960) pp.168–169; E Paice, *Tip and run* (2007) p.250
27. R Anderson, *Forgotten front* (2004) pp.138–139
28. IWM: MSS 98/1/1 Charlewood, p.10; E Paice, *Tip and run* (2007) p.245; C Hordern, *Military operations* (1941) pp.379–381
29. DP Tidy, 'They mounted up as eagles (A brief tribute to the South African Air Force)' in *South African Military History Journal* 5:6 (1982)
30. CJ Nöthling, *Suid-Afrika in die Eerste Wêreldoorlog (1914–1918)* (1994) pp.59–61; HA Jones, *War in the air* (1931) pp.15–16
31. JOEO Mahncke, 'Aircraft operations in the German colonies, 1911–1916: The Fliegtruppe of the Imperial German Army' in *South African Military History Journal* 12:2 (2001)

32. CJ Nöthling, *Suid-Afrika* (1994) pp.61–63; HA Jones, *War in the air* (1931) pp.14–19
33. JOEO Mahncke, 'Aircraft operations' (2001)
34. JOEO Mahncke, 'Aircraft operations' (2001)
35. E Paice, *Tip and run* (2007) pp.229–230
36. HA Jones, *War in the air* (1931) p.21
37. AE Capell, *2nd Rhodesian Regiment* (1922) p.39
38. AE Capell, *2nd Rhodesian Regiment* (1922) p.41
39. AMD Howes, 'Twenty-five years of flying' (1958) p.40; HA Jones, *War in the air* (1931) p.22
40. E Paice, *Tip and run* (2007) p.204
41. TNA: CAB 45/35, p.49
42. HA Jones, *War in the air* (1931) pp.21–68 contains exploits of the air services in East Africa
43. CJ Thornhill, *Taking Tanganyika* (2004) pp.146–147
44. AE Capell, *2nd Rhodesian Regiment* (1922) p.39; Lettow-Vorbeck in HA Jones, *War in the air* (1931) p.23
45. E Paice, *Tip and run* (2007) p.353
46. Frank Contey to B Garfield, *The Meinertzhagen mystery: The life and legend of a colossal fraud* (2007) pp.126–127,281–282; R Anderson, *Forgotten front* (2004) p.249; E Paice, *Tip and Run* (2007) pp.347–350
47. W Lloyd-Jones, *KAR* (1926) p.200
48. GL King, *A study of the operations in German East Africa during the World War 1914–1918* (1930) pp.14–15
49. IWM: MSS 98/1/1 Charlewood, p.16
50. R Anderson, *Forgotten front* (2004) p.231

Chapter 6   East Africa, 1915–1917

1. KP Adgie, *Askaris, asymmetry, and small wars: Operational art and the German East Africa campaign 1914–1918* (2001)
2. B Farwell, *Great War* (1987) p.201
3. J Listowell, *Tanganyika* (1965) p.56
4. Bennett in BM Du Toit, *The Boers* (1998) p.100; IWM: PP/MCR/62, GB Buxton, f.109; H Fecitt, *The death of Lance Corporal Otto Faber, 2nd Rhodesian Regiment* and *The East Africa Maxim Gun Company 1915–1916* [online: kaiserscross]; The regiment was raised in South Rhodesia in November 1914, sailed from Beira on 10 March 1915 and landed at Mombasa on 14 March 1915.
5. RH: MSS Micr Afr 599 Noel Smith, 7 Nov 1914 from Uasin Gishu; also in CJ Thornhill, *Taking Tanganyika* (2004) p.74

6. MPK Sorrenson, *Origins of European settlement in Kenya* (1968) pp.182–183
7. E Trzebinski, *Kenya pioneers* (1985) pp.182–183
8. ES Thompson, 'A machine gunner's odyssey through German East Africa: the diary of ES Thompson, Part 1, 17 Jan–24 May 1916' in *South African Military History Journal* 7:4 (1988)
9. IWM: MSS 87/47/8 Smith-Dorrien, 20 Dec 1915 Smith-Dorrien to my dear Asquith
10. P von Lettow-Vorbeck, *My reminiscences* (nd) pp.69–72
11. E Paice, *Tip and run* (2007) pp.80–83
12. C Hordern, *Military operations* (1941) pp.199–202; E Paice, *Tip and run* (2007) pp.94–97; Royal Naval Society, 'A backwater' (1921) pp.287–337
13. E Paice, *Tip and run* (2007) pp.108–109; C Hordern, *Military operations* (1941) pp.183–186; C Harding, *Frontier patrols* (1938) p.230
14. AJ Wills, *Central Africa* (1985) p.237
15. IWM: MSS 87/47/8 Smith-Dorrien; H Smith-Dorrien, *Memories of 48 years service* (1925) p.483; R Anderson, *Forgotten front* (2004) p.107; AJ Smithers, *The man who disobeyed* (1970)
16. Earl Buxton, *Botha* (1924) pp.293–295; R Anderson, *Forgotten front* (2004) p.110
17. R Anderson, *Forgotten front* (2004) pp.110–111
18. JA Brown, *They fought for king and Kaiser: South Africans in German East Africa, 1916* (1991) pp.73–79; AE Capell, *2nd Rhodesian Regiment* (1922)
19. IWM: MSS 87/47/8 Smith-Dorrien, File B letter to War Office, 31 Jan 1916
20. E Paice, *Tip and run* (2007) p.194fn
21. TNA: CAB 42/8/1, 3 Feb 1916 War Cabinet Meeting, p.12; PA: MSS Dav 8/83, 18 Mar 1916 Buxton to Bonar Law; F Brett Young, *Marching on Tanga with General Smuts in East Africa* (Glasgow, 1917)
22. JP Cann, 'Moçambique, German East Africa and the Great War' (2001) p.125; Cann has the date wrong. It should be 23 February 1916; R Anderson, *Forgotten front* (2004) p.117
23. IWM: MSS 87/47/8 Smith-Dorrien, File A, 18 Dec 1915 Instructions; R Anderson, *Forgotten front* (2004) p.111
24. E Paice, *Tip and run* (2007) p.192
25. C Hordern, *Military operations* (1941) pp.263–264
26. WE Wynn, *Ambush* (1937) pp.233–234
27. JP Cann, 'Moçambique, German East Africa and the Great War' (2001) pp.120–127
28. R Anderson, *Forgotten front* (2004) p.125
29. TNA: FO 371/2596/75000, 3 Apr 1916 Carnegie to Grey
30. TNA: FO 371/2596/67473, 9 Apr 1916 McDonnell, Lorenço Marques (rec 8pm)

31. JP Cann, 'Moçambique, German East Africa and the Great War' (2001) p.127
32. TNA: FO371/2599/72511, 17 Apr 1916 Carnegie
33. IWM: PP/MCR/C17, Northey war diaries; R Anderson, *Forgotten front* (2004) pp.117–118,138–139; C Hordern, *Military operations* (1941) pp.480,499–500
34. H Fecitt, *The Uganda Volunteer Reserve 1914–1916* [online: kaiserscross]; Royal Naval Society, 'A backwater' (1921) pp.287–337
35. R Anderson, *Forgotten front* (2004) pp.122–123; H Fecitt, *The Uganda Volunteer Reserve 1914–1916* [online: kaiserscross]; C Hordern, *Military history* (1941) pp.208,400–402
36. R Anderson, *Forgotten front* (2004) pp.124–125
37. P von Lettow-Vorbeck, *My reminiscences* (nd) pp.137–139,143,211; Mahiwa was the last battle fought in German East Africa.
38. R Anderson, *Forgotten front* (2004) p.136
39. JP Cann, 'Moçambique, German East Africa and the Great War' (2001) p.132; R Anderson, *Forgotten front* (2004) p.121; E Paice, *Tip and run* (2007) p.269
40. R Anderson, *Forgotten front* (2004) p.122; E Paice, *Tip and run* (2007) p.267
41. R Anderson, *Forgotten front* (2004) p.140; E Paice, *Tip and run* (2007) p.208 refers to Botha's visit being 7 July; Earl Buxton, *Botha* (1924) p.290; K Hancock and J van der Poel, *Smuts papers vol 3* (1966) pp.384,391 has Botha in East Africa from late June to 6 August. He toured and visited the wounded and sick, falling ill himself.
42. WK Hancock, *Smuts: The sanguine years 1870–1919 vol 1* (1962) p.551
43. D Fewster, *The Journals of Dan Fewster: A First World War British Army Battery Sergeant's account of his experiences in German East Africa and France* [online: www.jfhopkin.karoo.net] 11 Aug 1918
44. R Anderson, *Forgotten front* (2004) pp.139–144,152
45. C Harding, *Frontier patrols* (1938) pp.270–272
46. PA: Bonar Law 50/1/41, 22 Aug 1916, Fiddes to Bonar Law; R Anderson, *Forgotten front* (2004) pp.140–144; P von Lettow-Vorbeck, *My reminiscences* (nd) p.158; E Paice, *Tip and run* (2007) p.251; During the struggles to occupy the Central railway the only Victoria Cross to be awarded to a South African in East Africa was won by Captain WA Bloomfield of van Deventer's Scouts following an encounter at Kisagala Hill, Mlali, in the Uluguru Mountains. H Fecitt, *Captain WA Bloomfield VC* [online: kaiserscross]
47. R Anderson, *Forgotten front* (2004) pp.134–135; E Paice, *Tip and run* (2007) pp.228–229,242–243; JE Helmreich, *Belgium and Europe* (1976) pp.183,192
48. B Farwell, *Great War* (1987) p.289
49. TNA: FO 371/2599/80269, 27 Apr 1916 F Villiers to Grey; FO 371/2599/85501, 4 May 1916 private Villiers to A Nicholson (FO) 4 May 1916 Villiers to Grey; E Paice, *Tip and run* (2007) p.316

50. CJ Thornhill, *Taking Tanganyika* (2004) pp.186–187
51. R Anderson, *Forgotten front* (2004) pp.135,144ff
52. South African *Herald*, 2 Feb 1918, report 18 Jan 1918; R Anderson, *Forgotten front* (2004) p.149; E Paice, *Tip and run* (2007) p.294; JA Brown, *For king and Kaiser* (1991) pp.331–332
53. South African *Herald* (Johannesburg) 26 Jan 1918; E Paice, *Tip and run* (2007) p.289
54. TNA: CO 691/3/53827, 9 Nov 1916, Instructions; R Anderson, *Forgotten front* (2004) p.161
55. C Hordern, *Military operations* (1941) p.509
56. R Anderson, *Forgotten front* (2004) pp.207–208
57. R Anderson, *Forgotten front* (2004) p.157; E Paice, *Tip and run* (2007) pp.243–244
58. H Fecitt, *On the way to Tunduru* {online: kaiserscross}
59. 'Times History' in E Paice, *Tip and run* (2007) p.270
60. E Paice, *Tip and run* (2007) p.270
61. E Paice, *Tip and run* (2007) pp.270–272; J Gus Liebenow, *Colonial rule and political development in Tanzania: The case of the Makonde* (1971) p.84
62. R Anderson, *Forgotten front* (2004) pp.164–165; E Paice, *Tip and run* (2007) p.271
63. EP Hoyt, *The Germans who never lost* (1970) p.208
64. E Paice, *Tip and run* (2007) pp.272–274; FR de Meneses, 'Parliament and the army in Portugal, 1914–1918' in *Journal of Contemporary History* 33:1 (1998); On 22 December 1917 Sidonio Pais, the new Prime Minister, sent Gil's reports to the press
65. JP Cann, 'Moçambique, German East Africa and the Great War' (2001) pp.132,136; R Anderson, *Forgotten front* (2004) p.189
66. R Anderson, *Forgotten front* (2004) p.166
67. R Anderson, *Forgotten front* (2004) p.169
68. P von Lettow-Vorbeck, *My reminiscences* (nd) p.170
69. TNA: FO 371/2856/4468, 8 Jan 1917 Oliphant minute
70. R Anderson, *Forgotten front* (2004) pp.175–178
71. TNA: CO 691/9/2231, 8 Jan 1917 SoSW to Smuts; R Anderson, *Forgotten front* (2004) pp.176–177; E Paice, *Tip and run* (2007) pp.293–294
72. WK Hancock, *Smuts: Sanguine years* (1962) p.223
73. WO 33/858, No 1500, 11 Jan 1917 in R Anderson, *Forgotten front* (2004) p.177
74. TNA: CO 691/9/4108, EGM minute 22 Jan 1917; R Anderson, *Forgotten front* (2004) pp.178–179; E Paice, *Tip and run* (2007) pp.293–298
75. R Anderson, *Forgotten front* (2004) p.215

76. TNA: WO 158/477, 19 Mar 1917 MacDonell to Hoskins in R Anderson, *Forgotten front* (2004) p.216; E Paice, *Tip and run* (2007) p.318

77. TNA: CO 691/9/4108, 22 Jan 1917 EGM note, 20 Jan 1917 CIGS to GOC EA; E Paice, *Tip and run* (2007) p.298

78. Thornton papers in E Paice, *Tip and run* (2007) p.298fn

79. TNA: CAB 23/2 WC, 5 Mar 1917; R Anderson, *Forgotten front* (2004) p.195

80. TNA: CO 691/9/14847, 22 Mar 1917, EGM note

81. P von Lettow-Vorbeck, *My reminiscences* (nd) pp.190–193; R Anderson, *Forgotten front* (2004) pp.184,192

82. GL Simpson, 'British perspectives on Aulihan Somali unrest on the East Africa Protectorate, 1915–1918' in *Northeast African Studies* 6.1:2 (1999) pp.7–43

83. E Paice, *Tip and run* (2007) pp.309–315; H Fecitt, *4th Battalion 4 KAR in the Great War* [online: kaiserscross]

84. R Anderson, *Forgotten front* (2004) pp.188–189, 191

85. TNA: CAB 23/2, War Cabinet meeting 124, 23 Apr 1917, p.2; CO 691/10/23789, 3 Mar 1917 SoSW to Hoskins; CO 691/10/24055, 10 May 1917 Buxton to SoS Colonies and 11 May 1917; LHC: MSS GB99 KCLMA Robertson 8/2/46, 23 Apr 1917 Robertson to Smuts

86. TNA: CAB 23/2, 23 Apr 1917 War Cabinet meeting 124

87. WO 33/953, 22 May 1917 CIGS to van Deventer in R Anderson, *Forgotten front* (2004) p.212

88. TNA: CAB 23/3, 24 Jul 1917 WC 24; E Paice, *Tip and run* (2007) p.303

89. R Anderson, *Forgotten front* (2004) pp.212–218

90. P von Lettow-Vorbeck, *My reminiscences* (nd) p.202; E Paice, *Tip and run* (2007) pp.329–330

91. E Paice, *Tip and run* (2007) p.363

92. E Paice, *Tip and run* (2007) p.363

93. R Anderson, *Forgotten front* (2004) pp.236–237; DN Reach, 'The uses of colonial history and history of Mozambique' in *Cahiers d'Etudes Africaines* 104, 26:4 (1986) pp.707–713

94. WD Downes, *With the Nigerians in East Africa* (1919)

95. R Anderson, *Forgotten front* (2004) pp.248–249

96. HC Clifford, *The Gold Coast Regiment in the East African campaign* (1920)

97. P von Lettow-Vorbeck, *My reminiscences* (nd) pp.210–211; H Fecitt, *Lukuledi mission* [online: kaiserscross]

98. E Paice, *Tip and run* (2007) p.332

99. EP Hoyt, *The Germans who never lost* (1970) pp.226–227; P von Lettow-Vorbeck, *My reminiscences* (nd) pp.220–221

100. P von Lettow-Vorbeck, *My reminiscences* (nd) p.221

101. E Paice, *Tip and run* (2007) pp.332–337; P von Lettow-Vorbeck, *My reminiscences* (nd) p.220
102. R Anderson, *Forgotten front* (2004) pp.255,257; PJ Pretorius, *Jungle man* (1947) pp.182–185; P von Lettow-Vorbeck, *My reminiscences* (nd) pp.220–228; E Paice, *Tip and run* (2007) pp.339–342
103. P von Lettow-Vorbeck, *My reminiscences* (nd) p.236
104. R Anderson, *Forgotten front* (2004) pp.261,263
105. P von Lettow-Vorbeck, *My reminiscences* (nd) p.235
106. South African *Herald*, 26 Jan 1918, p.12
107. P von Lettow-Vorbeck, *My reminiscences* (nd) pp.241–242
108. P von Lettow-Vorbeck, *My reminiscences* (nd) p.234

Chapter 7   Personal, personnel and material

1. RJ Marrion & DSV Fosten, *The British Army 1914–1918* (1978) pp.1–5; SM Miller, *Volunteers on the Veld: Britain's Citizen-Soldiers and the South African War, 1899–1902* (2007)
2. RH: MSS Meinertzhagen; general EA histories
3. PA: MSS Dav 27/59, 1 Dec 1915 Buxton to Bonar Law; AJ Smithers, *The man who disobeyed* (1970)
4. PA: MSS Dav 28/83, 18 Mar 1916 Buxton to Bonar Law
5. E Trzebinski, *Kenya pioneers* (1985) p.187; JA Brown, *For king and Kaiser* (1991); papers and biographies used throughout
6. E Paice, *Tip and run* (2007) p.193
7. Bod: MSS Harcourt 471, 6 Nov 1914, f.66
8. E Paice, *Tip and run* (2007) p.326
9. P von Lettow-Vorbeck, *My reminiscences* (nd) pp.58–60
10. U Schulte-Varnedorff, *Kolonialheld* (2006) p.17; CB Quale, *To live like a pig and die like a dog: Environmental implications for World War 1 in East Africa* (2002) p.40
11. CAC: MSS Hankey HNKY 1/3, 16 Jun 1918, p.240; S Roskill, *Hankey vol 1* (1978) p.563
12. Lettow-Vorbeck in E Paice, *Tip and run* (2007) p.263
13. EP Hoyt, *The Germans who never lost* (1970) p.222; U Schulte-Varendorff, *Kolonialheld* (2006) pp.46–47,76–77
14. R Anderson, *Forgotten front* (2004) p.150
15. Messum in E Paice, *Tip and run* (2007) p.265
16. R Anderson, *Forgotten front* (2004) p.188
17. P von Lettow-Vorbeck, *My reminiscences* (nd) p.142
18. W Lloyd-Jones, *KAR* (1926) pp.198–199

19. P von Lettow-Vorbeck, *My reminiscences* (nd) p.249
20. Think of his attitude towards Gandhi on the India issue pre-1910 and the 1913/1914 strikes.
21. CAC: MSS Hankey HNKY 1/3, 14 Jun 1918, p.240
22. BLM: Buxton, 8 Sep 1919 Buxton to Milner
23. Earl Buxton, *Botha* (1924) p.290; various biographies on Botha and Smuts
24. I Liebenberg, *Sociology, biology or philosophy of a warrior? Reflections on Jan Smuts, guerrilla-being and a politics of choices* (nd) [online: http://www0.sun.ac.za]
25. TNA: FO371/2857/105917, 25 May 1917; R Anderson, *Forgotten front* (2004) pp.210,216
26. LHC: Robertson WR 7/5/59, 5 Apr 1917 Smuts to Robertson
27. LHC: MSS Robertson WR 8/2/46, 23 Apr 1917 Robertson to Smuts
28. LHC: MSS Robertson WR 8/2/47, 1 May 1917 Smuts to CIGS enclosing cables
29. E Paice, *Tip and run* (2007) p.345
30. E Paice, *Tip and run* (2007) p.345
31. B Farwell, *Great War* (1987) p.269
32. BM Du Toit, *The Boers* (1998) pp.2,4,41–42,45,59
33. *East African Standard*, 5 Aug 1914
34. MPK Sorrenson, *Origins of European settlement in Kenya* (1968) p.66; E Trzebinski, *Kenya pioneers* (1985) supports
35. BM Du Toit, *The Boers* (1998) pp.85–86
36. TNA: CAB 45/44, Private diary of Col CP Fendall, 4 Dec 1917, f.70
37. WE Wynn, *Ambush* (1937) pp.233–234
38. TNA: CO 533/161/35755, 12 Aug 1915 note by Read
39. TNA: FO 371/1882/37617, 18 Aug 1914 Grey comment on Sperling minute
40. TNA: CO 525/57/38176, 6 Oct 1914 note on cover
41. D Killingray, 'African voices from two world wars' in *Historical Research* 74:186 (2001) pp.425–443
42. P von Lettow-Vorbeck, *My reminiscences* (nd) p.287
43. M von Herff, *They walk through fire like the blondest Germans: African soldiers serving the Kaiser in German East Africa (1885–1914)* (1991)
44. P von Lettow-Vorbeck, *My reminiscences* (nd) pp.22–24; E Paice, *Tip and run* (nd) pp.287–288
45. TNA: CAB 45/27 pp.2–3; W Lloyd-Jones *KAR* (1926) p.186
46. WE Wynn, *Ambush* (1937) p.88; A Grundlingh, *Fighting their own war* (1987); G Hodges, *Kariakor* (1999); JB Gewalt, *Colonial warfare: Hehe and World War One, the wars besides Maji Maji in south-western Tanzania* (2005)

47. C Hordern, *Military operations* (1941) p.131fn; E Paice, *Tip and run* (2007) chapter 19; H Fecitt, *Cole's Scouts 1914–1915* [online: kaiserscross]
48. IWM: PP/MCR/150 Norman King diaries; GL Simpson, 'Aulihan Somali unrest' (1999) pp.7–43
49. E Paice *Tip and run* (2007) pp.213–223; W Lloyd-Jones *KAR* (1926) p.210; M Page, *KAR* (1998) chapter 2; TNA: CO 533/160/7814, 15 Feb 1915 Wapshare to WO (rec 3.55pm); WO 32/25822, 18 Feb 1916 CIGS to Smuts; Aga Khan, *India in transition: A study in political evolution* (1918)
50. BM Du Toit, *The Boers* (1998) p.95; E Paice, *Tip and run* (2007) chapter 19
51. PJ Pretorius, *Jungle man* (1947) pp.176–177
52. CJ Thornhill, *Taking Tanganyika* (2004) p.142; PJ Pretorius, *Jungle man* (1947)
53. R Meinertzhagen, *Army Diaries, 1899–1926* (1960); CJ Thornhill, *Taking Tanganyika* (1937); PJ Pretorius, *Jungle man* (1947); A Wienholt, *Lion hunt* (nd)
54. TNA: CAB 45/27 Report 15 Jun 1933, pp.6,9
55. P von Lettow-Vorbeck, *My reminiscences* (nd) p.20; C Hordern, *Military operations* (1941) p.16
56. P Lettow-Vorbeck, *My reminiscences* (nd) p.143; A Wienholt, *Lion hunt* (nd)
57. PJ Pretorius, *Jungle man* (1947) pp.170–171
58. PJ Pretorius, *Jungle man* (1947) p.174; AE Capell, *2nd Rhodesian Regiment* (1922) p.91
59. P von Lettow-Vorbeck, *My reminiscences* (nd) p.150
60. P von Lettow-Vorbeck, *My reminiscences* (nd) pp.137,264,306
61. WE Wynn, *Ambush* (1937) p.88
62. CJ Thornhill, *Taking Tanganyika* (1937) pp.140–141
63. P von Lettow-Vorbeck, *My reminiscences* (nd) pp.193–194
64. RH: MSS Afr S 2051 HM Stirling, 15 Jul 1917, f.199, 3 Oct 1917, f.212
65. R Anderson, *Forgotten front* (2004) p.230
66. G Corrigan, *Sepoys* (1999); G Hodges, *Kariakor* (1999)
67. H Strachan, *War in Africa* (2007) pp.103–104; JL Keene, 'The problem of munitions supply in the First World War and its effects in the Union Defence Force' in *South African Military History Journal* 6:4 (1984)
68. RH: MSS Afr s. 1715 (144) WG Hughes, f.8
69. CJ Thornhill, *Taking Tanganyika* (2004) p.178
70. E Paice, *Tip and run* (2007) p.136
71. JL Keene, 'Munitions supply' (1984)
72. E Paice, *Tip and run* (2007) p.270; chapter 25
73. ES Thompson, 'A machine gunner's odyssey through German East Africa: The diary of ES Thompson part 2' in *South African Military History Journal* 7:5 (1988)

NOTES 259

74. G Hodges, *Kariakor* (1999)
75. W Lloyd-Jones, *KAR* (1926) pp.183–189; A Skinner, *Tanzania and Zanzibar* (nd) p.285; E Paice, *Tip and run* (2007) pp.80–83,108–109; JA Brown, *For king and Kaiser* (1991) pp.124,151; C Hordern, *Military operations* (1941) pp.183–186; C Harding, *Frontier patrols* (1938) p.230
76. D Steinbach, 'Defending the Heimat: The Germans in South West Africa and East Africa during the First World War' in H Jones, J O'Brien, C Smidt-Supprian (eds), *Untold war: New perspectives in First World War studies* (2008); D Steinbach, 'Challenging colonial supremacy: the internment of "enemy aliens" in German East Africa during the First World War' in L Rowe, A Miller, J Kitchen (eds), *Other combatants, other fronts: Competing histories of the First World War* (2011). The focus is mainly on missionaries; EP Hoyt, *The Germans who never lost* (1970) p.236
77. WP Schutz, 'A distant field revisited: Captain WA Bloomfield VC' in *South African Military History Review* 10:3 (1996)
78. IWM: MSS Wapshare 88/61 newscuttings; RH: MSS Meinertzhagen; W Stevenson, *Ghosts of Africa* (1980), a novel, shows the effects of the propaganda and myths which developed around the campaign
79. CJ Thornhill, *Taking Tanganyika* (2004) p.138; PJ Pretorius, *Jungle man* (1947) pp.151–161; AE Capell, *2nd Rhodesian Regiment* (1922) pp.23–24; RV Dolbey, *Sketches of East Africa* (1918); EP Hoyt, *The Germans who never lost* (1970) pp.226–227; P von Lettow-Vorbeck, *My reminiscences* (nd) pp.220–221
80. C Cato, *The navy everywhere* (1919) pp.54–57
81. F Harris, 'Marched 600 miles with fleeing Germans' in *The New York Times*, 16 Sep 1917
82. P von Lettow-Vorbeck, *My reminiscences* (nd) p.239
83. P von Lettow-Vorbeck, *My reminiscences* (nd) pp.320–321
84. G Hodges, *Kariakor* (1999) pp.108–109
85. P von Lettow-Vorbeck, *My reminiscences* (nd) p.106; D Reitz, *Trekking on* (1933) p.140
86. U Schulte-Varnedorff, *Kolonialheld* (2006) p.35; P von Lettow-Vorbeck, *My reminiscences* (nd) p.170
87. P von Lettow-Vorbeck, *My reminiscences* (nd) pp.155,221
88. R Anderson, *Forgotten front* (2004) p.159
89. P von Lettow-Vorbeck, *My reminiscences* (nd) p.99
90. P von Lettow-Vorbeck, *My reminiscences* (nd) pp.289,298–299
91. E Paice, *Tip and run* (2007) p.257
92. WV Brelsford, *Northern Rhodesia Regiment* (1990) p.59
93. RH: MSS Afr S 2051 HM Stirling, 26 Oct 1917, ff.214–216
94. F Harris, '600 miles' 16 Sep 1917

95. P von Lettow-Vorbeck, *My reminiscences* (nd) p.155; JS Brown, 'On battle and disease: The East Africa campaign of 1914–1918' in *Parameters, Journal of the US Army War College* 12:2 (1982) pp.16–24; F Brett Young, *Marching on Tanga* (1917)

96. IWM: MSS PP/MCR/62, GB Buxton, f.98

97. H Fecitt, *The 17th Cavalry East Africa Squadron 1915–1916* [online: kaiserscross]

98. C Cato, *The navy everywhere* (1919) p.57

99. C Cato, *The navy everywhere* (1919) p.58

100. E Paice, *Tip and run* (2007) p.199

101. C Hordern, *Military operations* (1941) p.455fn; D Steinbach, 'Defending the Heimat' (2008); D Steinbach, 'Challenging colonial supremacy' (2011); B Farwell, *Great War* (1987) p.289

102. GW Hatchell, 'The British occupation of the south-western area of Tanganyika' in *Tanganyika Notes and Records* 51 (1958)

103. P von Lettow-Vorbeck, *My reminiscences* (nd) p.133

104. IWM: HL Duff, *Nyasaland in the World War* (1951)

105. TNA: CAB 45/24, 7 Jan 1918 van Deventer to General Staff

106. GW Hatchell, 'British occupation of south-western Tanganyika' (1958) pp.150–153; Byatt became the first Governor of Tanganyika on 22 July 1920

107. Bod: MSS Harcourt 475, 11 Oct 1916 & 11 Jan 1917, ff.13,21

108. G Lukas, *The Young Indiana Jones* shows an extreme case of the confusion

109. LHC: Robertson WR 7/2/36, 11 Nov 1915 Callwell to Robertson

110. E Trzebinski, *Kenya pioneers* (1985) pp.193–196

111. TNA: CAB 45/24 & CO 533/175/36355, 31 Jul 1916

112. LHC: MSS Robertson WR 4/4/30, 29 Jul 1916 Robertson to Smuts; WR 4/4/32, 11 Aug 1916 Smuts to Robertson

113. M Page, 'Recruitment of blacks: Malawians and the Great War: Oral history in the reconstructing of Africa's recent past' in *The Oral History Review* 8 (1980)

114. RH: MSS Afr s. 1715 (144) WG Hughes, f.6

115. RH: MSS Afr s. 2051 HM Stirling, 27 May 1917, f.197

116. C Hordern, *Military operations* (1941) p.265; WD Downes, *With the Nigerians* (1919); HC Clifford, *Gold Coast Regiment* (1920)

117. LHC: MSS Robertson WR 7/5/56, 15 Mar 1917 Smuts to Robertson; M Dixon-Fyle & GR Cole, *New perspectives on the Sierra Leone Krio* (2006)

118. P Lettow-Vorbeck, *My reminiscences* (nd) p.143; R Anderson, *Forgotten front* (2004) p.159

119. C Hordern, *Military operations* (1941) p.35

120. P von Lettow-Vorbeck, *My reminiscences* (nd)
121. Various private letters refer
122. AE Capell, *2nd Rhodesian Regiment* (1922) p.24
123. Various autobiographies, private letters and photos
124. RH: MSS Meinertzhagen; CJ Thornhill, *Taking Tanganyika* (2004); AE Capell, *2nd Rhodesian Regiment* (1922) pp.33–34
125. RH: MSS Micr Afr 599 Noel Smith, 14 Sep 1914, 7 Nov 1914
126. Carbutt in TJ Stapleton, *No insignificant part: The Rhodesia Native Regiment and the East Africa Campaign of the First World War* (2006) p.131
127. IWM: MSS Erskine 06/35/1, p.33, 20 May 1918
128. AE Capell, *2nd Rhodesian Regiment* (1922) p.88
129. Foreword by Cranworth in A Buchanan, *Three years of war in East Africa* (nd) vii
130. Dan Fewster diary in CB Quale, *To live like a pig* (2002) p.56
131. RH: MSS Afr S 2051 J Harry Miller Stirling
132. E Paice, *Tip and run* (2007) p.308
133. H Fecitt, *Cole's Scouts* (supplied by author)
134. H Fecitt, *The East Africa Maxim Gun Company 1915–1916* [online: kaiserscross]

Chapter 8   Last days, 1918

1. The other events being the decision to send ships – the *Marie* and *Kronborg* – to run the blockade; HH Herwig, 'The German victories 1917–1918' and T Travers, 'The Allied victories 1918' in H Strachan (ed), *Illustrated First World War* (1998)
2. P von Lettow-Vorbeck, *My reminiscences* (nd) p.244
3. R Anderson, *Forgotten front* (2004) pp.268,273–274; E Paice, *Tip and run* (2007) pp.365,368,371; H Fecitt, *Mbalama Hill, Portuguese East Africa 1918 and the Gold Coast Regiment advance from Port Amelia* [online: kaiserscross]
4. E Paice, *Tip and run* (2007) p.372
5. P von Lettow-Vorbeck, *My reminiscences* (nd) p.264
6. R Anderson, *Forgotten front* (2004) pp.280 281; E Paice, *Tip and run* (2007) p.373
7. E Paice, *Tip and run* (2007) pp.364–365
8. Boyle in E Paice, *Tip and run* (2007) p.376
9. P von Lettow-Vorbeck, *My reminiscences* (nd) pp.272–276
10. E Paice, *Tip and run* (2007) p.376
11. R Anderson, *Forgotten front* (2004) p.283; E Paice, *Tip and run* (2007) pp.377–378

12. P von Lettow-Vorbeck, *My reminiscences* (nd) pp.281–282
13. P von Lettow-Vorbeck, *My reminiscences* (nd) pp.277,280
14. H Fecitt, *Lioma, 30–31 August 1918* [online: kaiserscross]
15. H Fecitt, *The last shots in Portuguese East Africa* [online: kaiserscross]
16. R Anderson, *Forgotten front* (2004) pp.264–265,270–271; P von Lettow-Vorbeck, *My reminiscences* (nd) p.305
17. R Anderson, *Forgotten front* (2004) pp.290–291; E Paice, *Tip and run* (2007) pp.382,384; P von Lettow-Vorbeck, *My reminiscences* (nd) pp.303–305
18. E Paice, *Tip and run* (2007) p.384
19. E Paice, *Tip and run* (2007) p.383
20. U Schulte-Varnedorff, *Kolonialheld* (2006) p.34; P von Lettow-Vorbeck, *My reminiscences* (nd) p.294; E Michels, *Lettow-Vorbeck* (2008) p.227
21. BM Du Toit, *The Boers* (1993) p.3
22. E Paice, *Tip and run* (2007) p.383
23. E Paice, *Tip and run* (2007) p.384
24. P von Lettow-Vorbeck, *My reminiscences* (nd) pp.306–311; H Fecitt, *November 1918 in East Africa* [online: kaiserscross]
25. E Paice, *Tip and run* (2007) pp.385–386
26. E Paice, *Tip and run* (2007) pp.385–386; Croad in WV Brelsford, *Northern Rhodesia Regiment* (1990) p.61
27. W Lloyd-Jones, *KAR* (1926) pp.193–196
28. E Paice, *Tip and run* (2007) p.386; P von Lettow-Vorbeck, *My reminiscences* (nd) pp.313–314
29. H Fecitt, *November 1918 in East Africa* [online: kaiserscross]
30. Croad in WV Brelsford, *Northern Rhodesia Regiment* (1990) p.61
31. E Paice, *Tip and run* (2007) pp.386–387; P von Lettow-Vorbeck, *My reminiscences* (nd) p.316
32. P von Lettow-Vorbeck, *My reminiscences* (nd) p.318; Croad in WV Brelsford, *Northern Rhodesia Regiment* (1990) p.62
33. AJ Wills, *Central Africa* (1985) p.240
34. E Paice, *Tip and run* (2007) p.388
35. E Paice, *Tip and run* (2007) pp.398–399
36. BM Du Toit, *The Boers* (1998) p.98
37. SE Kanzler, *Expelled from a beloved country: German settlers in Southern Namibia between Colonial War and World War* (2006)
38. TNA: WO 158/907; E Paice, *Tip and run* (2004) pp.388–389
39. E Paice, *Tip and run* (2004) p.289
40. P von Lettow-Vorbeck, *My reminiscences* (nd) pp.321–322
41. E Paice, *Tip and run* (2007) p.390

Chapter 9   Behind the scenes, 1915–1918

1. TNA: CAB 45/27, 15 Jun 1933, Report pp.6,9
2. TNA: WO 106/572, 17 Sep 1914; CO 616/12/27492, 22 Sept 1914; CO 616/4/36299, 22 Sep 1914
3. TNA: FO 371/1882/71865, 17 Nov 1914 Sperling
4. AJ Wills, *Central Africa* (1985) p.509fn
5. TNA: CO 525/57/38176, 14 Aug 1914 GG Nyasaland to CO
6. A Samson, *Britain, South Africa and East Africa* (2006) p.51; TNA: CO 525/64/1136, 9 Jan 1915 Read to Anderson; 7 Jan 1915 CO minute and letter WO to CO
7. A Samson, *Britain, South Africa and East Africa* (2006) pp.51–52; TNA: CO 525/64/1496, 13 Jan 1915 Harcourt; CO 525/64/9325, 24 Jan 1915 CO minute; DD Phiri, *Let us die for Africa* (1999)
8. TNA: WO 32/5321, 9 Oct 1915 HCSA to SoS Colonies; FO 371/2232/149353, 12 Oct 1915 Lambert to WO; WV Brelsford, *Northern Rhodesia Regiment* (1990); TJ Stapleton, *No insignificant part* (1990); AE Capell, *2nd Rhodesian Regiment* (1922) p.35
9. TNA: WO 32/5321, 9 Oct 1915 HC SA to SoS Colonies (rec 1.55pm); FO 371/2232/149353, 12 Oct 1915 secret CO to FO
10. AJ Wills, *Central Africa* (1985) p.238
11. P McLaughlin, *Ragtime soldiers* (1980); TNA: CO 417/543
12. Bod: MSS Harcourt 474, 15 May 1914 Buxton to Harcourt, f.244
13. TNA: CO 616/27/34016, 23 Jul 1915 GG SA to SoS Colonies (rec 1.10am); WO 106/572, 23 Jul 1915 GG SA to SoS Colonies; CO 616/27/32634, 16 Jul 1915 CO minute by Sperling; WO 106/572, 20 Jul 1915 telegram SoS Colonies to HC South Africa; P McLaughlin, *Ragtime soldiers* (1980) p.17
14. TNA: CO 616/27/34016, 23 Jul 1915 GG SA to SoS Colonies (rec 1.10am); WO 106/572, 23 Jul 1915 GG SA to SoS Colonies; CO 616/27/32634, 16 Jul 1915 CO minute by Sperling; WO 106/572, 20 Jul 1915 telegram SoS Colonies to HC SA
15. TNA: FO 371/2600/256826, 9 Aug 1916 Kilmarnock to Grey; FO 371/2600/156921, 11 Aug 1916 Stratchey minute, 9 Aug 1916 private and secret Kilmarnock to Langley
16. TNA: FO 371/2600/256826, 9 Aug 1916 Kilmarnock to Grey; FO 371/2600/156921, 11 Aug 1916 Stratchey minute, 9 Aug 1916 private and secret Kilmarnock to Langley; FO 371/2600/69525, 13 Apr 1916 Carnegie enclosing Extract from *L'Etoile du Congo* (Elizabethville) 12 Feb 1916; SE Katzenellenbogen, *Railways and the copper mines of Katanga* (1973) pp.2,90
17. S Marks, *Innocent abroad: Belgium and the Paris peace conference, 1919* (1981) pp.46–47

18. E Paice, *Tip and run* (2007) pp.174, 243

19. Chapter 6, East Africa 1915–1916

20. R Anderson, *Forgotten front* (2004) pp.191–193

21. R Anderson, *Forgotten front* (2004) pp.193,232,236,251–252

22. DE Krieger, *Britain and the fate of German Africa: The debate over the future of the German colonies in Africa during the First World War, 1914–1918* (1973) pp.91–92 Renkin to Tombeur 27 Mar 1916 in *Archives Generales du Royume* Brussels; WR Louis *Ruanda-Urundi 1884–1919* (1963)

23. DE Krieger, *Britain and the fate of German Africa* (1973) pp.91–92 Renkin to Tombeur 27 Mar 1916 in *Archives Generales du Royume* Brussels; WR Louis, *Ruanda-Urundi 1884–1919* (1963)

24. R van Overstraeten (ed), *The war diaries of King Albert: King of the Belgians* (1954) p.79

25. S Marks, *Innocent abroad* (1981) pp.24,47; R van Overstraeten (ed), *King Albert I* (1954) pp.89–91 meeting 8 Feb 1916 King Albert and Colonel House

26. E Paice, *Tip and run* (2007) pp.143,322

27. TNA: FO 371/2859/28361, 26 Jan 1917 Carnegie to Balfour; FO 371/2859/137060, 7 Jul 1917 Langley

28. E Paice, *Tip and run* (2007) p.275

29. TNA: WO 158/469, 24 Sep 1917 Sheppard to MacDonell; R Anderson, *Forgotten front* (2004) p.237

30. R Anderson, *Forgotten front* (2004) pp.237–238

31. TNA: FO 371/2599/223719, 7 Nov 1916 Carnegie (rec 7pm); FO 371/2599/72511, 17 Apr 1916 Carnegie

32. TNA: FO 371/2599/223719, 7 Nov 1916 Carnegie (rec 7pm); FO 371/2857/27899, 29 Nov 1917 Carnegie (rec 20 Nov, 8am)

33. E Paice, *Tip and run* (2007) p.322

34. E Paice, *Tip and run* (2007) p.144

35. C Hordern, *Military operations* (1941) p.364

36. TNA: FO 371/3128, 2 Jan 1918, FO to Carnegie; E Paice, *Tip and run* (2007) p.365

37. FO 371/2859/195455, 16 Oct 1917 Snow minute; FO 371/2859/238022, 14 Dec 1917 WO to CO

38. TNA: FO 371/2599/72511, 16 Apr 1916 Carnegie; FO 371/2599/76116, 20 Apr 1916 CO to FO; CO 525/70/17881, 14 Apr 1916 Fiddes minute; FO 371/2856/4468, 8 Jan 1917 Oliphant minute

39. TNA: CO 533/174/16811, 7 Apr 1916 CO minutes; 11 Apr 1916 Balfour to Grey refers to Portugal's not wanting any territory in a dispatch by Carnegie of 28 Oct 1915

40. E Paice, *Tip and run* (2007) pp.141,267
41. R Anderson, *Forgotten front* (2004) p.190
42. E Paice, *Tip and run* (2007) pp.320–321
43. FR de Meneses, 'Too serious a matter' (1998) p.94
44. E Paice, *Tip and run* (2007) p.364
45. TNA: WO 150/475, van Deventer memo 1 Oct 1918 in E Paice, *Tip and run* (2007) pp.365–366
46. E Paice, *Tip and run* (2007) p.318
47. FR de Meneses, 'Too serious a matter' (1998) p.90
48. E Paice, *Tip and run* (2007) p.319
49. E Paice, *Tip and run* (2007) p.335
50. BLM: Bertie MSS ADD 63040, 3 Jan 1916 Bertie to Grey, ff.128–138
51. TNA: FO 371/2597/39073, 24 Feb 1916 Bertie to Grey; VH Rothwell, *British war aims and peace diplomacy, 1914–1918* (1971) p.11 refers CAB 42/9/3, 22 Feb 1916 War Committee meeting, pp.18–20
52. TNA: FO 371/2597/39073, 24 Feb 1916 Bertie to Grey
53. TNA: FO 371/2597/39073, 24 Feb 1916 Bertie to Grey; VH Rothwell, *British war aims* (1971) p.11 refers CAB 42/9/3, 22 Feb 1916 War Committee meeting, pp.18–20
54. TNA: FO 371/2600/116357, 15 Jun 1916 French Ambassador, London to FO; FO 371/2600/12599, 28 Jun 1916 French Ambassador, London to FO; FO 371/2600/136422, 13 Jul 1916 WO to FO
55. R Anderson, *Forgotten front* (2004) pp.127,165
56. SANA: MSS Smuts, vol 12 f.31
57. SANA: MSS Smuts, vol 12 f.84
58. SANA: MSS Smuts, vol 12 f.60
59. SG Millen, *General Smuts, vol 1* in MW Swanson, 'South West Africa' (1967) p.635
60. Bod: MSS Harcourt papers 474, 11 Mar 1915 letter from Harcourt to Buxton, f.29
61. H Strachan, *War in Africa* (2007) p.64
62. H Strachan, *War in Africa* (2007) p.64; MW Swanson, 'South West Africa' (1967)
63. SANA: GG 5/59/190, War 1914–1918 GSWA PM Minute 1947; J Silvester et al, 'Trees never meet!' (1998) p.7
64. SAL,CT: MSC 15/44/121 Merriman 5 Jun 1916 Merriman to Smuts
65. P Lewsen (ed), *JX Merriman* (1969) Sep 1916 Merriman to Botha, pp.279–280
66. P Lewsen (ed), *JX Merriman* (1969) 17 Dec 1916 Merriman to Bryce, p.289; GH Calpin, *Indians in South Africa* (1949)
67. BM Du Toit, *The Boers* (1998) p.81

68. BM Du Toit, *The Boers* (1998) p.86
69. WSA: MSS Long 947/598, 22 Jan 1917 H Wilson-Fox to Jameson
70. A Samson, *Britain, South Africa and East Africa* (2006) pp.54,66–67
71. P Lewsen (ed), *JX Merriman* (1969) 14 May 1918 Merriman to Bryce, p.308
72. SANA: MSS Smuts, vol 18, f.386
73. P Lewsen (ed), JX *Merriman* (1930) letter to Basil Williams, pp.392–393; Lettow-Vorbeck had been a Rhodes scholar
74. IOR: Chelmsford MSS EUR E 264/34, 29 Sep 1916 Chelmsford and others to Chamberlain, p.2; IOR: Curzon MSS EUR F 112/180, 26 Feb 1917 IWC GT 171 f.41; Aga Khan, *India in transition* (1918), pp.115–117, 128
75. PA: MSS Dav 12, 25 Mar 1915
76. South African *Herald*, 16 Mar 1918
77. Aga Khan, *India in transition* (1918), pp.115–8,127–128,130–131
78. AB Keith (ed), *Speeches and documents on Indian policy 1750–1921 vol III* (1922) p.116
79. IOR: Montagu MSS EUR D 523/2, 23 Dec 1918 Montagu to Chelmsford, p.2; Curzon MSS EUR F 112/180, An undated note between paper 26 Feb 1917 and Second Report of the Sub-committee on Territorial Desiderata 22 Mar 1917, f.42; H Lüthy, 'India and East Africa' in *Journal of Contemporary History* 6:2 (1971) pp.58–9
80. IOR: Chelmsford MSS EUR E 264/3, 9 May 1917 Chamberlain to Chelmsford, no 27, p.110; Montagu became SoS India in July 1917; IOR: Montagu MSS EUR D 523/2, 23 Dec 1918 Montagu to Chelmsford, p.2
81. TNA: CO 532/95/51785, 22 Oct 1917 Note by C Lucas

Chapter 10   The war in London, 1915–1917

1. TNA: FO 371/1882/81461, 9 Dec 1914 Callwell to Nicholson
2. TNA: FO 371/1882/82994, 18 Dec 1914, Sperling; R Anderson, *Forgotten front* (2004) pp.58–59
3. A Samson, *Britain, South Africa and East Africa* (2006) p.59
4. P von Lettow-Vorbeck, *My reminiscences* (nd) pp.32–33; H Moyse-Bartlett, *King's African Rifles* (1956); W Lloyd-Jones, *KAR* (1926); M Page, *KAR* (1998)
5. TNA: CO 533/160/4689, 1 Feb 1915, various CO minutes
6. See chapters covering 1914
7. Various biographies on Kitchener
8. TNA: CO 616/15/32010, 22 Aug 1914; CO 616/15/32203; CO 626/15/32583/ CO 25/8/14; TJ Stapleton, *No insignificant part* (2006)
9. TNA: CO 533/260/5719, 1 Feb 1915 Wapshare to WO (rec 9.35pm)

10. RH: MSS Micr Afr 599 Noel Smith
11. E Trzebinski, *Kenya pioneers* (1985) p.180
12. TNA: CO 533/160/4013, 24 Jan 1915 WO to Wapshare (sent 2.55pm), 26 Jan 1915 CO Bottomley minute; CO 533/160/4269, 22 Jan 1915 WO to IO
13. TNA: CO 533/160/2491, 13 Jan 1915 Wapshare to WO (rec 10.16am), 13 Jan 1915 WO to Wapshare (sent 12.50pm); CO 533/160/1910, 14 Jan 1915 Fiddes; 22 Jan 1915 WO to IO; WO 33/714, 12 Jan 1915 SoS War to Wapshare in GH Cassar, *Kitchener's war: British strategy from 1914–1916* (2004) p.159; Lord Cranworth, *Kenya chronicles* (1939) p.182; IWM: MSS Wapshare 88/61/1, diary entry 13 Feb 1915
14. Lord Cranworth, *Kenya chronicles* (1939) p.185
15. IWM: MSS Henry Wilson HHW 2/75/12, 22 Oct 1914 Charles [Callwell] to Henry [Wilson] (the letter is incorrectly dated. It should read 22 Nov 1914); GH Cassar, *Kitchener's war* (2004) p.159; C Hordern, *Military operations* (1941) pp.132–134; Lord Cranworth, *Kenya chronicles* (1939) p.186
16. Lord Cranworth, *Kenya chronicles* (1939) p.207
17. TNA: CO 533/161/35755, 12 Aug 1915 Read note; E Huxley, *White man's country vol 2* (1953) pp.20–21; R Meinertzhagen, *Army diary* (1960) p.110; GH Cassar, *Kitchener's war* (2004) p.160
18. E Trzebinksi, *Kenya pioneers* (1985) p.184
19. TNA: WO 374/20803, JJ Dough
20. G Corrigan's *Sepoys* deals with religion and Indian loyalty. Although for the Western Front, it is helpful to understand some of the African issues concerning Indian troops.
21. TNA: CO 533/160/5554, 31 Jan 1915 WO to CiC India (sent 11.50am); 2 Feb 1915 CiC India to WO (rec 6.10pm); CE Callwell, *Small wars* (1906)
22. TNA: CO 533/160/5554, 3 Feb 1915 Pedley to CO, 4 Feb 1915 CO various minutes; 5 Feb 1915 Just minute; Francis Brett Young, a doctor with the East Africa forces in 1916, had nothing but praise for these and the other Indian troops in his book *Marching on Tanga* (1917)
23. TNA: WO 32/5822, 18 Feb 1916 CIGS to Smuts
24. IOR: Curzon MSS EUR F 112/180, CID 22 Mar 1917; TNA: PRO 30/57/80, envelope 31, pp.55–58 Harcourt to Kitchener; CO 533/160/5554, 31 Jan 1915 WO to CiC India
25. TNA: PRO 30/57/80, 4 Mar 1915 letter Harcourt to 'My dear Kitchener', envelope 31, pp.55–58; O Ransford, *Livingstone's Lake* (1966) pp.229–236; DD Phiri, *Let us die for Africa* (1999)
26. TNA: CO 533/162/53599, 17 Nov 1915 telegram CIGS to Earl Kitchener (sent 4.55pm) 19 Nov 1915 CO minute by Fiddes
27. AM Gollin, *Proconsul in politics: A study of Lord Milner in power and opposition* (1964) p.237

28. Various letters to/from Grey; FH Hinsley, *British foreign policy under Sir Edward Grey* (1977)
29. LH Gann, *A history of Northern Rhodesia* (1964) p.178
30. CAC: MSS Hankey HNKY 1/3, p.165
31. HH Asquith, *Memories and reflections vol 2* (1928)
32. J Pollock, *Kitchener* (2000) pp.185,372
33. RH: MSS Afr 195/1 Stephen Butler, f.27
34. IWM: MSS Wilson 2/75/12, 22 Oct [Nov] 1914 Charles to Henry
35. IWM: MSS Wilson 2/75/54, 28 Oct 1914 Charles to Henry
36. IWM: MSS Wilson 2/75/54, 16 Jul 1915 Charles to Henry
37. GH Cassar, *Kitchener's war* (2004) p.37
38. CAC: HNKY 4/7, 2 Jan 1915 Balfour to Hankey
39. P Magnus, *Kitchener: Portrait of an imperialist* (2000) p.307
40. TNA: PRO 30/57/98 Kitchener
41. *East African Standard*, 15 Aug 1914, Songhor Notes, p.7
42. P Magnus, *Kitchener* (1958) pp.308–309; Majors McMurdo, Fitzgerald and Leggett were partners; Kitchener held 50% of the shares
43. P Magnus, *Kitchener* (1958) p.307; TNA: CO 533/485/8
44. J Pollock, *Kitchener* (2000) p.50
45. R Coupland, *The exploitation of East Africa* (1968) pp.470–476; P Magnus, *Kitchener* (1958) p.92; C Hordern, *Military operations* (1941) p.4; HA Jones, *War in the air* (1930) p.1
46. Various Kitchener biographies
47. TNA: FO 371/2234/94558, 9 Jul 1915 SoS Colonies to Governor Nyasaland (sent 12.43pm)
48. TNA: CO 533/161/35755, 12 Aug 1915 Steel-Maitland; Bod: MSS Harcourt 472, 18 May 1915; BL: MSS Buxton dep 9930 File May 1915, 15 May 1915 Buxton to Harcourt
49. SANA: GG 667 9/93/7, 10 Aug 1915 secret minute 1037
50. R Anderson, *Forgotten front* (2004) p.102; K Hancock and J van der Poel, *Smuts papers vol 3* (1966) p.310
51. See earlier chapters
52. PA: MSS Dav 27/27, 3 Sep 1915 Bonar Law to Buxton; TNA: CO 616/28/40569, 23 Aug 1915 private and personal SoS Colonies to GG SA (sent 6.10pm); 1 Sep 1915 secret and immediate to WO
53. TNA: CO 616/28/40569, 10 Aug 1915 GG SA to SoS Colonies
54. Earl Buxton, *Botha* (1924) pp.246–56; R Keiser, *The South African Governor General* (1975) p.294; PA: MSS Dav 27/21, 11 Aug 1915 Buxton to Bonar Law, MSS Dav 27/27, 3 Sep 1915 Bonar Law to Buxton
55. TNA: CO 616/28/40569, private and personal 28 Aug 1915 GG SA to SoS Colonies (rec 7.50pm); CO 616/28/44145, 28 Aug 1915 minute 1136; CO

525/65/31423, 9 Jul 1915; CO 616/32/52611, 9 Jul 1915 SoS Colonies to GG SA (sent 8.50pm); CO 616/27/32634, 15 Jul 1915 HC SA to SoS Colonies (rec 1.45pm)

56. Newland, *Tarlton's Monthly*, 6:7 (Dec 1915) p.1; Earl Buxton, *Botha* (1924) pp.246–255

57. TNA: CO 616/28/40569, 1 Sep 1915 secret and immediate Fiddes to Secretary WO and 15 Sep 1915 SoS Colonies to GG SA (sent 3.45pm); CO 533/161/41573, 3 Sep 1915 GOC SA to WO (rec 3.5pm); R Keiser, *The South African Governor General* (1975)

58. H Spender, *Botha* (1919) p.345

59. PA: MSS Lloyd George F 32/5/16, 16 Jan 1918 Buxton to Long

60. TNA: CAB 42/4/5 Appendix I. Attendees: Percy (FO), Fiddes (CO), Major CH Leveson (WO) and Captain Earl Percy (WO). The Belgian government had proposed a feint landing on the German East Africa coast to draw attention away from the actions planned for Lake Tanganyika. The demonstration became Spicer-Simson's expedition to Lake Tanganyika. C Hordern, *Military Operations* (1941) p.211

61. CAC: MSS Hankey HNKY 1/1, 10 & 11 Nov 1915, p.100

62. TNA: CAB 42/5/15, 10 Nov 1915 Terms of Reference for a sub-committee to 'consider the question of future operations in East Africa'; 18 Nov 1915 CID Paper. The members of the committee were Percy (FO), Steel-Maitland (CO), Fiddes (CO), Colonel CH Selwyn (IO), Leveson (WO) and Captain HW Grant (Adm); WO 32/5324.

63. CAC: MSS Hankey HNKY 1/1, 6 Nov 1915, f.98, Churchill believed an armoured car attack would work

64. A Samson, *Britain, South Africa and East Africa* (2006) p.65; TNA: CAB 42/6/8, 15 Dec 1915 War Council, pp.12–15; WO 106/310, file 1

65. TNA: CAB 42/6/8, 15 Dec 1915 War Council, pp.12–15; WO 106/310, file 1

66. TNA: CAB 42/6/8, 15 Dec 1915 War Council, 14 Dec 1915 Kitchener minute

67. TNA: CO 533/162/54132, 23 Nov 1915 Cubbitt to Under SoS Colonies; CO 533/162/53599, 23 Nov 1915 secret WO to GOC EA (sent 5.45pm); R Anderson, *Forgotten front* (2004) p.105

68. TNA: CAB 42/6/14, 28 Dec 1915 War Committee, p.11; CAC: MSS Hankey HNKY 1/1, 16 Dec 1915, p.120; ML Dockerill & D French, *Strategy and intelligence: British policy during the First World War* (1996); D French, *Strategy of the Lloyd George coalition 1916–1918* (1995); D Lloyd George, *War memoirs* (1932); W Robertson, *From private to field-marshal* (1921); J Turner, *British politics and the Great War: Coalition and conflict 1915–1918* (1992); R Anderson, *Forgotten front* (2004) p.106

69. CAC: MSS Hankey HNKY 1/1, 16 Dec 1915, p.123
70. IWM: MSS Smith Dorrien 87/47/8 file B
71. IWM: MSS Smith Dorrien 87/47/8 file B, 20 Dec 1915 Smith-Dorrien to My dear Prime Minister
72. LHC: MSS Robertson 4/3/15, 25 Jan 1916 Wedgwood to Prime Minister
73. TNA: FO 371/2599/66746, 4 Apr 1916 Smuts to WO (rec 7.45pm); CO 533/174/16, 7 Apr 1916 Fiddes minute
74. TNA: CO 533/173/18420, 15 Apr 1916 Carnegie and Villiers
75. PA: MSS Dav 29/111, Aug 1916 paper by CH Rodwell; TNA: CO 533/175/39324
76. TNA: FO 608/219 Registry No 1501, File No 803/2/1, 6 Feb 1919 Meinertzhagen; FO 371/2299/170926, 29 Aug 1916 CO to FO; FO 371/2599/176732, 31 Aug 1916 WO to FO, 5 Sep 1916 CO to WO; FO 371/2856/19021, 19 Jan 1917 Long to Balfour, Butler note, Villier's private 2 Jan 1917 in WSA: MSS Long 947/532; CO 533/174/16811, 7 Apr 1916 CO minutes
77. TNA: FO 371/2299/170926, 29 Aug 1916 CO to FO; FO 371/2599/176732, 31 Aug 1916 WO to FO, 5 Sep 1916 CO to WO; FO 371/2856/19021, 19 Jan 1917 Long to Balfour, Butler note, Villier's private 2 Jan 1917 in WSA: MSS Long 947/532; CO 533/174/16811, 7 Apr 1916 CO minutes
78. TNA: FO 371/2599/80269, 28 & 29 Apr 1916 Strachey minute
79. R Anderson, *Forgotten front* (2004) pp.139–140,152
80. R Anderson, *Forgotten front* (2004) p.152; E Paice, *Tip and run* (2004) p.243
81. TNA: FO 371/2856/157, 11 Jan 1917 FO to Villiers; FO 371/2857/72437, 21 Mar 1917 Villiers to Balfour; E Paice, *Tip and run* (2004) p.316
82. E Paice, *Tip and run* (2004) p.316
83. DE Krieger, *Britain and the fate of German Africa* (1973) p.74; Grey note in FO 371/2598, No 117797
84. FH Hinsley, *Sir Edward Grey* (1977)
85. TNA: CAB 42/16/12, 31 Jul 1916 Smuts to CIGS; BLM: Balfour MSS ADD 49748, 8 Aug 1916 Steel-Maitland to Balfour
86. TNA: CAB 42/17/1, 1 Aug 1916 War Committee
87. TNA: CAB 42/17/11, 3 Aug 1916 Fiddes memorandum; CAB 42/16/5, 11 Jul 1916 War Committee
88. P von Lettow-Vorbeck, *My reminiscences* (nd) p.158
89. IOR: Curzon MSS EUR F 112/180, CID, 22 Mar 1917 G-118a ff.54–87; E Goldstein, *Winning the peace* (1991) pp.13–15
90. WK Hancock, *Smuts: Sanguine years* (1962) p.223
91. A Samson, *Britain, South Africa and East Africa* (2006) pp.234–240
92. TNA: CAB 29/1, Imperial War Cabinet, 28 Apr 1917, P-16, ff.325,333; IOR: Curzon MSS EUR F 112/180, 28 Mar 1917 CID G118a & G118b, the

committee consisted of L Mallett (Chairman), W Tyrrell, G Clerk, Lieut-Gen
AH McMahon, HJ Read, C Stratchey, H Lambert, TW Holderness, Lord
Islington, GMW Macdonogh, F Maurice, Adm AK Wilson, WF Nicholson,
H Llewellyn Smith, H Fountain (BoT), P Ashley (BoT); JM Ferreira, *Portugal
na Conferência da Paz Paris 1919* (1992) p.17; The Portuguese delegate to the
Peace Discussions refuted this allegation at the first meeting he attended

93. CAB 29/1, Imperial War Cabinet, 28 Apr 1917; IOR: Curzon MSS EUR F
    112/180, 28 Mar 1917 CID G118b; 19 Apr 1917
94. CAB 29/1, Imperial War Cabinet, 28 Apr 1917
95. DE Krieger, *Britain and the fate of German Africa* (1973) p.56 refers Harcourt,
    6 Aug 1914
96. DE Krieger, *Britain and the fate of German Africa* (1973) p.57; CO 537/28,
    7 Aug 1914
97. DE Krieger, *Britain and the fate of German Africa* (1973) p.65; TNA: CO
    537/526; CO 537/28, 7 Aug 1914; FO 371/1882, File 71865, 17 Nov 1914
98. Bod: MSS Harcourt 474, f.34
99. LHC: MSS Robertson WR 8/5/53, 24 Nov 1917 Long to Robertson
100. LHC: MSS Robertson WR 8/5/54, 26 Nov 1917 Robertson to Long

Chapter 11   All for what?

1. G Mead, *The Doughboys: America and the First World War* (2000)
2. J Tomes, *Balfour and foreign policy* (1997)
3. A Walworth, *Wilson and his peacemakers: American diplomacy at the Paris
   peace conference, 1919* (1986) pp.64–65
4. TNA: FO 800/199 53b, 5 Jan 1918 PM's speech; CAB 23/5, 4 Jan 1918
   WC 314 Appendix 4
5. WSA: MSS Long 947/604, 27 Aug 1918 Long to Buxton; TNA: CAB 23/7,
   15 Aug 1918 WC 459/IWC 32 (also CAB 23/42); CAB 23/42, 20 Dec 1918
   IWC 44, p.7; SAL,CT: MSC 15/52/665 Merriman, 21 Dec 1918 EIB Gordon
   at British War Cabinet; SANA: MSS Smuts A1 291/2/64, 14 Jan 1919 Smuts
   to PM; J Barnes & D Nicholson (eds), *The Leo Amery diaries vol 1 1869–1929*
   (1980); Foreign Relations of the United States Diplomatic Papers, *Paris peace
   conference, vol V*, 5 May 1919, document 180.03401/144; IC 181-B, p.472
6. P Lewsen (ed), *JX Merriman* (1969) pp.289,392–393
7. BLM: Balfour MSS ADD 49775, 15 Aug 1918 Amery; TNA: FO 800/207
   (PA: MSS Dav 70/14), 15 Jun 1918 Amery
8. TNA: CAB 23/7, 14 Aug 1918 WC 458/IWC 31
9. J Barnes & D Nicholson, *The Leo Amery diaries* (1980) 29 Oct 1918, p.239;
   Colonel House was Wilson's chief confidant; Sir Maurice Hankey was
   Secretary to the British War Cabinet and later to the peace conference.

10. K Hancock and J van der Poel, *Smuts papers vol 3* (1966) p.683
11. ED Morel, *Africa and the peace of Europe* (1917) p.xxii in DE Krieger, *Britain and the fate of German Africa* (1973) p.29
12. DE Krieger, *Britain and the fate of German Africa* (1973) p.29
13. K Hancock and J van der Poel, *Smuts papers vol 3* (1966) p.389
14. CAC: MSS Hankey HNKY 1/3, 14 Jun 1918, p.240
15. BLM: Bertie MSS ADD 63043, 11 Aug 1916 memo, ff.29–35; also 24 Aug 1916 to Hardinge shown to Cambon, ff.81–96; BLM: Bertie MSS ADD 63045, 28 Feb 1917 Bertie to Balfour, ff.129–131; AG Lennox, *Diary of Lord Bertie of Thame 1914–1918* (2 vols) (1924) entry of 2 Oct 1917, p.194 contains an assessment of Smuts
16. RS Baker, *Woodrow Wilson and world settlement vol 1* (1958) pp.265–266; Secretary of State Lansing was the exception on the American delegation – he actually proposed the USA acquire colonies.
17. TNA: CAB 23/7, 14 Aug 1918 WC 458/IWC 31; IOR: Curzon MSS EUR F 112/122B, 25 Nov 1918 Smuts to Curzon; my emphasis; Curzon MSS EUR F 112/122A, 28 Nov 1918 Long to Curzon
18. JRM Butler, *Lord Lothian (Philip Kerr) 1882–1940* (1960) p.74 (memo 16 Dec 1918); MD Callahan, *Mandates and Empire: The League of Nations and Africa, 1914–1931* (1999) p.24; G Curry, 'Woodrow Wilson, Jan Smuts and the Versailles settlement' in *American Historical Review* 66:4 (1961) pp.968–988; M Mazower, *No enchanted palace: The end of empire and the ideological origins of the United Nations* (2008)
19. WK Hancock and J van der Poel, *Smuts papers vol 3* (1966) p.609
20. CAC: MSS Hankey HNKY 1/5, 20 Dec 1918
21. MD Callahan, *Mandates and empire* (1999) pp.31–32; *Paris Peace Conference vol III*, 30 Jan 1919 Document reference 180.03101/24, BC-19 Annex A
22. Lord Hankey, *The supreme control at the Paris peace conference 1919: A commentary* (1963) p.62
23. A Samson, *Britain, South Africa and East Africa* (2006) pp.154–155
24. S Marks, *Makers of the modern world: The peace conferences of 1919–1923 and their aftermath: Paul Hymans* (2010) chapter 4
25. *Paris peace conference vol V*, 7 May 1919, document reference 180.03401/147; IC 181-E, pp.498,500 and 180.03401/149; IC 181-G, p.506; WR Louis, 'The US and African peace settlement' in *Journal of African History* 4:2 (1963) p.246
26. S Marks, *Paul Hymans* (2010) pp.79–80
27. TNA: FO 608/216, registry no 9546, file 724/1/1, 8 May 1919 Villliers to Balfour, 10 May 1919 Hankey note
28. WR Louis, *Great Britain and Germany's lost colonies 1914–1919* (1967) p.150

29. Bod: MSS Milner 390, 29 May 1919 memo, 26 May 1919 Milner to Orts
30. WR Louis, *Ruanda-Urundi* (1963) p.257. The land was returned to Belgium in 1923. Significantly, at no point during any of these discussions was the future or sovereignty of the Sultan of Zanzibar's ten mile-wide strip north of Umba discussed or taken into account at the peace discussions. Germany had bought its strip of land (south of the Umba) from the Sultan in 1895 whereas Britain leased its section. In 1917 Britain tried to purchase the land to impose conscription but the Sultan objected. He again objected during 1919 when Britain asked for the territory. Britain dropped the issue to avoid French interference and the anomalous position of the land was only resolved on independence in the 1960s. J Brennan, 'Lowering the Sultan's flag: Sovereignty and decolonisation in coastal Kenya' in *Comparative studies in society and history* 50:4 (2008) pp.831–864
31. FO 608/216 (registry no 18287; file no 724/1/1) 24 Aug 1919, f.106 & 27 Sep 1919, f.123; *Paris peace conference vol III*, 30 Jan 1919, Document ref 180.03101/25; BC-18; IC-128, pp.808–813; NS Teixeira, *O Poder e a Guerro 1914–1918: Objectivos Nacionais e Estratégias Políticas na Entrada de Portugal na Grande Guerre* (1996)
32. MD Callahan, *Mandates and empire* (1999) pp.31–32
33. J Silvester, 'Beasts, boundaries and buildings: The survival and creation of pastoral economies in Southern Namibia, 1915–1935' in P Hayes et al, *Namibia under South African rule* (1998) p.105
34. BLM: MSS Buxton, 2 Jul 1919 FS Malan to Buxton
35. BLM: MSS Balfour ADD 49734, 23 Jul 1923

Chapter 12   Conclusions

1. DE Krieger, *Britain and the fate of German Africa* (1973) p.71
2. E Paice, *Tip and run* (2007) p.399
3. A Clark, *The donkeys* (1964)
4. P Lewsen (ed), *JX Merriman* (1969) p.289
5. B Farwell, *Great War* (1987) p.355
6. AJ Wills, *Central Africa* (1985) pp.240–241
7. H Strachan, *War in Africa* (2007) p.62
8. TNA: CAB 45/27 Report 15 Jun 1933, pp.6,9
9. C Walker, 'The women's suffrage movement' in C Walker (ed) *Women and gender in South Africa to 1945* (1990) pp.330–332
10. E Trzebinski, *Kenya pioneers* (1985) pp.182–183
11. AMD Howes, 'Twenty-five years of flying' (1958)
12. AE Capell, *2nd Rhodesian Regiment* (1922)

13. TJ Stapleton, *No insignificant part* (2006) p.2
14. V Bickford-Smith, E van Heyningen, N Worden, *Cape Town in the twentieth century* (1999) p.54
15. B Garfield, *Meinertzhagen* (2007) p.170 quoting Lettow-Vorbeck, *Mein Leben*
16. H Fecitt, *November 1918 in East Africa* [online: kaiserscross]; E Paice, *Tip and run* (2007) p.387

BIBLIOGRAPHY

Bodleian Library, Oxford

Department of Special Collections and Western Manuscripts (Bod)

MSS Lewis Harcourt, 1st Viscount Harcourt (1863–1922) (Harcourt)

New College, Oxford

MSS Milner 390 Alfred Milner

Rhodes House Library (RH)

MSS Richard Meinertzhagen
MSS Afr s. 2175 Sir George Farrar
MSS Micr Afr 599 Noel Smith
MSS Afr s 2051 HM Stirling
MSS Afr s. 1715 (144) WG Hughes
MSS Afr 195/1 Stephen Butler

British Library

India Office Records

MSS EUR E420 – Barrow (Edmund George), General Sir
MSS EUR E264 – Lord Chelmsford
MSS EUR F112 – Lord Curzon
MSS EUR D523 – Lord Montagu

Manuscripts Department

MSS Arthur Balfour

MSS Buxton (Sydney Charles) Earl Buxton
MSS Bertie of Thame

Cambridge University Library Archive (CUL)

MSS Robert Offley Ashburton Crewe-Milnes (1858–1945), 1st marquess of Crewe (Crewe)
MSS Charles, 1st Baron Hardinge of Penshurst (1858–1944) (Hardinge)

Churchill Archives Centre, Churchill College, Cambridge

MSS HNKY Maurice Hankey papers

Imperial War Museum Archive (IWM)

MSS 06/88/1 Private Papers of LES Ward
MSS PP/MCR/150 Private Papers of Norman King
MSS PP/MCR/62 Private Papers of GB Buxton
MSS Misc 164 (2541) Diary of an unidentified Petty Officer Stoker in HMS Weymouth
MSS 87/47/8 Smith Dorrien
MSS 98/1/1 Private Papers of C J Charlewood
MSS PP/MCR/C17, P 5 Private Papers of Sir Edward Northey
MSS 88/61 Private Papers of Richard Wapshare
MSS 06/35/1 Lieutenant P Erskine
MSS 73/1/1-9 Private Papers of Henry Wilson
Duff, HL, *Nyasaland in the World War, 1914–1918* (1951)

Liddell Hart Centre for Military Archives, King's College London (LHC)

MSS GB99 KCLMA Robertson W R

Parliamentary Archives, House of Lords, London (PA)

MSS Davidson; John Campbell (1889–1970); Politician; 1st Viscount Davidson (Dav)
MSS BL The Bonar Law Papers
MSS F 32/5/16 Lloyd George papers

South African Defence Force Archive, Pretoria

DC 744 box 1717

South African National Library, Cape Town Manuscripts (SAL,CT)

MSS John X Merriman Collection

South African National Archives, Pretoria (SANA)

UG 10 (1915) CD 7874, *Report on the outbreak of Rebellion and the policy of the government with regard to its suppression*

UG 46 (1916) *Report of the Judicial Committee relating to the recent Rebellion in South Africa*

DC/2/74/1717, 26 Nov 1915 Report

Governor General Series GG

Prime Minister Series PM

Smuts papers A1

The National Archives, Kew (TNA)

ADM – Admiralty

CAB – Cabinet Office

CO – Colonial Office

FO – Foreign Office

WO – War Office

PRO 30/57/80 – Kitchener papers

Wiltshire & Swindon Archives (WSA)

Walter Long collection 947

Newspapers

East Africa
East Africa Standard
The East African Leader
South African
Bloemfontein Post
De Burger
De Volkstem (Pretoria)
Herald (Johannesburg)
Matatiele Mail
Newland, *Tarlton's Monthly*

Published Material

Adgie, KP, *Askaris, asymmetry, and small wars: Operational art and the German East Africa campaign 1914–1918* (Fort Leavenworth, 2001)

Aga Khan, *India in transition: A study in political evolution* (London, 1918)

Alhadeff, Vic, *South Africa in two World Wars: A newspaper history* (Cape Town, 1979)

Anderson, Ross, *The forgotten front: The East African campaign 1914–1918* (Stroud, 2004)

Asquith, HH, *Memories and reflections vol 2* (London, 1928)

Baker, RS, *Woodrow Wilson and world settlement vol 1* (University of Michigan, 1958)

Barnes, J, & Nicholson, D (eds), *The Leo Amery diaries vol 1 1869–1929* (London, 1980)

Belgian Government, *The Belgian campaigns in the Cameroons and German East Africa* (London, 1917)

Bickford-Smith, V, van Heyningen, E, & Worden, N, *Cape Town in the twentieth century* (Cape Town, 1999)

Brelsford, WV, (ed), *The story of the Northern Rhodesia Regiment* (Bromley, 1990)

Brennan, J, 'Lowering the Sultan's flag: Sovereignty and decolonisation in coastal Kenya' in *Comparative studies in society and history* 50:4 (2008) pp.831–864

Brett Young, Francis, *Marching on Tanga with General Smuts in East Africa* (Glasgow, 1917)

Brien, Michael, *An uneasy anger: De la Rey and the Foster Gang* (Newlands, 2009)

Brown, James Ambrose, *They fought for king and Kaiser: South Africans in German East Africa, 1916* (Rivonia, 1991)

Brown, JS, 'On battle and disease: The East Africa campaign of 1914–1918' in *Parameters, Journal of the US Army War College* 12:2 (1982)

Buchanan, Angus, *Three years of war in East Africa* (Uckfield, nd)

Butler, J, 'The German factor in Anglo-Transvaal relations' in Gifford, P & Louis, WMR, *Britain and Germany in Africa: Imperial rivalry and colonial rule* (New Haven, 1967)

Butler, JRM, *Lord Lothian (Philip Kerr) 1882–1940* (London, 1960)

Buxton, Earl, *Botha* (London, 1924)

C Lucas, *The empire at war vol 5* (1921)

Calitz, GJ, *Deneys Reitz (1882–1944) Krygsman, avonturier en politikus* (Thesis: University of Pretoria, 2008)

Callahan, MD, *Mandates and Empire: The League of Nations and Africa, 1914–1931* (Sussex, 1999)

Callwell, CE, *Small wars* (London, 1906)

Calpin, GH, *Indians in South Africa* (London, 1949)

Cann, JP, 'Angola and the Great War' in *Small wars & insurgencies* 12:1 (2001) pp.145–160

Cann, JP, 'Moçambique, German East Africa and the Great War' in *Small wars & insurgencies* 12:1 (2001) pp.114–143

Capell, AE, *The 2nd Rhodesian Regiment in East Africa* (London, 1922)

Cartwright, AP, *The first South African: The life and times of Sir Percy Fitzpatrick* (Cape Town, 1971)

Cassar, GH, *Kitchener's war: British strategy from 1914–1916* (Washington, 2004)

Cato, C, *The navy everywhere* (1919)

Charlewood, CJ, 'Naval action on the Tanganyika coast, 1914–1917' parts 1 and 2 in *Tanganyika Notes and Records* 54 & 55 (1960)

Clark, Alan, *The donkeys* (London, 1964)

Clifford, HC, *The Gold Coast Regiment in the East African campaign* (London, 1920)

Cloete, B, *Die lewe van Senator FS Malan (President van die Senaat)* (Johannesburg, 1946)

Clothier, Norman, *Black valour: The South African Native Labour Contingent 1916–1918 and the sinking of the Mendi* (Pietermaritzburg, 1998)

Collyer, JJ, *Official History: Campaign in German South West Africa, 1914–1915* (Nashville, 1937)

Connaughton, R, 'The First World War in Africa (1914–1918)' in *Small wars & insurgencies* 12:1 (2001) pp.111–113

Corbett, JS, *Official history of the war: Naval operations vol 1* (London, 1920)

Corbett, JS, *Official history of the war: Naval operations vol 2* (London, 1923)

Cornwell, R, 'The war for independence' in Cilliers, J, & Dietrich, C (eds) *Angola's war economy: The role of oil and diamonds* (2000) [online: www.issafrica.org]

Corrigan, G, *Mud, blood and poppycock* (London, 2003)

Corrigan, G, *Sepoys in the trenches* (Staplehurst, 1999)

Coupland, R, *The exploitation of East Africa* (London, 1968)

Cranworth, Lord, *Kenya chronicles* (London, 1939)

Curry, G, 'Woodrow Wilson, Jan Smuts and the Versailles settlement' in *American Historical Review* 66:4 (1961) pp.968–988

Davenport, R, *South Africa* (Hampshire, 1991)

Davenport, Rodney, & Saunders, Christopher, *South Africa: A modern history* (5th ed) (Basingstoke, 2000)

Davies, A, & Robertson, HJ, *Chronicles of Kenya* (London, 1928)

de Meneses, Filipe Ribeiro, 'Parliament and the army in Portugal, 1914–1918' in *Journal of Contemporary History* 33:1 (1998)

de Meneses, Filipe Ribeiro, 'Too serious a matter to be left to the Generals? Parliament and the army in wartime Portugal, 1914–1918' in *Journal of Contemporary History* 33:1 (1998) pp.85–96

de Meneses, Filipe Ribeiro, *Makers of the modern world: The peace conferences of 1919–1923 and their aftermath: Afonso Costa, Portugal* (London, 2010)

Dixon-Fyle, M, & Cole, GR, *New perspectives on the Sierra Leone Krio* (New York, 2006)

Dockerill, ML, & French, D, *Strategy and intelligence: British policy during the First World War* (London, 1996)

Dolbey, Robert V, *Sketches of the East Africa campaign* (1918) or *The bush war doctor: The experiences of a British army doctor during the East African campaign of the First World War* (London, 2007)

Downes, WD, *With the Nigerians in East Africa* (London, 1919)

Du Toit, Brian M, *The Boers in East Africa: Ethnicity and identity* (Connecticut, 1998)

Durschmied, Erik, *The hinge factor: How chance and stupidity have changed history* (Philadelphia, 2003)

Engelenberg, FV, *General Louis Botha* (London, 1929)

Fecitt, H, *The soldier's burden: Harry's Africa* [online: http://www.kaiserscross. com/188001/home.html] for all articles listed by Fecitt, copies supplied by author for reference

Farwell, Byron, *The Great War in Africa 1914–1918* (Middlesex, 1987)

Ferreira, JM, *Portugal na Conferência da Paz Paris 1919* (Lisboa, 1992)

Fewster, Dan, *The Journals of Dan Fewster: A First World War British Army Battery Sergeant's account of his experiences in German East Africa and France* [online: www.jfhopkin.karoo.net/DanFewster/Diary.html accessed 30 May 2011]

Foden, Giles, *Mimi and Toutou go forth: The bizarre battle of Lake Tanganyika* (London, 2005)

Foreign Relations of the United States Diplomatic Papers, *Paris peace conference vol V*

Forster, Kent 'The quest for East African neutrality in 1915' in *Africa Studies Review* 22:1 (1979) pp.73–82

French, D, *Strategy of the Lloyd George coalition 1916–1918* (Oxford, 1995)

Gann, LH, *A history of Northern Rhodesia* (1964)

Garfield, Brian, *The Meinertzhagen mystery: The life and legend of a colossal fraud* (Washington, 2007)

Gewalt, JB, *Colonial warfare: Hehe and World War One, the wars besides Maji Maji in south-western Tanzania* (Leiden, ASC working paper 63/2005)

Gilbert, Martin, *First World War* (London, 1994)

Goldstein, E, *Winning the peace* (Oxford 1991)

Gollin, AM, *Proconsul in politics: A study of Lord Milner in power and opposition* (London, 1964)

Grundlingh, Albert, *Fighting their own war: South African blacks and the First World War* (Johannesburg, 1987)

Grundy, KW, *Soldiers without politics: Blacks in the South African armed forces* (California, 1983)

Hance, WA, & van Dongen, IS, 'Lorenço Marques in Delagoa Bay' in *Economic Geography* 33:3 (1957) pp.238–256

Hancock, WK, & van der Poel, Jean, *Selections from the Smuts papers June 1910–November 1918 vol 3* (Cambridge, 1966)

Hancock, WK, *Smuts: The fields of force 1919–1950 vol 2* (Cambridge, 1968)

Hancock, WK, *Smuts: The sanguine years 1870–1919 vol 1* (Cambridge, 1962)

Hankey, Lord, *The supreme control at the Paris peace conference 1919: A commentary* (London, 1963)

Harding, C, *Frontier patrols: A history of the British South African Police and other Rhodesian forces* (London, 1937)

Hardinge, C, *My Indian years 1910–1916: The reminiscences of Lord Hardinge of Penshurst* (London, 1948)

Harmer, Harry, *Makers of the modern world: The peace conferences of 1919–1923 and their aftermath: Friedrich Ebert* (London, 2008)

Harris, F, 'Marched 600 miles with fleeing Germans' in *The New York Times*, 16 Sep 1917

Harvey, Kenneth J, *The Battle of Tanga: German East Africa, 1914* (Thesis for MA Military Art and Science, Fort Leavenworth, 2003)

Hatchell, GW, 'Maritime relics of the 1914–1918 war' in *Tanganyika Notes and Records* 36 (1954) pp.1–21

Hatchell, GW, 'The British occupation of the south-western area of Tanganyika' in *Tanganyika Notes and Records* 51 (1958)

Helmreich, Jonathan E, *Belgium and Europe: A study in small power diplomacy* (The Hague, 1976)

Henderson, WO, *The German Colonial Empire 1884–1919* (Bath, 1993)

Herff, M von, *They walk through fire like the blondest Germans: African soldiers serving the Kaiser in German East Africa (1885–1914)* (MA thesis, McGill University: Montreal, 1991)

Hinsley, FH *British foreign policy under Sir Edward Grey* (Cambridge, 1977)

Hodges, Geoffrey, *Kariakor: The Carrier Corps* (Nairobi, 1999)

Holtom, Ernest Charl, *Two years' captivity in German East Africa, being the personal experiences of surgeon ECH, Royal Navy* (nd)

Hordern, Charles, *Military operations East Africa, August 1914–September 1916 vol 1* (Nashville, 1941/1990)

Howes, AMD, 'Some details of the first twenty-five years of flying in Tanganyika, 1914–1939 in *Tanganyika Notes and Records* 50 (1958) pp.39–47

Hoyt, Edwin P, *The Germans who never lost* (London, 1970)

Huxley, Elspeth, *White man's country vol 2* (London, 1953)

Hyam, Ronald, *The failure of South African expansion, 1908–1948* (New York, 1972)

Ingham, K, *A history of East Africa* (3rd ed) (London, 1965)

Jones, HA, *Official history: The war in the air vol 3* (London, 1930)

Kanzler, SE, *Expelled from a beloved country: German settlers in Southern Namibia between Colonial War and World War* (Namibia, 2006)

Katzenellenbogen, SE, *Railways and the copper mines of Katanga* (Oxford, 1973)

Keegan, John, *The First World War* (1999)

Keene, JL, 'The problem of munitions supply in the First World War and its effects in the Union Defence Force' in *South African Military History Journal* 6:4

Keiser, R, 'The South African Governor General 1910–1919' (Thesis, Rhodes House, Oxford University, 1975)

Keith, AB (ed), *Speeches and documents on Indian policy 1750–1921 vol III* (London, 1922)

Killingray, D, 'African voices from two world wars' in *Historical Research* 74:186 (2001) pp.425–443

King, GL, *A study of the operations in German East Africa during the World War 1914–1918* (1930)

Kleynhans, WA, *Election manifestos* (1987)

Krieger, DE, *Britain and the fate of German Africa: The debate over the future of the German colonies in Africa during the First World War, 1914–1918* (Doctorate of Philosophy, University of California: Davis, 1973)

Langhorne, RTB, 'Anglo-German negotiations concerning the future of the Portuguese colonies, 1911–1914' in *Historical Journal* 16:2 (1973) pp.361–387

Layman, RD, *Naval aviation in the First World War: Its impact and influence* (London, 1994)

Lennox, AG, *Diary of Lord Bertie of Thame 1914–1918* (2 vols) (London 1924)

Lettow-Vorbeck, Paul von, *My reminiscences of East Africa: The campaign for German East Africa in World War 1* (Nashville, nd)

Lewsen, P (ed), *Selections from the correspondence of JX Merriman 1905–1924* (South Africa, 1969)

Liebenberg, BJ, & Spies, SB (eds), *South Africa in the 20th Century* (Pretoria, 1993)

Liebenberg, I, *Sociology, biology or philosophy of a warrior? Reflections on Jan Smuts, guerrilla-being and a politics of choices* (Pretoria, nd) [online http://www.sun.ac.za/sdorm/index2.php?option=com_docman&task=doc_view&gid=83&Itemid=26; accessed 25 Feb 2011]

Liebenow, J Gus, *Colonial rule and political development in Tanzania: The case of the Makonde* (Evanston, 1971)

Listowell, J, *The making of Tanganyika* (London, 1965)

Lloyd George, D, *War memoirs* (London, 1932)

Lloyd-Jones, W, *KAR: Being an unofficial account of the origin and activities of The King's African Rifles* (London, 1926)

Louis, WR, 'The US and African peace settlement' in *Journal of African History* 4:2 (1963)

Louis, WR, *Great Britain and Germany's lost colonies 1914–1919* (Oxford, 1967)

Louis, WR, *Ruanda-Urundi 1884–1919* (Oxford, 1963)

Lukas, G, *The Young Indiana Jones* (Lucasfilm Ltd & Paramount Pictures, 2008)

Lüthy, H, 'India and East Africa' in *Journal of Contemporary History* 6:2 (1971)

Macdonald, T, *Ouma Smuts: The first lady of South Africa* (London, nd)

Magnus, P, *Kitchener: Portrait of an imperialist* (Middlesex, 1958)

Mahncke, JOEO, 'Aircraft operations in the German colonies, 1911–1916: The Fliegtruppe of the Imperial German Army' in *South African Military History Journal* 12:2 (2001)

Maritz, Manie, *My lewe en strewe* (1939)

Marks, Sally, *Makers of the modern world: The peace conferences of 1919–1923 and their aftermath: Paul Hymans, Belgium* (London, 2010)

Marks, Sally, *Innocent abroad: Belgium and the Paris Peace Conference, 1919* (Carolina, 1981)

Marrion, RJ, & Fosten, DSV, *The British Army 1914–1918* (1978)

Matten-Klodt, W, (translator: Oakley Williams) *A fugitive in South West Africa, 1908–1920* (1931)

Mazower, Mark, *No enchanted palace: The end of empire and the ideological origins of the United Nations* (Princeton, 2008)

McLaughlin, P, *Ragtime soldiers: The Rhodesian experience in the First World War* (1980)

Mead, G, *The Doughboys: America and the First World War* (London, 2000)

Mehrotra, SR, *India and the Commonwealth, 1885–1929* (London, 1965)

Meinertzhagen, R, *Army Diary 1899–1926* (London, 1960)

Michels, Eckard, *Der held von Deutch-Ostafrika: Paul von Lettow-Vorbeck, ein preußischer Kolonialoffizier* (Paderborn, 2008)

Miller, Stephen M, *Volunteers on the Veld: Britain's Citizen-Soldiers and the South African War, 1899–1902* (Norman, 2007)

Monick, S, 'The third man: Willy Trick and the German Air Force in South West Africa in World War One' in *South African Military History Journal* 5:3 (1988)

Moyse-Bartlett, H, *The King's African Rifles: A study in the military history of East and Central Africa, 1890–1945* (Aldershot, 1956)

Muller, CFJ, *500 years: A history of South Africa* (Pretoria, 1990)

Nasson, Bill, *Springboks on the Somme: South Africa in the Great War 1914–1918* (Rosebank, 2007)

Nöthling, CJ, *Suid-Afrika in die Eerste Wêreldoorlog (1914–1918)* (Silverton, 1994)

Overstraeten, R van (ed), *The war diaries of King Albert: King of the Belgians* (London, 1954)

Packenham, T, *The scramble for Africa 1897–1912* (Johannesburg, 1992)

Page, M, 'Recruitment of blacks: Malawians and the Great War: Oral history in the reconstructing of Africa's recent past' in *The Oral History Review* 8 (1980)

Page, Malcolm, *KAR: A history of the King's African Rifles* (London, 1998)

Page, Melvin E, *The Chiwaya war: Malawians and the First World War* (Colorado, 2000)

Paice, E, *Tip and run: The untold tragedy of the Great War in Africa* (London, 2007)

Paris Peace Conference vol III

Paris peace conference vol V

Paterson, H, 'First allied victory: the South African campaign in German South West Africa, 1914–1915' in *South African Military History Journal* 13:2 (2004)

Pélissier, R, 'Campagnes militairies au Sud-Angola (1885–1915)' in *Cahiers D'etudes Africaines* 33:9 (1969) p.97

Phiri, DD, *Let us die for Africa: An African perspective on the life and death of John Chilembwe of Nyasaland/Malawi* (Blantyre, 1999)

Pollock, J, *Kitchener* (London, 2000)

Porter, Bernard, *The lion's share: A short history of British imperialism 1850–1995* (3rd ed) (London, 1997)

Power, PF, 'Gandhi in South Africa' in *Journal of Modern African Studies* 7:3 (1969) pp.441–455

Pretorius, Frans Johan, *Life on commando* (Cape Town, 1999)

Pretorius, PJ, *Jungle man* (London, 1947)

Quale, CB, *To live like a pig and die like a dog: Environmental implications for World War 1 in East Africa* (Fort Leavenworth, 2002)

Ransford, O, *Livingstone's Lake* (London, 1966)

Reach, DN, 'The uses of colonial history and history of Mozambique' in *Cahiers d'Etudes Africaines* 104 26:4 (1986) pp.707–713

Reitz, Deneys, *Trekking on* (London, 1933)

Ritchie, EM, *The unfinished war: The drama of Anglo-German conflict in Africa in relation to the future of the British Empire* (London, 1940)

Robbins, Keith, *The First World War* (Oxford, 1993)

Roberts, Andrew, *A history of Zambia* (London, 1976)

Robertson, W, *From private to field-marshal* (London, 1921)

Roskill, S, *Hankey: Man of secrets 1877–1918 vol 1* (1978)

Rothwell, VH, *British war aims and peace diplomacy, 1914–1918* (London, 1971)

Round Table, *Commonwealth Quarterly* 17 (Dec 1914) pp.491–496

Royal Naval Society, 'A backwater: Lake Victoria Nyanza during the campaign against German East Africa' in *Royal Naval Review* 9:2 (1921) pp.287–337

Sampson, PJ, *The capture of de Wet, 1914* (London, 1915)

Samson, Anne, *Britain, South Africa and the East Africa campaign 1914–1918: The Union comes of age* (London, 2006)

Sanderson, GM, 'Gunfire on Nyasa' in *The Nyasaland Journal* 10:2 (1957) pp.25–39

Schulte-Varnedorff, Uwe, *Kolonialheld für Kaiser und Führer: General Lettow-Vorbeck – Mythos und Wirklichkeit* (Berlin, 2006)

Schutz, WP, 'A distant field revisited: Captain WA Bloomfield VC' in *South African Military History Review* 10:3 (1996)

Seegers, Annette, *The military in the making of modern South Africa* (London, 1996)

Shankland, P, *The phantom flotilla* (London, 1968)

Shepperson, George A, & Price, Thomas, *Independent African: John Chilembwe and the Nyasaland rising of 1915* (2000)

Silvester, J, 'Beasts, boundaries and buildings: The survival and creation of pastoral economies in Southern Namibia, 1915–1935' in Hayes, Patricia; Silvester, Jeremy; Wallace, Marion & Harman, Wolfram (eds) *Namibia under South African rule: Mobility and containment 1915–1946* (Oxford, 1998)

Silvester, J, Wallace, M, & Hayes, P, 'Trees never meet: mobility and containment: an overview 1915–1946' in Hayes, Patricia; Silvester, Jeremy; Wallace, Marion & Harman, Wolfram (eds) *Namibia under South African rule: Mobility and containment 1915–1946* (Oxford, 1998)

Simons, HJ & Simons, RE, *Class and colour in South Africa 1850–1950* (1969)

Simpson, GL, 'British perspectives on Aulihan Somali unrest in the East African Protectorate 1915–1918' in *Northeast African Studies* 6:1–2 (1999) pp.7–43

Skinner, A, *Tanzania and Zanzibar* (Cadogan Guides)

Smith, Ken, & Nöthling, FJ, *North of the Limpopo: Africa since 1800* (Pretoria, 1993)

Smith-Dorrien, H, *Memories of 48 years service* (1925)

Smithers, AJ, *The man who disobeyed: Sir Horace Smith-Dorrien and his enemies* (London, 1970)

Sorrenson, MPK, *Origins of European settlement in Kenya* (1968)

Southern, Paul, 'German border incursions into Portuguese Angola prior to the First World War' in *Portuguese Journal of Social Science* 6:1 (2007)

Spender, Harold, *General Botha* (London, 1919)

Stapleton, TJ, *No insignificant part: The Rhodesia Native Regiment and the East Africa Campaign of the First World War* (California, 1990)

Stassen, Nicol, *Afrikaners in Angola, 1928–1975* (Pretoria, 2009)

Steinbach, Daniel, 'Challenging colonial supremacy: the internment of "enemy aliens" in German East Africa during the First World War' in Rowe, L, Miller, A, & Kitchen, J (eds), *Other combatants, other fronts: Competing histories of the First World War* (Newcastle, 2011)

Steinbach, Daniel, 'Defending the Heimat: The Germans in South West Africa and East Africa during the First World War' in Jones, H, O'Brien, J, & Smidt-Supprian, C (eds), *Untold war: New perspectives in First World War studies* (Brill: Leiden, 2008)

Stevenson, William, *The ghosts of Africa* (London, 1980)

Steyn, JC, *Trowe Afrikaners* (Cape Town, 1987)

Strachan, Hew (ed), *The Oxford illustrated history of the First World War* (1998)

Strachan, Hew, *The First World War in Africa* (Oxford, 2007)

Stratford, DO, 'Naval ships move overland up Africa' in *South African Military History Journal* 1:4 (1969)

Sutton, J, *Wait for the wagon: The story of the Royal Corps of Transport and its predecessors, 1794–1993* (London, 1998)

Swanson, MW, 'South West Africa in Trust 1915–1919' in Gifford, P, & Louis, WMR *Britain and Germany in Africa: Imperial rivalry and colonial rule* (New Haven, 1967)

Swart, SS, *The rebels of 1914: Masculinity, republicanism & the social forces that shaped the Boer rebellion* (MA Dissertation: University of Natal, 1997)

Teixeira, NS, *O Poder e a Guerro 1914–1918: Objectivos Nacionais e Estratégias Políticas na Entrada de Portugal na Grande Guerre* (Lisbon, 1996)

Thompson, ES, 'A machine gunner's odyssey through German East Africa: The diary of ES Thompson part 3, 18 September 1916–26 February 1917' in *South African Military History Journal* 7:6 (1988)

Thompson, ES, 'A machine gunner's odyssey through German East Africa: the diary of ES Thompson, Part 1, 17 January–24 May 1916' in *South African Military History Journal* 7:4 (1988)

Thompson, ES, 'A machine gunner's odyssey through German East Africa: The diary of ES Thompson, Part 2' in *South African Military History Journal* 7:5 (1988)

Thornhill, Christopher J, *Taking Tanganyika: Experiences of an Intelligence Officer 1914–1918* (Uckfield, 2004)

Tidy, DP, 'They mounted up as eagles (A brief tribute to the South African Air Force)' in *South African Military History Journal* 5:6 (1982)

Tomes, J, *Balfour and foreign policy* (Cambridge, 1997)

Townsend, ME, *The rise and fall of Germany's colonial empire, 1884–1918* (New York, 1930)

Truter, E, *Tibbie: Rachel Isabella Steyn, 1865–1955: Haar lewe was haar boodskap* (Cape Town, 1997)

Trzebinksi, Errol, *The Kenya pioneers* (London, 1985)

Turner, J, *British politics and the Great War: Coalition and conflict 1915–1918* (New Haven, 1992)

van der Waag, Ian, 'Rural struggles and the politics of a colonial command: The South African Mounted Rifles of the Transvaal Volunteers, 1905–1912' in Miller, Stephen M (ed), *Soldiers and settlers in Africa, 1850–1918* (Leiden, 2009)

Vincent-Smith, JD, 'The Anglo-German negotiations over the Portuguese colonies in Africa, 1911–1914' in *Historical Journal* 17:3 (1974) pp.620–629

Walker, C, 'The women's suffrage movement' in C Walker (ed), *Women and gender in South Africa to 1945* (Oxford, 1990)

Walker, Eric A, *A History of Southern Africa* (3rd ed) (London, 1957)

Wallace, L, 'Northern Rhodesia and the last phase of the Great War' in Lucas, C, *The empire at war* (1926)

Walworth, A, *Wilson and his peacemakers: American diplomacy at the Paris peace conference, 1919* (London, 1986)

Webb, HS, *The causes of the rebellion* (Pretoria, 1915)

Weber, C, & Lint, D, (exec producers) *The jungle navy* (National Geographic Television, 1999)

Wheeler, D, 'The Portuguese army in Angola' in *The Journal of Modern African Studies* 7:3 (1969)

Wienholt, Arnold, *The story of a lion hunt; with some of the hunter's military adventures during the war* (London, nd)

Wills, AJ, *An introduction to the history of Central Africa: Zambia, Malawi and Zimbabwe* (4th ed) (Oxford, 1985)

Wilson Fox, H, 'The development of Rhodesia from a geographical standpoint' in *The Geographical Journal* 48:4 (1916) pp.302–303

Wingate, R, 'In Memoriam: Sydney Charles, Earl Buxton, GCMG (Sometime Governor General of South Africa and for Twelve Years President of the African Society)' in *Journal of the Royal African Society* 34:134 (1935) pp.1–6

Wynn, WE, *Ambush* (London, 1937)

FORCES INDEX

British Empire

2nd Rhodesian Regiment 57, 67, 109,
    153, 169, 170, 230
Rhodesian Native Police 67
1st Rhodesian Native Regiment 117
Royal Naval Reserve 66
Scouts 47, 137, 141, 142
    Arnoldi 138
    Berkeley Cole 156
    Bowker 138
Shortcol 160
Somali Field Force 140
Somali Mounted Scouts 140, 156
South African Division (Delville Wood)
    97
South African Infantry Brigade 198
South African Mounted Rifles 75
2nd South African Rifles 169
Uganda Police Active Service Unit 48
Uganda Railway Volunteer Reserve 48
2/West India Regiment 152, 156
Zanzibar Volunteer Defence Force 141

South West Africa

No 4 Division (McKenzie) 77

Belgian

2nd Battalion 56

Portuguese

Expeditionary Forces

1st (Pereora d'Eca) 85, 127, 177, 178
2nd (Moura Mendes) 113, 127
3rd (Jose Gil) 115, 127
4th (Thomas Rosa) 121, 127, 178

German forces

See Names index for commanders

PERSON INDEX

PLACE INDEX

GENERAL INDEX

German navy
  Adjutant 102, 103
  Dix Tonne 100
  SMS *Emden* 61, 62, 65
  Feldmarshall (Later *Transvaler*) 51,
    165
  Graf von Gotzen 100, 102, 103
  Hedwig von Wissmann 58
  Helmuth 63
  Herman von Wissmann 58
  Kingani (later *Fifi*) 100, 102
  Koenig 51
  SMS *Königsberg* 1, 47, 50, 62, 65,
    66, 98, 99, 100, 101, 106, 119,
    121
  Marie 103, 104, 107, 142
  Möwe 51
  Netta 100
  Peter 100
  Tabora 51
  Wami 102
Nazi 7
Neutrality 28, 30, 35, 46, 50,
    51, 54, 59, 60, 71, 141,
    169, 175
Niassa Company 36, 129, 176, 178

Order Pour le Mérite 147

Peace 7, 83, 104, 116, 119, 157, 160,
    161, 165, 174, 179, 181, 183,
    185, 188, 193, 200, 201, 205,
    210, 211, 213, 214, 215, 216,
    217, 220, 225, 226, 227, 230
Planes 66, 83, 99, 102, 105, 106, 107,
    146, 223
  Curtis 66
  Naval Air Service Detachment 106
  Royal Flying Corps 105
  Sea 99, 103, 105, 106
  Sopworth 99
  South African Air Force 105
  Zeppelin 107, 108

Police 37, 40, 41, 42, 48, 52, 55, 57,
    59, 66, 67, 73, 75, 84, 85, 111,
    149, 156
Ports 7, 28, 40, 51, 62, 65, 72, 78, 119,
    159, 175, 179
Press 46, 72, 77, 79, 87, 93, 94, 123,
    145, 159, 182, 190
Prisoners (internment camp) 47, 76, 84,
    142, 148

Railways 33, 41, 42, 45, 62, 63, 65, 104,
    116, 118, 182, 204
  Benguela 41
  Cape Town to Cairo 65, 203, 230
  Central (Tanganyika) 52, 102, 117, 150
  Lorenço Marques 32
  Uganda 27, 47, 48, 53, 109, 127, 172,
    195
  Usambara 27, 52, 64, 104
Recruitment 52, 57, 90, 91, 94, 95, 96,
    131, 138, 146, 149, 150, 177,
    189

Scouts – see Forces Index
Senussi 97
South Africa
  Air Force (see Planes)
  Defence Act 1912 39, 74, 105
  Defence Force 39, 40, 71, 72, 73, 74,
    75, 145
  Department of the Interior 39
  Election 37, 68, 86, 87, 89, 90, 92,
    93, 94, 95, 197, 198, 199, 224,
    225
  Governor General – see Buxton,
    Gladstone
  High Commissioner 26, 42, 55, 57,
    66, 168, 169, 170, 224
  Land Act 1913 90
  Political Parties
    Labour 38, 92
    National 37, 38, 70, 73, 92, 93,
      94, 199